CHAUCER AND CHAUCERIANS

Critical Studies in Middle English Literature

CHAUCER
AND
CHAUCERIANS

CRITICAL STUDIES IN
MIDDLE ENGLISH LITERATURE

Edited by

D. S. BREWER

Lecturer in English at the University of Cambridge,
Fellow of Emmanuel College, Cambridge

NELSON

THOMAS NELSON AND SONS LTD
36 Park Street London W 1
P.O. Box 336 Apapa Lagos
P.O. Box 25012 Nairobi
P.O. Box 21149 Dar es Salaam
77 Coffee Street San Fernando Trinidad

THOMAS NELSON (AUSTRALIA) LTD
597 Little Collins Street Melbourne

THOMAS NELSON AND SONS (SOUTH AFRICA) (PROPRIETARY) LTD
P.O. Box 9881 Johannesburg

THOMAS NELSON AND SONS (CANADA) LTD
81 Curlew Drive Don Mills Ontario

THOMAS NELSON AND SONS
Copewood and Davis Streets Camden 3, N.J.

———

First published 1966
Reprinted 1967

Printed in Great Britain by
Thomas Nelson (Printers) Ltd, London and Edinburgh

CONTENTS

Chaucer's Life and Works	Other Literary Events	National Events
	c.1300 Machaut born	
	1304 Petrarch born	
		1307 accession of Edward II
	c.1313 Boccaccio born	
	c.1320 Wycliffe born	
	1321 Dante died	
	1326 Trevisa born	
		1327 accession of Edward III
	c.1330 Gower born	
		1337 declaration of war against France (Hundred Years' War)
c.1340 Chaucer born	c.1340 Auchinleck MS written	
	c.1346 Deschamps born	1346 Crecy
	1348-58 Boccaccio's Decameron	1348-9 Black Death
	c.1352 Winner and Waster	
		1356 Poitiers
1357 page to Countess of Ulster		
1359-60 military service		1360 Treaty of Bretigni
	c.1362 first (A text) version of Piers Plowman	
c.1366 married		
1367 Yeoman in King's Household		
	c.1368 Hoccleve born	
1369 Campaign in France The Book of the Duchess		1369 war with France renewed
	c.1370 Lydgate born	
1372-3 journey to Italy		
1374 Comptroller of Customs	1374 death of Petrarch	
1374-80 The House of Fame		
	1375 death of Boccaccio	
	1377 death of Machaut	1377 accession of Richard II
	c.1377 second (B text) version of Piers Plowman	
1378 second Italian journey		

Chaucer's Life and Works	Other Literary Events	National Events
	c.1380 *Sir Gawain and the Green Knight*	
		1381 The Peasants' Revolt
c.1382 *The Parliament of Fowls*		1382 Richard marries Anne
1382-5 translation of Boethius' *Consolation*; *Troilus and Criseyde* *Palamon and Arcite* (*The Knight's Tale*)		
	1384 death of Wycliffe	
1385 appoints permanent deputy. J.P. in Kent		
1385-6 *The Legend of Good Women*		
1386 Knight of the Shire for Kent, then loses controllerships	1386-90 Gower's *Confessio Amantis*	1386 Council of Regency: impeachment of Suffolk
c.1387-1400 *The Canterbury Tales*		
	1388 Thomas Usk executed	1388 The Merciless Parliament
1389 Clerk to the King's Works		1389 restoration of Richard's power
	c.1390 third (C text) version of *Piers Plowman*	
1391 relinquishes Clerkship: appointed Subforester		
		1392 death of Anne
1399 grants confirmed by Henry IV		1399 deposition of Richard and accession of Henry IV
1400 dies		

FOREWORD

The following essays are not the work of a specially convened group, nor the product of collaboration. They have been independently contributed at the editor's request by a number of American and English scholars and critics whose various approaches to fourteenth- and fifteenth-century literature were felt to have something in common. Of course, many other distinguished scholars and critics might also have been asked to contribute.

The most important development in medieval literary studies recently has been a new critical sophistication, a sharpened literary sense of the language the poet actually uses. Each contributor was therefore asked to begin his work from a consideration of the language and rhetoric of the poetry. After this first request there has been no attempt to avoid conflicting arguments and conclusions. In fact, an impressive coherence, though not uniformity, will be obvious to the reader, and such disparities and disagreements as there are will no doubt stimulate him to further thought. The essays are not summaries of recent work on Chaucer and his disciples, but they take it into account, and make a further contribution to criticism which is now laid before the expert and the common reader.

In addition to the mainly critical essays by various hands on the poetry, the editor has contributed a mainly historical introduction placing Chaucer in his English and European setting; and a mainly historical final chapter showing how Chaucer has been received and understood up to the twentieth century.

Each chapter with its footnotes is complete in itself, but it should be noticed that all references to Chaucer's works are to the edition by F. N. Robinson, *The Complete Works of Geoffrey Chaucer*, 2nd ed., 1957.

D. S. Brewer

The relationship of Chaucer to the English and European traditions

D. S. BREWER

CHAUCER, the 'father of English poetry' as he used to be called, is often thought to be without English ancestry. New material for poetry, new attitudes, new verse-forms, all drawn from the more sophisticated French or Italian cultures, are as characteristic of Chaucer as they are of T. S. Eliot. Like Wordsworth and Eliot, Chaucer began a revolution in poetic diction. Sometimes he is thought to have been so much influenced by French writing that it was almost an accident that he wrote in English. Chesterton talks of 'the faint trail of Anglo-Saxon traditions and various dialects like Middle English'—whatever that may mean, for Chaucer's language *was* Middle English, the lineal descendant of Old English or Anglo-Saxon. The truth is that Chaucer inherited a particular English style, which he enriched by his borrowings from French and Italian and Latin.

All poets need a prepared language and an accepted tradition to begin to write in, or they could not begin at all; a poet's stock-in-trade is words, not 'life' or 'feelings' or 'ideas'. A medieval poet was particularly dependent on a formed verbal tradition; he needed it to help himself, and also to fulfil that other essential demand of the rhetoric of poetry, to communicate with the audience. No poet could stand up in his pulpit before the audience, as medieval poets did,[1] if he was not prepared to use a poetic language with which his audience was reasonably familiar, and which it could be expected to understand and even to like. Such concepts of a recognisable, indeed conventional style, appropriate

[1] See the famous 'Troilus frontispiece' of Corpus Christi College, Cambridge, MS No. 61, many times reproduced, most recently in D. S. Brewer, *Chaucer in his Time*, 1963.

to both subject-matter and audience, consciously chosen with the desire to communicate interest and pleasure, are remote from most modern theories of poetry. They are the concepts of medieval rhetoric. Before condemning them we should realise that some sort of rhetoric is the basis of any poetry.

In order to recognise Chaucer's inherited style we must look at his earliest piece of independent writing, *The Book of the Duchess*, which must have been composed soon after the death in 1369 of Blanche, Duchess of Lancaster and first wife of John of Gaunt, whom it commemorates. Chaucer was between twenty-five and thirty when he wrote it. The poem is heavily indebted for its subject-matter to the French poet Machaut, and, like Machaut's work, it is written in the general tradition of *Le Roman de la Rose*, of which poem there are several actual reminiscences in the text. But our concern here is with the poetc language. The first fifteen lines are closely imitated from *Le Paradys d'Amour* by Chaucer's contemporary, the chronicler and poet Froissart, who also wrote in the tradition of *Le Roman de la Rose*. Chaucer's poem is thus well within the French tradition. Here are Froissart's and Chaucer's openings side by side.

Je siu de moi en grant merveille	I have gret wonder, *be this lyght*
Comment je vifs quant tant je veille	How that I lyve, for *day ne nyght*
Et on ne point en veillant	I may nat slepe *wel nygh noght*;
Trouver de moi plus traveillant,	I have so many an ydel thoght
Car bien sacies que par veillier	*Purely* for defaute of slep
Me viennent souvent travillier	That, *by my trouthe* I take no kep
Pensees et merancolies	Of nothyng, how hyt *cometh or*
Qui me sont ens au coer liies	*gooth*,
Et pas ne les puis deslyer,	Ne me nys nothyng *leef nor looth*
Car ne voeil la belle oublyer	Al is ylyche good to me—
Pour quele amour en ce travail	*Joye or sorowe*, wherso hyt be—
Je sui entres et tant je veil.[1]	For I have felyng in nothyng,
	But, as yt were, a mased thyng
	Alway *in poynt* to falle a-doun;
	For sorwful ymagynacioun
	Ys always hooly in my mynde.

There is no attempt at close translation. Chaucer has taken the subject-matter from the French, but not the style. Already we

[1] *Oeuvres de Froissart*, ed. M. A. Scheler, Brussels 1870, I, p. 1.

have the characteristic Chaucerian tone of voice, self-confidently self-deprecatory, the half-humorous 'I'. What a contrast with Froissart's style! Froissart has written a direct, well-articulated sentence that winds its way gracefully through the octosyllabic rhyme-scheme. If not notably concise, it is not padded; it is sober, well-languaged, flat. In contrast, Chaucer's style is lively, conversational, emphatic, dramatic, stuffed with doublets and alternatives, asseverations that are mild oaths, expletives and parentheses. He seems even to avoid French words. Froissart uses *merveil*, and *marvel* had been long enough borrowed from French to make it easily available, but Chaucer prefers the Old English *wonder*, a more powerful word for amazement, with undertones of distress and atrocity. Mersand emphasises 'the overwhelmingly Anglo-Saxon proportion' of the poem's vocabulary.[1] Wherever Chaucer uses a French word, it is because there is no English equivalent available. The deliberately *chosen* quality of this apparently slack style may be judged by comparison with the Middle English *The Romaunt of the Rose*, a translation of part of *Le Roman de la Rose*. The earlier part of the *The Romaunt* is probably by Chaucer. The opening passage is notably different in tone from that of *The Book of the Duchess*, with few additional phrases, presumably because the aim was a close translation.

Where did Chaucer get such a style? It often seems to be assumed that he carved it out of French, or that he invented it. Of course he invented it in the sense that only his unique individual genius could have put the words together in precisely that way; but he did not invent English. Nor did he invent the collocations that I have italicised in my quotation of the first few lines of *The Book of the Duchess*. Nor did he invent the general tone of the style. This tone resides in the language as it had been

[1] J. Mersand, *Chaucer's Romance Vocabulary*, New York 1937, p. 91. Neither Mersand nor I distinguish here between Anglo-Norman (that dialect of French spoken in England) and Continental French, since the immediate point here is the native *English* origin of Chaucer's style, and the main point later will be the influence of Continental French. Chaucer's consciousness of the difference between Anglo-Norman and Continental French is suggested by his satirical reference to the Prioress's ignorance of 'French of Paris' (*The Canterbury Tales*, 1126). That Anglo-French had begun to be old-fashioned even by the beginning of the century is suggested by Miss M. D. Legge in her valuable *Anglo-Norman Literature and its Background*, 1963, p. 6.

spoken and evolved in the country for nearly a thousand years, and in that artistic formalisation of the language which is found in what may be called the Middle English rhyming romances. Chaucer's acquaintance with these romances is well known through his sparkling parody of some of their characteristics in *Sir Thopas*, and some scholars have pointed out how his poetry, being, like the romances, to some extent intended for oral delivery, has a number of their stylistic traits.[1] But it cannot be assumed that Chaucer took his parody from his amused discovery in his maturity of naive rubbish.[2] The romances are in fact very mixed, and some of them are poor stuff; perhaps Chaucer did come to despise them: if he did, he was biting the hand that fed him.

In the opening lines of *The Book of the Duchess* (and continually through the poem, too extensively to quote) he shows the romances to be the source of his first poetic nourishment. The collocation *day-night*, for example, is the most frequently repeated phrase in all the romances. The early couplet version of *Sir Guy of Warwick* (to be referred to as *Guy* I), has six instances.[3] That is not a fault of undue repetitiousness in a poem of 7,036 lines, but along with similar repeated collocations it helps to mark its characteristic diction. The charming Breton lay *Sir Degaré* has two instances of *day-night* in its 1,073 lines,[4] while the later *Sir Degrevant* has no less than fourteen in a total of just under two thousand lines.[5] It is needless to multiply examples. Throughout his work Chaucer uses the phrase, in

[1] See especially Ruth Crosby, 'Oral Delivery in the Middle Ages', *Speculum*, XL (1936) 88-110; and 'Chaucer and the Custom of Oral Delivery' *Speculum* XIII (1938) 413-32. Cf. also A. C. Baugh, 'Improvisation in the Middle English romance', *Proceedings of the American Philosophical Society* CIII (1959), who illustrates very copiously the frequent formulas in the metrical romances.

[2] As seems to be assumed in the valuable essays by L. H. Loomis, 'Chaucer and the Auchinleck MS.', *Essays and Studies in Honor of Carleton Brown*, New York 1940.

[3] *Guy of Warwick*, ed. J. Zupitza, EETS, ES 42, 49, 59, (1875-91), ll. 512, 521, 626, 1707, 1716, 4235.

[4] The most convenient collection of romances is that edited by W. E. French and C. B. Hale, *Middle English Metrical Romances*, New York 1930. See *Sir Degaré*, ed. French and Hale, ll. 3, 712.

[5] *Sir Degrevant*, ed. French and Hale, ll. 28, 44, 49, 60, 111, 412, 495, 534, 708, 740, 784, 1119, 1645, 1790.

one form or another, over forty-five times.[1] By contrast Gower, who seems to have been little influenced by the romances, uses the phrase only rarely. Chaucer's loose phrase *wel nygh noght* I have not found in the romances, but it is very typical of their style, which abounds in such redundant phrases as *never nought, wel god sped, ryght noght, never none*. Chaucer's phrase *by my trouthe* is again the type of asseveration in which both the romances and the whole of Chaucer's work abound. A hard-swearing romance is *Guy* I—

'God', quod Gij, 'we ben y-nome!'   (we are captured

l. 1337

Guy's beloved swears *bi mi trewthe* (l. 405), and Guy himself *bi treuthe mine* (l. 4687). The king in *Degaré* also swears *bi my trewthe* (l. 559). The phrase occurs in the alliterative romances of the Northern and Western tradition, but is used in a different way, and there is no sign that Chaucer was much, if at all, influenced by this literature. Gower, a Kentish man, uses the phrase like Chaucer.[2] The romances have many other similar phrases: *bi me leute*, frequent in *Guy* I,[3] *by my feyth* in *Eglamour*,[4] and so forth. Chaucer's *cometh or gooth* is a doublet phrase of a type common in the romances. The more usual phrase is *ride or go*, but *comen and goon* occurs in the romances of the second half of the century, though it is also found in other writings. *Leef nor looth* is a pretty example of the long-lasting continuity of English poetic phrases, though it is not confined to the romances. It is first recorded in *Beowulf*, usually thought to have been composed in the eighth century, and by the fourteenth century it was widely diffused in English poetry.[5] *In poynt* is recorded in the fourteenth century only in the rhyming romances, its first recorded use in prose being by Mandeville about 1400.

[1] Crosby, *Speculum*, XIII, 422.

[2] *Confessio Amantis* IV, l. 2747, in *Works*, ed G. C. Macaulay, 1901.

[3] E.g. ll. 916, 1512, 1634, etc., ed. cit.

[4] E.g. *Sir Eglamour*, ed. cit. ll. 440, 442, 1066, etc.

[5] *Beowulf*, l. 511; *Havelok*, ed. Skeat and Sisam, (1915) l. 2379; 'Song of Lewes', l. 38, and *Bestiary*, l. 86 (both ed. Dickins and Wilson, *Early Middle English Texts* (1951)); 'On the Death of Edward III', ed. Sisam, *Fourteenth Century Verse and Prose*, 1921. Frequent in Gower.

I have left to the last the phrase in the very first line of *The Book of the Duchess*, *be this lyght*. It is a type of asseveration very common in the romances, and is the same type of phrase as *by my truth*. There is another phrase of great frequency, *on a day*, normally used in the romances as an introduction. *By this (day) light* would be a natural conflation of the asseveration and the introductory phrase, suitable enough for a first line, and this is no doubt how the collocation came to be made. It looks commonplace enough, but the earliest quotation in the *NED* is from an interlude of 1510. Though rhymes with *light* are very common in the romances, considerable search has failed to find any other instances of this deliberately mild oath, and it does indeed look as if Chaucer was unique in its literary use for a hundred and fifty years. The later quotations of *by this light* are from colloquial contexts, and this example, trifling in itself, suggests that Chaucer was more colloquial on occasion than even his earliest masters, the romance-writers.

The romances show great delight in the lively rendering of personal speech. Compare with the opening of *The Book of the Duchess* such turns of phrase as these from the romances:

'Y have wondur, by Goddys myght'	*Toulouse* l. 884
'Swiche liif Y lede, day and night'	*Guy* I, ll 512 and 521
'Ichot for sothe he wil me sle	(I know
And that schal turn me al to blis,	
When Y schal dye, for sothe, y-wis.	(indeed
Henne forward ne reche Y me	(care
Of me liif, whare it be,	
No of mi deth, never the mo,	
No reche Y never where Y go.'	
He ferd as he were mat,	(he behaved as if he were mad
Adoun he fel aswowne with that.	(he fell down in a faint

Guy I, 590-8

This is the very true gallop of Chaucer's earlier metre and style, though Chaucer betters instruction. One might quote more passages where the 'doublet' style of *day ne nyght, cometh or gooth, joye or sorowe* is paralleled, such as the introduction to *Lai le Freine*, which is almost identical with that of *Sir Orfeo*. There is no question of 'source-hunting' here. Chaucer was not borrowing specific passages; he was using a traditional style, which he had found in these and other poems. The romances which come nearest to the style of *The Book of the Duchess* are *Guy* I, *Degaré*, both in short couplets, and *Eglamour*, which is a tail-rhyme romance. Both *Guy* I and *Degaré* are in the Auchinleck Manuscript, which will be discussed later, and which, it has been plausibly argued, Chaucer himself may have actually handled.[1] The influence of *Guy* I may be even greater and more direct. The exaggerated feeling expressed in the beginning of *The Book of the Duchess*, where the poet is 'yn poynt to falle a-doun' reminds one of the doughty Sir Guy's tendency to swoon for love. There is no hint of it in Froissart. Sir Guy is also very much of a prototype for Troilus in his tendency to despair for love, to swoon at crucial moments, in his chastity, and in his military prowess. Troilus is nearer Sir Guy than he is to his apparent model, Boccaccio's Troilo.[2]

Another link with the romances is Chaucer's technique of entry into a poem, though, once again, he improved on his masters almost out of all recognition. One need read only a few of the introductions, especially to the tail-rhyme romances, with their confident yet ingratiating tone of personal address to the audience, to see something similar, though very much better, in Chaucer's mode of beginning a poem. Thus in *The Earl of Toulouse*, probably contemporary with Chaucer, the poet begins:

> Jhesu Cryste, yn Trynyte,
> Oonly God and persons thre,
> Graunt us wele to spede,   (to get on well
> And gyf us grace so to do,
> That we may come thy blys unto,
> On rode as thou can blede!   (cross
> Leve lordys, Y schall you telle   (dear
> Of a tale, some tyme befelle,
> Farre yn unkowthe lede: (unknown country
> How a lady had grete myschefe,

---

[1] Cf. L. H. Loomis, art. cit.

[2] Cf. K. Young, 'Chaucer's *Troilus and Criseyde* as Romance', *PMLA*, LIII (1938) 38-63, who emphasises the differences from Boccaccio in terms of French romance but neglects the English romances. Sir Guy's qualities are to a large extent attributable to the Anglo-Norman original, *Gui de Warewic*.

And how sche covyrd of hur grefe,   (recovered from
Y pray yow take hede!

(l. 1-12, normalised from French and Hale,
Middle English Metrical Romances, New York, 1930)

The romances are often clearly designed for oral delivery,
sometimes, at least, by the 'minstrels that walken far and wide'
who are referred to in the second stanza of *Emaré*. We know from
both internal and external evidence that at least Chaucer's earlier
poems were written with oral delivery of a similar type in mind.
In such circumstances the narrator must strike in at once to
capture the interest of his audience. He must whet their appetite
in the first few lines, but he must not waste essential parts of his
story before he has their full attention. Chaucer had a further
advantage and disadvantage. He was not, as must often have been
the case with the romances, an unknown minstrel hired to recite
a poem by an unknown author, before an unknown audience, at
a rich merchant's feast. He was the familiar courtier, envoy,
negotiator, king's pensioner, Geoffrey Chaucer, speaking to a
group of nobles and royal persons who knew him well. In
whatever light he might present himself in description in the
course of his poem while he was actually speaking the poem, his
audience *knew* who he was, they could *see* the actual Narrator.
The text of the poems alone makes this clear. For this reason
Chaucer's poetry has a special quality even apart from his genius,
as Milton's or Shakespeare's poetry has not. It is to some extent
in a special *genre* of its own; specially written by a unique poet
for a unique audience. The beginning of *The Book of the Duchess*
shows that even at this early stage of his career Chaucer was
regarded as something of a humourist—it was a time that
cherished court-fools. Chaucer, as he begins his poem, clearly
expects his audience to smile a little, and he has to defer to this
response, though it must be dangerous to the ultimate effect of
his poem, granted its melancholy occasion; he has to indulge
and flatter this response a trifle, before he can sufficiently dominate
his audience to lead them towards his more serious purpose. This
process of indulgence, flattery, and ultimate domination reaches
its extreme of elaboration in the marvellously subtle beginning to

the *Troilus*. Far as Chaucer carried this technique of entry into a poem, its origins lie with the rhyming romances.

How was it that these poems came to be the first source of Chaucer's literary inspiration, and what is the significance of his development from them? To answer such questions will illuminate many of the factors that make for great literature in any age, as well as show more clearly the nature of Chaucer's achievement.

It must first be recalled that at the Conquest the English language, the most highly developed vernacular of Northern Europe, was displaced as the language of the dominant classes by French and Latin. The process was slow; slowest in the West and North, least slow in the South and East, which was the richest and most favoured part of the country then as now, and also nearest the home of the Norman invaders. The result of this displacement was that almost the whole of the 'cultural superstructure' that had been developed in the Old English language gradually perished; that is, most of the general terms, the abstractions, the subtle poetic and prose diction, the words of government, the terms of art, disappeared. What remained was the main hull of the language, the words we cannot live without—*eat, drink, love, sleep, live, die, fight, plough, build, man, woman, child, father, mother, God, light, dark, day, night, wonder, truth*, and indeed, among thousands of others, almost all the words in the first fifteen lines of *The Book of the Duchess*. Gradually the conquered absorbed their masters, most of whom, after the first generation, learnt some English. The story of the language for the next few centuries is the story of how it created, largely by borrowing, a new superstructure of abstractions, words for new things, new ideas, new feelings, new arts, that were built on to the continuing basic language, and were modified to its essential, though changing, nature. When the language came to be written down again over a fairly wide area, in the Middle English of the thirteenth century, it was still English, and though impoverished compared with Old English (except in some religious prose like *Ancrene Wisse*), it was steadily on the way to enriching itself again. The language of the court in the thirteenth century and in the first half of the fourteenth century was French, which now had the prestige of an extraordinarily rich culture; but there is some evidence to suggest that even most of the gentry spoke English as their first language. By the middle of the fourteenth century English was established in government circles, and we know for certain that in one school (and, to judge from the rapid loss of knowledge of French, probably in many more) the language of instruction became English.[1] From the thirteen-sixties onwards the very existence of Chaucer's poetry proves that the language of the court was English, and that the standard of literary culture was as high as it has ever been in any English court, and a good deal higher than it has been in most.

Literature is the formalisation of language at its greatest intensity of meaning. English literature in both prose and verse inevitably reflects the state and status of the English language. I shall discuss the verse before the prose. In verse there are several discernible streams, which sometimes partly mingle. There was the aristocratic Northern and Western alliterative verse, close in spirit and metre to Old English verse, which so astonishingly appears in the fourteenth century. There was a tradition of witty and sophisticated vernacular verse which appears to have been written mostly by and for clerics, of which the best-known examples are the remarkable *Owl and the Nightingale*, composed about 1200, and the famous Harley Lyrics, composed about 1300.[2] But Chaucer was grounded in yet another tradition, that considerable body of secular fiction, of which the core is composed of the Middle English rhyming romances. These seem to be centred on the eastern part of the country, towards the south (as opposed to the alliterative poetry), and to have been designed for a secular, middle- and upper-class audience, thereby differing from the clerical-vernacular tradition.

The earliest of the romances extant are *King Horn*, *Havelok*, and *Floris and Blauncheflor*, all written in 'octosyllabic' couplets about the middle of the thirteenth century. The first two are on English subjects but, equally significantly, there had been earlier poems on these subjects in French. English was under tutelage. To judge

[1] For details see A. C. Baugh, *A History of the English Language*, 2nd ed. 1959.
[2] *The Owl and the Nightingale*, ed. E. G. Stanley, Nelson's Medieval and Renaissance Library, 1960: *The Harley Lyrics*, ed G. L. Brook, 1948.

from the language, the English poems were written in the eastern part of the country, probably about the middle part, though *Havelok* is about the supposed founder of Grimsby. The audience must mainly be judged by the nature of the poems themselves, and such clues as the poets' addresses to the hearers. There is an interest in chivalry, and a strong prejudice in its favour, which argues an upper-class audience. On the other hand, the authors write without much intimate knowledge of the specifically courtly life, while the sports of all classes of people are described with relish and knowledge. The audience is not likely, therefore, to have been closely associated with the King's court. *Floris and Blauncheflor* seems the most sophisticated, *Havelok* the least courtly. *Havelok* begins:

> Herkneth to me, gode men,
> Wives, maydnes, and alle men,

which suggests a range coming between the aristocrat and the peasant. With some variation in degree, the sort of audience that is suggested by the romances as a whole is what we would think of as upper-class. They were people with some degree of education above the common, and especially above the illiterate peasantry, who probably comprised ninety per cent of the population. They had enough wealth to hire a professional entertainer for the halls of their own houses, or to have a manuscript copied which a clerk or a clever son or daughter could read aloud. Sometimes they could afford large and expensive manuscripts, like the Auchinleck Manuscript. They were people who could enjoy the sort of festival that the author of *Havelok* attributes to his happy king, which included jousting, wrestling, playing with dice, harping, piping, telling of stories, and 'romance-reading on the book' (ll. 2322-9). This is that middle group of society which has given a backbone to many centuries of English life, and has provided great writers, clerics, scientists, and other intellectual persons. It is 'middle-class' in the way it has bridged, with its manifold degrees, the gap between high and low, and has always merged easily into the higher class, in the fourteenth century as in other centuries. It can be called *bourgeois* since it has always been primarily town-dwelling, but the word has unfortunately acquired contemptuous overtones. It is remarkable that many of the English romances which it is supposed were written for this ill-defined English *bourgeoisie* were based on French romances which were designed for a courtly audience, and which treated the French *bourgeois* characters with rough contempt. The English romances moderate this contempt, and one reason may well be that the class-distinction between courtly and *bourgeois* in England was not at all clear. In the late fourteenth century, for example, the Earl of Salisbury became the third husband of the daughter of a rich London mercer. There has usually been in England not so much a class distinction between upper, middle and lower, as between gentry and non-gentry.[1] Just as the twice-widowed mercer's daughter could marry the Earl of Salisbury, so Elizabeth Bennet, with no money to speak of, and relations in 'trade', could marry the rich Darcy, whose ancestors were in part titled nobility. When Lady Catherine de Bourgh remonstrated, Elizabeth replied 'He is a gentleman; I am a gentleman's daughter. So far we are equal'.[2] As Chaucer might have said, 'There is namoore to say'. The nature of the audience for the romances is further suggested by some of the manuscripts in which they have been preserved. Some of these manuscripts are small, and might perhaps have gone into a minstrel's saddle-bag. But some of them are large books, such as the Auchinleck and Thornton Manuscripts. The Auchinleck Manuscript has some dozen and a half romances, with as many more mainly religious pieces.[3] It is a large book, written somewhere about 1340, possibly in a commercial bookshop in London, and though not the kind of book that was the glory of princes, it must have been extremely expensive by modern standards. It can only have been bought by a lover of romances who was a rich man. The Thornton Manuscript was written a century later, and is known by the name of its compiler and first owner, a gentleman called Robert Thornton, lord of the manor of East Newton,

---

[1] Cf. Peter Laslett, 'The World We Have Lost', *The Listener* LXIII (1960) pp. 607ff., 657ff., 699ff.

[2] Jane Austen, *Pride and Prejudice*, Chapter lvi.

[3] For a description, cf. besides L. H. Loomis, art. cit., her article 'The Auchinleck MS. and a possible London Bookshop of 1330-1340', *PMLA* LVII (1942) 595-627, and A. J. Bliss, 'Notes on the Auchinleck MS.', *Speculum* XXVI (1951) 652-8.

Yorkshire.[1] It is more miscellaneous than the Auchinleck Manuscript, and contains theonly surviving text of *Syr Percyvelle*, which Chaucer refers to in *Sir Thopas*, and which must have been composed some time about the middle of the fourteenth century. Thornton himself is clearly gentry, and a lover of the romances, while Chaucer's reference to *Syr Percyvelle* makes it clear that even the audience of the King's court could be expected to know it. The list of books apparently belonging to John Paston, which was compiled during the reign of Edward IV (1461-83), includes several romances.[2] One might further add that as late as 1613 the London audience of Shakespeare's and Fletcher's play *Henry VIII*, which may have been meant for a royal occasion, was expected to recognise references to the adventures of Sir Guy of Warwick.[3] To sum up, the audience of the English romances, from the thirteenth to the sixteenth centuries, always included, and was probably chiefly made up of, persons who must be called gentry. At latest by the second half of the fourteenth century, this audience will often have included the aristocracy and the court.

The location of the audience is also of some interest. Many of the romances are tail-rhyme romances, of the sort of which *Sir Thopas* is a cruel but not altogether unjust parody. These have been convincingly located by Trounce mainly in the East Midlands.[4] *Guy of Warwick* suggests the spread to the Central Midlands; Thornton, in Yorkshire, marks about the northern-most boundary of the typical romances, and he has many characteristics of language and subject-matter which show he is

---

[1] *The Thornton Romances*, ed. J. O. Halliwell, Camden Society, 1844.

[2] *The Paston Letters*, ed. J. Gairdner, 6 vols., 1904, VI, pp. 65-7; also in Everyman's Library Edition, n.d. II, p. 232.

[3] *Henry VIII*, ed. J. C. Maxwell, New Cambridge Shakespeare, 1962, V. iv. 22 (apparently by Fletcher). Another romance hero, Bevis of Southampton, is mentioned, I. i. 38, apparently by Shakespeare.

[4] A. McI. Trounce, 'The English Tail-Rhyme Romances', *Medium Ævum*, I (1932) 87-108; 168-82; II (1933) 34-57; III (1934) 30-50, especially 49-50. Trounce over-emphasises the 'popular' quality, but has made a valuable study. For a text of a fourteenth-century tail-rhyme romance, with valuable introduction, see Thomas Chestre's *Sir Launfal*, ed. A. J. Bliss, Nelson's Medieval and Renaissance Library, 1960, though Bliss seems to me to over-emphasise the peasant quality as against 'middle-class' quality of the audience.

near the Northern and Western alliterative verse. The Pastons in East Anglia are right in the middle of the area. This geographical distinction of poetic styles between North and West on one side and South and East on the other was clearly recognised in the fourteenth century. Chaucer makes his Parson say:

> But trusteth wel, I am a Southren man,
> I can nat geeste 'rum, ram, ruf,' by lettre.
> *The Canterbury Tales* X 42-3

The author of the alliterative poem, *Winner and Waster*, is clearly aware of the regional difference, though he puts it in terms of honesty rather than style![1] One must not push the distinction too far. There was always overlapping, and though London was predominantly an East Midland area it offered a greater mixture of poetic styles than any other part of the country, as the London-based, but alliterative, poem *Piers Plowman* shows. Nevertheless the rhyming romances offer a fairly cohesive body of verse fiction, mostly East Midland, directed to an upper-class audience, with characteristic styles and ethos. Even in *Horn*, *Havelok*, and *Floris*, these styles seem well established, with the simple, forceful narrative, the delight in dialogue, and perhaps especially the repeated tags which are the most obvious hallmark of the *genre*. These earliest poems already have *night and day*, *hende* (meaning courteous), *leef and loth* (six times in *Havelok*), and several others, of the kind that is so noticeable in *The Book of the Duchess*. Like Chaucer's poem, they are written in a rough octosyllabic couplet, though in the fourteenth century the twelve-line tail-rhyme stanza became equally favoured as the narrative form. Different poets use slightly different patterns of this stanza, but a good example is provided by the tail-rhyme continuation of *Sir Guy of Warwick*. In quality many of the romances have a patriotic note, especially both versions of *Sir Guy*, which seems to have been the most popular of all. When Guy fights the Danish giant Colbrond, he fights 'to make England free', and 'to save England's right'. There is a strong consciousness of the history of England back to Anglo-Saxon times. The romances, again, are notably decent, though

---

[1] *Winner and Waster*, ed. I. Gollancz, 1931, pp. 5-10.

they include a few *fabliaux*. Guy's bravery, nobility, and chastity in the first part have already been mentioned; the second part of the poem, in tail-rhyme, turns him into a pious, though hard-fighting, pilgrim. The liveliness, decency, piety, variety, and occasional patriotism of the romances as a body (of course, there are exceptions) are not enough to make them great literature. They are too simple. In any case only a tiny proportion of the literature of any age is likely to be great literature. But they had real literary virtues, and appealed to a large number of people in England, up to and including the King's court. Though many of their qualities may ultimately derive from Anglo-Norman, the evidence of style suggests that it was the English version or versions which offered the first poetic impulse to Chaucer, and in many ways set the tone of most of his verse writing.

Chaucer himself is a representative of what we may imagine to be the typical romance audience. He was of high bourgeois origin, from a rich merchant family, who had been gentry and connected with the King's court (though professionally, as wine-merchants) for at least two generations. All the records show his family firmly rooted in England, and in the very area where the romances most flourished, for the family had property in East Anglia (Ipswich) and in London. Chaucer, well-grounded in the romances, educated by his father's wealth and doubtless in his own tongue to be a member of the King's court, the cultural as well as political centre of the kingdom, was carrying on a well-established linguistic and literary process, as the English language itself rose higher in the social scale and was adopted into the King's court.

To suggest the English tap-root of Chaucer's poetry—English both in language and literature—is, however, to tell only half the story. Certainly, the first fifteen lines, and indeed all the rest of *The Book of the Duchess*, are written in what is essentially the style of the romances. Yet there are also great differences from that style. The lines already have a more spacious rhythm that is purely Chaucerian, flowing on from line to line; while to anyone familiar with the plain diction typical of the romances, the two lines:

> For sorwful ymagynacioun
> Ys always hooly in my mynde

are most strikingly different with their amplitude and their vigorous learned polysyllable. As one reads through *The Book of the Duchess* one is further struck by the fullness of mind with which it overflows. Some critics have even condemned the excess of information, the 'medieval didacticism', and they have some justification on purely aesthetic grounds. All the same, looked at historically the poem marks, just because of this fullness, an exciting moment: the moment when English secular poetry begins to deploy once again the forces of the European literary mind. There can be no great poetry which does not rest on the intellectual labours of many men, and which has not itself high intellectual status. The English romances lacked both intellectual material and intellectual status. The trouble was that intellectual matters in the thirteenth century—which, after all, saw one of the great climaxes in intellectual history with the triumph of scholasticism—were carried on in Latin; and furthermore, that purely intellectual Latin culture was hostile to the literary imagination, as some scientific intellectual culture is today. Even in the fourteenth century, as Professor Shepherd rightly suggests in the essay on *Troilus* (below, p. 65), English vernacular poetry never completely adapted itself to the dominant scholastic intellectual culture. But by the fourteenth century the literary imagination, as represented in European literature from Virgil, Cicero, and Ovid onwards, was able, even in the vernaculars, both to draw strength from, and to stand out against, the purely intellectual tradition. For the sake of recognising both the strength and weakness of vernacular medieval literature it is worth tracing, even in much simplified form, how this situation, with its interesting differences from and similarities with the situation today, came about.

Medieval vernacular literature in Europe begins with saints' lives, epics, and the courtly poetry of love. We are interested here specifically in secular literature, and must inevitably make crude distinctions which oversimplify the complexity of the actual situation. In the secular literature we may disregard the epics for our present purpose, since they belonged essentially to an older world, and for all their greatness gave little to the more modern courtly and secular literature. It is the love-poetry, beginning in the courts of Provence, which is most important from our present point of view. It was especially distinguished by the sophistication with which it treats love between a courtier and his lady. From the nature of courtly society the lady was almost inevitably the courtier's social superior, and very often married to someone else. This is the poetry of what scholars in the late nineteenth century called *amour courtois*, or *courtly love*. The more exact term was *fine amour*, or in Chaucer's words, 'the craft of fine loving'[1]: *fine amour* is the term used in this book, partly because it is more historical and precise, partly because the term *courtly love* has come to be more rigidly interpreted than is justified. *Fine amour* was love which treated the lady with the highest respect; by his experience of love the courtier or knight felt himself ennobled, irrespective of whether the lady looked on him with the 'mercy' or 'pity' which was all that he could claim. *Fine amour* took on many forms and varieties according to the time, the country, the general tradition, and the personal quality of the poet who was writing. Some poems portray love of tragic intensity and outcome; some as a merely flippant literary parlour game. Sometimes *fine amour* was the less, sometimes the more, important part of stories of love and adventure. Sometimes it was deeply hostile to the prevailing morality; more usually it was associated with marriage and devoutness. Interest in *fine amour* spread throughout European literature, and it provided the main force of most purely imaginative writing until sex was substituted for love in the twentieth century. In particular it inspired great literature in Germany, Italy and France in the twelfth and thirteenth centuries; but here we must concentrate on those parts of the tradition which ultimately concerned Chaucer. The centre of medieval vernacular culture was France, and perhaps the purest and certainly the most influential example of this literary tradition of refined feelings and beautiful descriptions is the first section of *Le Roman de la Rose*, as it was left unfinished by Guillaume de Lorris in the early part of the thirteenth century.

Besides the vernacular, secular, courtly literature there was produced in the twelfth century, also mainly in France, an intellectually much more impressive Latin literature, based on and

---

[1] *Prologue to the Legend of Good Women*, F. 544; cf. *The Parlement of Foulys*, ed. D. S. Brewer, Nelson's Medieval and Renaissance Library, 1961, pp. 21ff.

extending Classical Latin literature. The high point of twelfth-century Latin literature was achieved at the Cathedral School of Chartres, with such major European writers as Bernard Silvestris, Alan of Lisle, and John of Salisbury. Though the authors were clerics and much of the literature was religious, it was neither monkish and devotional, like the writings of St Bernard, nor incipiently scholastic, like the writings of Abelard. The writers of the School of Chartres were essentially literary and rhetorical. Among them, or associated with them, were the rhetoricians who had so much influence on later ages; Matthew of Vendôme, and the Englishmen John of Garland and Geoffrey of Vinsauf. It seems that the teachings of the rhetoricians were well received in England, where a number of their manuscripts are preserved, and where the most influential of all these authors, Alan of Lisle, was well known. It is easy to be irritated, and easier to be baffled, by the extreme artificiality of Alan's style. Those who understand him best perhaps like him least.[1] It is part of our Romantic heritage to dislike the idea of a consciously formulated style—though everyone consciously formulates his style. Professors Coghill and Muscatine in later essays in this book rightly refer t ⟩ the weaknesses and limitations of medieval rhetoric. Yet the production of so elaborate an instrument of communication as Alan's style is a high achievement of intellectual and literary culture. We owe to the medieval rhetoricians, whatever their weaknesses, the preservation of the very concept of 'style' in literature and in the arts generally. They inherited and maintained the work of the classical rhetoricians; and classical Latin rhetoric has been described as the most elaborate and effective codification yet made of language as an instrument of thought, of expression, of communication, and of persuasion.[2] It is the idea of persuasion which has come to dominate our concept of rhetoric, and which we now so much distrust, partly because of its misuse in so much dishonest advertising, but also because of the excessive emphasis in modern times on self-expression, and therefore on 'sincerity'

[1] Cf. C. S. Lewis, *The Allegory of Love*, 1936, and E. R. Curtius, *European Literature and the Latin Middle Ages*, translated by W. R. Trask, 1953.
[2] The medieval rhetoricians were edited by E. Faral, *Les Arts Poetiques du XIIe et du XIIIe Siècles*, Paris 1923; cf. also E. H. Gombrich, *Art and Illusion*, New York 1960, pp. 374-5.

in art. Yet persuasion need not be bad; it is a main element in all artistic communication, and what we need is not to deny rhetoric, but to know more about it; to see how we are persuaded, to what end. We shall find that good modern writers have their rhetoric, just as much as the ancients.[1]

The medieval rhetoricians deserve our gratitude, then, for preserving and extending the concept of style as literary choice, as capable of being learnt, and of maintaining the concept of persuasion, without which literature retreats into a little, private world of its own, afraid of the great issues of the public world, afraid even as a lover of trying to persuade his mistress. To recognise the artificiality of literature is to enable men both to live by it and distrust it—that strange paradox of literary culture. 'Teach us to care and not to care. Teach us to believe and not to believe. Teach us to see how it's done.' These are the demands we must make of the rhetorical, the literary teacher, whose reward will be to have his pupils outdo him in subtlety, learning and literature. Such was the reward of the rhetoricians of the late twelfth and early thirteenth centuries, who helped to shore up the ruins of the world with such fragments of the ancient classical rhetoric as they could get hold of and understand. We are naturally aware of their great deficiencies; later ages have— sometimes—done better. Their sometimes mechanical artificiality was part of their strength at their time, for often they had to work on men in whom the very idea of literature was like an old man's lust, a small fire in a large field. Their success is seen in the achievements of writers influenced by them, in many European languages, in prose as well as verse, including (besides Chaucer) Dante, Boccaccio and Petrarch. Moreover, the latest scholarly opinion sees the medieval rhetoricians of Italy as the stock from which sprang the Humanists, who created not only the Renaissance but the very idea of the Middle Ages and the Renaissance.[2]

To go so far ahead, however, is to look at the late products of the seed before knowing the fate of the flower, that is, the Latin literary culture of the twelfth century. It was soon blasted. The best scholar and one of the best writers of the School of Chartres,

---

[1] Cf. for example, Wayne Booth, *The Rhetoric of the Novel*, 1962.
[2] P. O. Kristeller, *Renaissance Thought*, Harper Torchbooks, New York 1961.

John of Salisbury, who became bishop of Chartres, had already to complain, towards the end of his life, that men were beginning to despise the study of literature. Curtius has re-told the story and shown its significance.[1] Literary studies were removed from university syllabuses and logic substituted. In the thirteenth century scholasticism and science reigned supreme, and literature was destroyed. Such, at least, was the case with Latin; Latin culture became mainly intellectual, logical, scientific, anti-humanist, anti-literary (always, it will be understood, with exceptions which do not affect the general truth).

By the thirteenth century, however, Latin had a rival. More lay people had become literate, and the lay vernaculars of the French and Italian courts, especially, now had a literary life of their own. The two cultures, one, the clerical and scientific Latin, the other the lay and literary vernaculars, overlapped and mingled to some extent, but did not lose their fundamental incompatibility, which emerges even in some great works of art, like the *Troilus*. The twelfth-century Latin literature was as a dammed stream in full flood, and it happily overflowed into the vernacular literature. The supreme example of this development is the second and far larger part of *Le Roman de la Rose*, added to the first part by Jean de Meun some time about 1270. The basis of Jean's enormous addition was Alan of Lisle's writing about the goddess Natura. *Le Roman* thus became a strange hybrid. The first part is courtly, brilliantly visualised, the first and best of courtly love-allegories; the second much stronger meat, discursive, energetic, full of popularised learning, anti-clerical satire, serious and radical intellectual propaganda, social and sexual comedy. The poem in its full length is unified only by its vernacular French and the almost infinitely stretchable allegorical scheme. Of these perhaps the language was the more important. The mixture met a widespread need of the developing lay mind knowing French but no Latin. The poem as a whole became the most popular and influential poem in all Europe. The appeal of Guillaume's first part is obvious; the entertainment value of much of Jean's second part has also been easily recognised. Less than justice has been done to Jean's thousands and thousands of lines of varied scientific and

[1] Op. cit., especially 591ff.

philosophic discussion. They are no worse poetry than the rest, which is not faint praise. In particular they must have provided laymen who knew only the vernacular with the intellectual nourishment for which, especially when enriched with the other qualities of poetry, they hungered.

The important vernacular poetry of the fourteenth century, based on *Le Roman de la Rose*, is characterised by a new intellectual content, some of which may be derived from the contemporary scholastic culture, but which is essentially based on the Latin of the writers of the School of Chartres, and, as schooling improved, on the writers of the older Latin tradition, Virgil, Ovid, Statius, Claudian, Cicero, Aulus Gellius, and others. In France, which concerns us most in speaking of Chaucer, the great poet was Machaut (c. 1300-77), who was also the leading musician of his day. In himself he illustrates the common-law marriage that could exist between the clerical and literary cultures. He was nominally a cleric, as at that time was almost inevitable for one who wrote much. Yet he led the adventurous, amorous, much-travelled life of a courtier. He wrote many poems continuing the tradition of *Le Roman de la Rose*, and his endless subject was *fine amour*. His verse is usually condemned today for its personifications and prolix subtilisings about love. His astonishing metrical ability, the smoothness and flexibility of his style, his extraordinary copiousness of language, are no longer appreciated, and he is praised only for his occasional passages of life-like realism. We are entitled to our own tastes, and there is no absolute reason why modern critics should

> read each work of wit
> With the same spirit that its author writ,

but if we wish to *understand* Machaut and Chaucer, rather than project our own fantasies upon them, we shall take warning when we find that Machaut, like Chaucer, was praised in his own day for his learning and his art. His nephew, disciple and successor to his fame, Eustache Deschamps (1340-1410) praised him as 'le noble rhethorique'.[1] In the *Prologue* to the *Dit dou Vergier*, in

---

[1] Cf. A. T. Kitchel, 'Chaucer and Machaut's *Dit de la Fontaine Amoureuse*', *Vassar Medieval Studies*, ed. C. F. Fiske, New Haven 1923, 219-31, and Deschamps, *Oeuvres*, ed. St Hilaire, SATF, I, 243-5.

which Machaut at the very end of his life reviews the whole of his poetic career,[1] he shows how he understood the quality of his own work. Nature, he says, granted him, as a poet, her three children *Scens* (inspiration), *Retorique* (that part of verbal art that can be taught), and *Musique* (the gift of song). Then he says that Love presented him with suitable subject-matter, Sweet Thought, Pleasure and Hope. This is a crude, but on the whole just summation of his work. Under *Retorique* may be classed the manner that was so much admired in Machaut—the allusions to classical mythology, references to classical fable, and such personifications as that of Nature, which, deriving from Alan of Lisle and Jean de Meun, has a fuller intellectual and emotional content than is sometimes realised. Nature came to Machaut bearing an immense load of meaning; he was not poet enough to release all that meaning in his verses (perhaps Spenser is the only poet who could), but even in Machaut the word has not lost all its original brightness to those who know something of its earlier uses.[2] Machaut's verse carries concept and information, as well as description of feeling.

The structure of *The Book of the Duchess*, its quality of feeling, and much of its actual material, come directly from Machaut.[3] Machaut had given the precedent, which Chaucer, already much better informed, took further, for the use of Ovid's story of Ceyx and Alcyone, and for all the informative references to Pythagoras and the rest. A good example of Chaucer's actual borrowing from Machaut can be seen in the description or 'portrait' of Blanche the Duchess. The origins of the literary portrait lie far back in Greek antiquity; the medieval rhetoricians developed its potentialities and set it on a career that lasted till the nineteenth century.[4] The literary portrait of the ideal lady was not quite unknown in England before Chaucer. It can be found in the Harley Lyrics, from the most elaborate of which comes the following piece of description:

[1] Machaut, *Oeuvres*, ed. E. Hoepffner, SATF (1908) I, 1ff. Cf. W. F. Patterson, *Three Centuries of French Poetic Theory*, Part I, Ann Arbor 1935, pp. 8off.
[2] See especially the Appendix to J. A. W. Bennett, *The Parlement of Foules*, 1958.
[3] See Robinson's notes for details.
[4] Cf. D. S. Brewer, 'The Ideal of Feminine Beauty', *Modern Language Review*, L (1955), and C. Schaar, *The Golden Mirror*, Lund 1955.

A suetly suyre heo hath to hold   (sweet neck she
With armes, shuldre ase mon wolde (as one would wish
Ant fyngers feyre forte holde   (fingers fair to hold

The Harley Lyrics, ed G. L. Brook, 1948, p. 49.

and here is an exactly corresponding piece of description from
The Book of The Duchess:

But swich a fairnesse of a nekke
Had that swete that boon nor brekke (blemish
Nas ther non sene that myssat.   (that was disproportionate
Hyt was whit, smothe, streght, and
 pure flat,
Withouten hole; or canel-boon   (collar-bone
As be semynge, had she noon.
Hyr throte, as I have now memoyre,
Semed a round tour of yvoyre,
Of good gretnesse, and noght to
 gret.
   (her name was White)
Ryght faire shuldres and body long
She had, and armes, every lyth   (limb
Fattysh, flesshy, not gret therwith;
Ryght white handes, and nayles
 rede,
Rounde brestes; and of good brede
Hyr hippes were; a streight flat bak.
  939-47, 952-7

In comparison with the writer of the Harley Lyric Chaucer has
learnt verbosity. To put it more historically, he has learnt what
the Elizabethans came to value highly as *copie*, copiousness. He
has learnt it from Machaut, and we have here the curious sight of
Machaut's copious elegance being translated a little clumsily into
the language of the English rhyming romances. Almost everything
in the passage here quoted except the actual diction is taken
directly from Machaut's *Jugement dou Roy de Behaingne*. Chaucer
has even learnt something of Machaut's irritating habit of piling
up adjectives. Machaut describes the lady's body as being not only
par mesure, but also

Gent, joint, joli juene, gentil, grasset,
Lonc, droit, faitis, cointe, apert et graillet.
   374-5

Of these riches Chaucer is content with *lonc* (long), *grasset* (fattysh, flesshy), and *graillet* (not gret)—to sum up, she was fat where she ought to be and thin where she ought to be. In comparison with the French writer, Chaucer is briefer and more vividly concrete. (The lady's red nails are a detail that seems never to appear in French catalogues of a lady's charms. She probably did indeed paint her nails, and this may be a detail from real life, but there is also a similar detail in the English romance *The Soudan of Babylone*.) But if from the French point of view Chaucer is briefer and more concrete, from the English point of view Chaucer is much more longwinded, though he still uses a typically English diction.

In fact, the contrast between the new European range of reading shown in *The Book of the Duchess* and the plain old-fashioned English of the diction is very marked. Even where the words Chaucer used are of ultimately French origin, nearly all of them were well established in his day. He recognises the limitations of his diction when he makes the Black Knight say:

Me lakketh both Englyssh and wit
898

All his life Chaucer felt the lack of English to be a hindrance to his poetry.[1] Yet even in this early poem he already begins to repair the lack, and to enrich or 'augment' English within the predominantly Anglo-Saxon diction. In this poem he introduces no less than fourteen French words into literary English, besides the two new Anglo-French compounds, *chambre-roof* and *maister-hunte*.[2] Five of the new words are taken from his sources; *fers*, *pervers*, *poune*, *soleyn*, and *trayteresse*. Of the others, *embosed*, *forloyn*, *founes*, *lymeres*, *rechased*, *relayes*, *soures*, are connected with hunting. *Rayed* and *tapite* are connected with the decoration of a room; like the words to do with hunting, they belong to the courtly life, and were doubtless in normal colloquial use. Fourteen new words in one poem is a considerable addition to the literary language. There are more to add, if we consider new meanings of words already established in the language. The word 'imagin-

---

[1] Cf. *The Complaint of Venus*, l. 80, written when he was old.
[2] Mersand, op. cit., counts twenty-one new words, but his details are not always unquestionable.

ation', already noted, appears to be used to mean 'desire', which Godefroy records first in Froissart's *Chronicles*, and is a sense of the word not noticed in the *NED*. *Imagination* was well established in fourteenth-century English, normally used in serious, often religious contexts, but Chaucer is using it in its most modern courtly sense, according to the most advanced usage of his day.

The sources of Chaucer's new words indicate their quality. The five borrowed direct from his sources give a literary tone, and *perverse* and *soleyn* and *trayteresse* convey a degree of abstraction, subtlety and generality of language which is lacking in the romances, though those that were clearly written late in the fourteenth century begin to have something of it. Chess had been played in the romances, and the earliest use of the word *chek* as Chaucer uses it in *The Book of the Duchess* is recorded in the tail-rhyme *Guy*. But *fers* and *poune*, like the words to do with hunting, suggest a new courtly level in the diction. These words, like Chaucer's use of the word *imagination*, are not due to any immediate literary source; they show that Chaucer tends to take his new vocabulary more from the spoken language of the court than from what was to him the latest literature.

There was a constant interaction between poetry and speech. Ever since Wordsworth's dictum about 'the real language of men' we have been especially aware of the strength poetry must take from contemporary speech if poetry is to prevail and survive. With this in mind we sometimes, like Wordsworth himself, condemn 'poetic diction' out of hand, identifying it with the formal abstract diction of the less successful poets of the late eighteenth century. But to condemn formality, abstraction, elaboration *as such* is to jump a stage in logic which may well make nonsense of our judgments. What about the suitability of diction to subject-matter and audience? Or, to put it in more modern terms, what if the *spoken* language itself is becoming *more* elaborate, courtly, formal, abstract? In such a case, if poetry is going to maintain its lifeline to the spoken language, is going to appeal to its audience, it too must take on this more polite and intellectual tone. We fail to see this immediately nowadays because the historical trend in the twentieth century has been in the opposite direction; the spoken language has become *less* formal, *less* polite, *less* abstract, *less* intellectual, at the cultura level which concerns poetry. Since the spoken language is usually in advance of the written language, we think of modern colloquial English as simpler, cruder, less mannered, often less well-mannered, than most written English, especially old-fashioned written English; but good modern poetry has naturally hastened to reflect the change because poetry *is* the language in an important sense.

The present situation, however, is not typical. Colloquial English has not always had the same tendencies as it has now. All through the sixteenth century, for example, colloquial English was steadily becoming more, not less, complicated, formal, elaborate and abstract, and it at least maintained these qualities in the seventeenth and eighteenth centuries. It is not necessarily an unconnected fact that in these centuries was written our greatest poetry, and that the more Wordsworth laboured over his greatest poem, the more he returned to that eighteenth-century diction which he had earlier condemned. In the late fourteenth century also, for at least a short time, the spoken language seems to have achieved a vocabulary and a syntax which made great poetry possible, by building on to the basis of the concrete firm-set words about the essentials of existence, a 'cultural superstructure' of great variety and intellectual power. Nothing would be more absurd than to attribute the marvellous flourishing of English poetry in the late fourteenth century—Chaucer, Langland, the *Gawain*-poet, and others—to a recrudescence of 'the folk', redolent of the soil. There were certainly patriotic elements, and certainly the language of the farmyard, so to say—truly basic English—was the foundation. But the romances had had this. What made the difference was the increasing use, as we can detect it in Chaucer's verse and elsewhere, of a language of wider vocabulary of ideas, of intellectual discriminations, of items of luxury, of more sophisticated entertainment, of deeper thought. The resulting potential was given actuality in the range of styles that, as Professor Muscatine shows in a later essay (p. 88), Chaucer was able to control in *The Canterbury Tales*. Chaucer revolutionised 'poetic diction' by 'augmenting' his English with a vast number of new words of Latin, French, and Italian origin.

At first many of these were derived from his literary sources. According to Mersand about seventy per cent of the words ultimately derived from French or Latin in his translation of *Le Roman de la Rose*, presumed to be amongst his earliest works, are from the source. But in *The Book of the Duchess* the proportion of such words is just under thirty per cent. In *The House of Fame*, the next of his important poems, though there are fifty-seven new words from French, Italian or Latin, only *two* were traced by Mersand to a literary source. The proportion in *The Parliament* is higher than in *The House of Fame*, but still lower than in *The Book of the Duchess*. In other words, the huge majority of words introduced by Chaucer into the literary language came from current usage. Mersand (p. 74) says it was ninety per cent. In his large vocabulary of just over eight thousand words, about four thousand are words of ultimately Latin source, and well over a thousand of these Chaucer seems to have been the first to use in the literary language.[1] Three-quarters of his innovations have been retained in the language, which in itself speaks well for his inwardness with the genius of English. Of course, the rhyming romances from which Chaucer started also had a good proportion of words of ultimately Latin derivation, having come through French; Chaucer only extends a practice inherent in the language, but the proportion in the romances seems to be much smaller than in Chaucer.

In respect of language, therefore, Chaucer grafts on to his basic English style, found in the romances, a new diction, more elaborate, learned and formal, though also colloquial. This new diction signalises Chaucer's progressive immersion in European literary culture, first in the poetry of the leading poet of his day, Machaut, and in the dominant poetic influence of his day, *Le Roman de la Rose*. Then there was a progressive broadening; Ovid, and to a less extent Virgil, Statius, and Claudian, were all doubtless cherished from schooldays, though Machaut seems to have given the key to their poetic utilisation. *Le Roman de la Rose* had pointed to other Latin authors whom Chaucer makes good use of, such as Macrobius and Boethius, late Romans, and the twelfth-century Alan of Lisle, opening the way to science and philosophy. Italian

[1] Mersand, op. cit., p. 53.

authors Dante and Boccaccio (though not with the *Decameron*)
came to swell the flood. Here is indeed the mighty pressure of the
European literary mind flooding English poetry.

These authors, and others, are not to be seen only as 'source
material'. They were important for that but their richness as
sources was dependent on other more general factors. First is the
intellectual power and the learning which their poetry rested
upon, and which, in a sense, it made immortal. Something has
already been said of this. Second, related to intellect and learning,
is the high status that was given to literature in most of these
poems. These poets were learned men, whose works were read
by princes. Virgil's *Aeneid* was produced to celebrate the greatest
empire the West had known. Dante's poetic 'arrogance' is well
known. Only when the status of literature and of literary studies
is high, it would seem, can great literature be produced. The
status of literature with the scholastic philosophers was very low;
and it was low for different reasons with the anonymous authors
of the English rhyming romances. Probably the status of literature
was never completely assured even in Richard II's court. There
are signs of strain in Chaucer's poetry, and the need he feels to
present himself mockingly is no doubt partly a defensive reaction
on his part. The speed with which high literary achievement
collapsed in the English court after Richard's and Chaucer's
deaths is another pointer. Lydgate, for all his virtues, was never a
true court poet; he was a monk who could be called on to produce
suitable poetry for a number of different occasions, by London
guilds, by noblemen, by private patrons. It is no denigration of
him in this context to think of him simply as a craftsman.
Chaucer's other immediate disciple was the amusing but undig-
nified Hoccleve, a minor Chancery clerk, on the fringes of the
court. Chaucer was not such a man. Whatever the insecurities of
his position, he eventually took up a position of great independence and dignity—no small achievement in a court full of
factions and feuds, with death the possible penalty for being in
the wrong faction, as Thomas Usk, another disciple, found.
Chaucer's mockery of his presumed patrons, however politely
disguised, in the later version of *The Prologue to the Legend of Good
Women*, and his satire of contemporaries, even if they did not

include the great, in *The Prologue to the Canterbury Tales*, shows how much he could assert himself. But the most striking assertion is, after all, earlier in his career, in that strange poem *The House of Fame*. He makes an unequivocal statement of his own independence of mind and sense of inner value, or of the value of his poetry:

I wot myself best how I stonde.

1878

Following Dante he invokes, to guide his 'little last book', Apollo, god of science (i.e., learning) and of light. And he sees holding up the pillars of the Hall of Fame the historians, and especially, the great poets—Virgil, Ovid, Homer, Lucan, and Statius, to give the list that he also gives towards the end of *Troilus*, and with whom, though modestly, he there associates himself. Chaucer does not make exclusive claims for literature, but he includes within it scientific, philosophical, and historical learning, as well as humour. For all its self-mocking comedy *The House of Fame* asserts the dignity of poetry. Even the Retraction of his 'translations and inditings of wordly vanities' at the end of *The Canterbury Tales* is based on the biblical 'All that is written is written for our doctrine'.

The third general factor in Chaucer's achievement that is to be attributed to the influence of 'the European literary mind' is his use of rhetoric. It is well known that he refers, half-mockingly, to Geoffrey of Vinsauf, in *The Nun's Priest's Tale*, written fairly late in life. Professional rhetoricians are rarely the best poets; just as the best trainers are rarely the best football players. For all that, rhetoric is important to Chaucer. The English rhyming romances of the earlier fourteenth century are innocent of all save the most elementary rhetorical devices, that are practically inseparable from the mere ability to make oneself understood. *The Book of the Duchess* has absorbed a good deal of rhetoric direct from Machaut, as for example in the portrait of the Lady already quoted, but it is mainly rhetoric by translation, and almost, as it were, by accident. *The House of Fame* is a rather similar case, even with the stirring sense of the high status of poetry; though here an important source is Dante. With *The Parliament of Fowls* all is different. Chaucer has broken away from the 'octosyllabic' line of the romances and of his earlier poems, and uses the fuller-breathed 'decasyllabic'. This enables him to begin the poem with a most artful and elaborate first stanza, full of rhetorical devices.[1] Rhetoric is well used; the sense of the speaking voice is never lost, communication never breaks down, and Chaucer in fact preserves the sense of his own personal presentation of the poem more vividly even than is done in the romances. It is possible even for those who think that poetry should speak sincerely from the heart to respond to such a beginning. Historically speaking it is a moment as exciting for English literature as *The Book of the Duchess*, which introduced such a mass of new material to English poetry. If *The Book of the Duchess* marks a new direction, *The Parliament* marks 'the point of take-off'; the fully-fledged flight begins. Rhetoric is not the end of poetry, and Chaucer comes to much more subtle uses of it, including the knowledge of when to refrain from ornamentation, but rhetoric is the art of writing, and here Chaucer shows a mastery in English verse that had not been seen in English since *Beowulf*. From this poem onwards Chaucer's mastery is complete, and goes beyond his masters, sometimes with a Shakespearian casualness and carelessness. Later essays in this book explore part of that mastery. Prose is a slightly different story, and to that we must now turn.

Prose, just as much as verse, is a formalisation of the spoken language. In some ways, because it has an even greater need of the physical basis of pens, ink, paper, or their equivalent, prose is even more artificial than verse. Hence it usually appears in history long after verse, and has a different relation to the general culture. Prose is closer to writing and depends on the diffusion of formal book-education and the preservation of libraries. It is essentially the instrument of an educated class, of administrators, teachers, scholars, scientists, philosophers, and so forth. An illiterate peasantry or aristocracy may have verse; they cannot have prose. Therefore prose is an index to the general level of intellectual culture as verse may not be. It is even more dependent than verse on the efforts of many men over a long period—that is, on a

[1] Cf. Brewer, ed. cit.

tradition—because it is not so easily memorised. For this reason Chaucer's prose, regarded as an instrument of communication, is at a disadvantage compared with his verse. It is common to find his verse easier to understand than his prose. English vernacular prose was a less practised instrument in his time, and Chaucer was among the pioneers of its use. Yet in recognising this we must not oversimplify. That Chaucer could write prose at all was in itself due to a tradition in vernacular English, and in French, Latin and Italian. This tradition could be much more sophisticated than a simple-minded modern may realise. Chaucer's prose is also difficult to understand because it arises out of this special tradition, which was very highly mannered, as Professor Schlauch shows in a later essay (below, p. 140). Though such formal prose was more or less familiar in Europe for two thousand years, its forms have now almost completely dropped from ordinary educated consciousness. Even more than verse we tend to value prose for its 'natural' expression, forgetting the years of schooling and the evidences of conscious and unconscious imitation in all our writing. The object of the next few paragraphs is to sketch in briefest outline the historical conditions that affected Chaucer's writing of prose.

As with verse, we must first make a distinction between the native vernacular on the one side, and Latin on the other. To take the vernacular first; what has been said about the English language in connection with verse naturally holds good in general for prose. At the time of the Conquest English prose was the most developed and flexible among European vernaculars. It was the instrument of government, of historiography, of various new kinds of imaginative literature, to some extent of education. The eventual substitution of French and the increase of Latin in the administrative and educational systems after the Conquest naturally weakened vernacular prose. The English *Chronicle* went out in a blaze of passion at Peterborough about 1160. But as R. W. Chambers long ago pointed out in his famous essay,[1] because

[1] R. W. Chambers, *On the Continuity of English Prose*, 1932. That there is true continuity of prose style, as argued by Chambers, is not part of my argument and would not be accepted by most scholars today. See especially R. M. Wilson, 'On the continuity of English Prose', *Mélanges de Linguistique et de Philologie*:

religious education had to be carried on, religious prose continued to be written in English. The authors were all clerics; they instructed the ignorant in the elements of the faith, they stimulated devotion and aquiescence. On their labours depended much of the maintenance of society and the progress of civilisation. Yet for all its value as a foundation such a tradition was limited in range of information, variety of purpose, and especially in intellectual challenge. Sometimes its limitations are reflected in a pedestrian style, but by no means always. The need, the passionate desire, the imperious demand, to communicate the message of salvation, often challenged the writer or speaker to heighten his style and employ all the devices of effective communication. The homiletic style in the vernacular, borrowing from the more sophisticated medieval Latin of the Church, learnt to employ all the artifices of oratory and persuasion, from the colours of rhetoric to the playing on conscious rhythms. When such potentialities of style united with genius and learning in the writer, and with an audience worthy of him, English vernacular prose could rise, as it did with *Ancrene Wisse* written for three well-born young ladies about 1200, to heights of artistry unequalled in English till the seventeenth century, while in the fourteenth century the writings of Richard Rolle and his followers, and of such mystics as Walter Hilton, achieved remarkably rich effects. Such works were meant for audiences with special interests, well-educated, on whom unusually high literary demands could be made, as is no doubt always the case with outstanding works of literature. Here were shown the possibilities of English prose. But the rather specialised circumstances left aside the majority of lay people.

Eventually there came a broadening of interest, due in the first place to the Church itself, in its care for men's minds as well as for their souls. Throughout the thirteenth and fourteenth centuries an enormous educational effort was made by the Church to increase the literacy which is fundamental to Christianity. In the middle of the fourteenth century at least one and probably more of the grammar schools in England changed their language of

---

Fernand Mossé In Memoriam, Paris 1959; and N. Davis, 'Styles in English Prose of the Late Middle and Early Modern periods', *Langue et Littérature*: *Bibliothèque de l'Université de Liège*, CLXI, Paris 1961, which I have not seen.

instruction from French to English. It seems very likely that the new currents in English literary culture, and especially in prose, that became apparent towards the end of the century were due to the cumulative effects of education, and especially to the education of laymen in English. Two main currents in English prose can be distinguished here, each rising from greater literacy among laymen.

The first new current is the appearance of vernacular prose on secular matters. An outstanding instance is the circular letter which was issued by John Ball at the time of the Peasants' Revolt in 1381.[1] It is mostly in prose, though part is in doggerel verse. What peasants were these, who could read and recognise the enigmatic and lightly allegorical style of this letter? Other examples of secular prose are Trevisa's translation of the thirteenth-century Latin encyclopaedia of Bartholomew the Englishman, and his translation of Higden's Latin history, the *Polychronicon*. Scientific prose, often well written, begins to appear. Chaucer is well to the front in these new developments, with the moral and political tract, *The Tale of Melibeus*, the scientific work *The Astrolabe*, and, if his, *The Equatorie of the Planetis*.[2]

Besides new secular subject-matter in English prose, we find another new current; the writing of religious prose by laymen. Such a development had already taken place in French and Anglo-Norman prose. When it took place in English it had far-reaching effects on the whole of later English history. The outstanding instance is the literature of Lollardy. Some of this may indeed have been written by clerics, but the force behind Lollardy was the working of lay minds, literate in English but not in Latin, passionately interested in religion, demanding access to the Bible, intellectually alert, yet not committed to the ecclesiastical intellectual tradition, which was, of course, in Latin. Such a movement can easily be conceived as arising from the Church's programme of elementary education in English. Many other forces coincided with the new lay spirituality. Wycliffe's honest, stubborn, polemical mind reflected from the scholastic side the new laity's

[1] Ed. K. Sisam, *Fourteenth Century Verse and Prose*, 1921.
[2] *The Equatorie of the Planetis*, ed. D. J. Price, 1955. The introduction briefly comments on other scientific writing of the period.

difficulties with doctrine, and he gave the movement an intellectual background, as well as inspiration for translating the Bible. English religious prose of the late fourteenth century suddenly woke up to sharp questioning and intellectual debate. Lollardy was a very complex movement, but there seems little doubt that the Bible in English, and the intellectual use of English prose, were very near the heart of it. The time was not quite ripe enough for such a degree of literacy as Anglicanism presupposes. At all events Lollardy was driven underground by persecution, until, as recent research seems to suggest, it joined up again in the sixteenth century with Continental movements which, through Wycliffe's influence on Huss, it had itself helped to inspire. With the Reformation it was finally possible in England to read the Bible in English without being burnt as a heretic.

It is natural for us, in view of such great issues, to notice the polemical prose especially. It was, however, accompanied by a quantity of less polemical religious prose which was ultimately perhaps more central and of equal importance. Such prose was certainly a testimony of the new spirit of enquiring lay spirituality, but it was not as revolutionary as so much Lollard prose. Its audience may well have been in part the audience who read *Piers Plowman* (which is hostile to Lollardy, though often similar in spirit), and included those who read the numerous volumes of entirely orthodox sermons produced in English, especially in the fifteenth century.[1] The tone of such prose is moralistic and devotional, like that of earlier sermons. Usually there is nothing remarkable about it, except that in a few cases we know for certain that the author was a layman and even a courtier. The outstanding example, of course, is Chaucer, as usual in the forefront of the developing literary culture of his day. Chaucer's genius and position in life make *The Parson's Tale* well worth reading today, both for its own sake and for what it tells us about the culture of his time. Chaucer was not alone except in his genius. Another example of the same tendencies is provided by the work of Sir John Clanvowe (1341-91), who probably wrote *The Cuckoo and the Nightingale*, better entitled *The Book of Cupid*, the best

[1] Cf. G. R. Owst, *Preaching in Medieval England*, 1926, and *Literature and Pulpit in Medieval England*, 1933.

English Chaucerian poem that is not by Chaucer.[1] Clanvowe was a contemporary of Chaucer's; certainly his disciple and associate; probably his friend. He was a member of a group of courtiers of a new type who made their careers at court, were given financial rewards, and were not feudal retainers. With considerable political and administrative responsibility they combined a taste for literature and Lollardy. This group, long known as 'the Lollard knights', were among Chaucer's closer associates. Clanvowe wrote more than *The Cuckoo and the Nightingale*. He also wrote, there is no reasonable doubt, the treatise ascribed to him in University College, Oxford, MS 97, so far not printed, and entitled *De Duabis Viis*.[2] In this he seems to identify himself as a Lollard, but essentially it is a moralising tract of no particular originality, written against the Devil, the Flesh, and the World, especially as summed up in that courtly life which all the other evidence would have suggested that he lived contentedly to the full. Not surprising in itself, it is astonishing for its authorship, and should make us look with fresh eyes at Chaucer, that truly remarkable phenomenon of learned, lay, devout, literacy. We shall realise anew that Chaucer wrote (mostly, to be sure, as translation) a considerable amount of religious prose, some of it now lost.

Clanvowe's prose, historically remarkable though it be, lacks distinction when compared with Chaucer's. Clanvowe lacks Chaucer's genius, and also the learning and art which Chaucer's genius enabled him to acquire. Clanvowe, for example, shows no deep knowledge of Latin. Chaucer's Latin may have been of the kind that—the Bible apart—always welcomed cribs in French or even in Italian, but he drew copiously on Latin writing of all periods of its greatness from the first century B.C. to the twelfth century A.D. Within the limits of his day he was, like most great poets, an astonishingly learned man, though not in the strict sense a scholar. With prose, as with verse, it was not merely a question of taking over subject-matter, but also of style. In so far as this

---

[1] Ed. W. W. Skeat, *Chaucerian Pieces*, 1897, and in an as yet unpublished Birmingham Dissertation, 1963, by V. J. Scattergood. Biographical details are collected by Scattergood, and found also in W. T. Waugh 'The Lollard Knights', *Scottish Historical Review*, XI (1913) 55-120.

[2] Transcribed by V. J. Scattergood, Birmingham Diss., 1963, pp. 226ff.

concerns vocabulary much the same is true of his prose as is true, *mutatis mutandis*, of his verse. According to Mersand, nearly a fifth of the words ultimately derived from Latin that are used in the translation of Boethius's *Consolation of Philosophy* are here used in English for the first time.[1] But there is another important aspect of prose style which has hardly ever received due attention in modern English. This is the deliberate use of certain prose rhythms well established in medieval Latin prose, but not often recognised in English. Here is the mannered prose that has been mentioned earlier.

The chief structural principle of prose rhythm lies in controlling the rhythm of the last part of a clause.[2] The orators of classical antiquity recognised and practised the art of rhythmical prose, whose theory was preserved for the Middle Ages by the rhetoricians and such well-known text-books as Martianus Capella's *De Nuptiis Philologiae et Mercurii*. Medieval men gave the art a characteristically practical turn by employing it especially for the Latin letter-writing of ecclesiastical and secular chancelleries. From the eleventh century onwards, especially in Italy, but all over Europe, a succession of instructional books were issued to help Latin secretaries write rhythmical prose. The instructions concentrated particularly on the various patterns of sound to be used in ending a clause, such rhythmical patterns being called *cursus*. The rhetoricians who had helped to elaborate the styles of verse in the late twelfth and thirteenth centuries also wrote on prose style. Geoffrey of Vinsauf wrote a *Scientiae Epictularis*, of which three manuscripts are extant in England, though none in France. John of Garland in his *Poetria* discusses also prose and its rhythms, distinguishing various types. He makes the familiar point, which Chaucer also makes in the preface to *The Astrolabe*, that style should be adapted to the persons who are being addressed. John also distinguishes technical prose, narrative prose (*hystorialis*), dictamen (the style used in courts and universities) and rhythmical prose (used in ecclesiastical writing). By the end of the fourteenth

---

[1] Op. cit., p. 67.
[2] What follows is based on M. Schlauch 'Chaucer's Prose Rhythms', *PMLA* LV (1950) 568-89, and N. Denholm-Young, 'The Cursus in England', in *Collected Papers on Medieval Subjects*, 1946, 26-55.

century in England the use of the *cursus* had become familiar in
Latin writing; a number of different patterns were recognised.
Stressed and unstressed syllables, not long and short syllables (as
in classical Latin) were accepted as forming the pattern, and the
differences between the various vernaculars, and the national
variants of medieval Latin, seem to have been at least partly noted.
Mr Denholm-Young comments on the popularity of the *cursus*:
'The modern contrast between the spoken and the written word
was unknown: the rhythm of a letter did not differ from that of
speech. This helps to explain the great popularity of the Cursus,
which reveals and elucidates the structure of the spoken sentence.
Not the papal chancery alone, but anyone who wished to issue a
manifesto, to write an important letter, or anyone who thought
he was writing literature, would employ it.'[1] One might wish to
qualify 'speech' here as 'formal speech', but the closeness of
literature to the spoken word is important.

Chaucer, an experienced diplomat, friend of many learned men
like the 'philosphical Strode', must have known, and had his ears
tuned, to the rhythm of *cursus*. His reference to *cadence* (in *The
House of Fame*, l. 623) suggests that he means rhythmic prose,
though this has been disputed.[2] Other writers of English prose,
like Rolle, earlier in the century had unquestionably used it. Of
course, the rhythms of English prose are not entirely similar to
those of Latin prose, and Chaucer must have made a fairly free
adaptation. There are difficulties of knowing degrees of stress;
where the stress fell in many words; whether final *-e* was pronounced in the prose; just as there are similar difficulties in
understanding Chaucer's verse metres. Even so, the general picture that Professor Schlauch draws of Chaucer's deliberate use of
rhythmical prose is convincing. There are examples of rhythmical
prose in English after Chaucer—for example, in the Prayer Book,
and in the writings of Sir Thomas Browne. No doubt our ears
recognise these cadences unconsciously, and certainly neither the
liturgy nor Sir Thomas Browne have lacked praise for their
rhythms, but our failure to recognise the consciously artistic
nature of such effects deprives us of one of the more sophisticated

[1] Art. cit. p. 44-5.
[2] Cf. P. F. Baum, *Chaucer's Verse*, North Carolina 1961, 5ff.

pleasures of the art of prose. Our difficulties are the greater in that we live in an age in which the fashion is for the short, unmodulated sentence, and flat, plain words. Other aspects of prose style apart from rhythm are, however, more easily recognised, and these, as discussed in Professor Schlauch's essay, need no introduction.

The earlier poems

JOHN LAWLOR

I

CHAUCER'S earlier poems present distinct problems. We know—or think we know—where we are with a work like *Troilus and Criseyde*, complete in design and clear in its refusal to pass judgment; or with the varied matter, comic and realistic or tender and pathetic by turns, of *The Canterbury Tales*. But what are we to make of the mixture of comedy with elegy in *The Book of the Duchess*; or the marked shift from Book I of *The House of Fame*, a dutiful recital of familiar story, to the comic and sometimes enigmatic events of the rest of the poem— a poem, moreover, unfinished? Even where the going is simpler, in *The Parliament of Fowls*, the matter, as we may discover under learned guidance, can be mightily complex; and where the poems are short, as in *Anelida* and *Mars*, we may find it hard to assess with any confidence their designed scope and distinctive effect. 'Explanations' which, in the end, tell us no more than that we are to accept these characteristics will not serve. Should we then treat these early works as poems *sui generis*, and withhold, for the moment, any comparison between them and later work? Yet there are certainly some relevant lessons in the critical history of *Troilus and Criseyde* and *The Canterbury Tales*. With both works, we have had to learn to attend by laying aside certain pre- dispositions. In *Troilus and Criseyde* we have grown aware of the presence and varied activity of a narrator who in the course of the telling moves away from dependence upon his authorities to growing realisation that the truth of the story is not so simple as they had made out. A responsible criticism must now concern itself with the overall balance of the poem, the varying weight of emphasis between the received story and the narrator's reactions to it, until in the end the story is referred back to its sources and the last perspective is one of entire release from a story that has grown too difficult to tell. Or, in *The Canterbury Tales*, some awareness of the rhetoric of the tales, in its widely varying degrees, has brought the realisation that tale and teller are not so simply or consistently related as had sometimes been assumed. Instead of the complex drama of many narrators on their 'movable stage'[1] we may see more clearly the width and variety of Chaucer's narrative art.

This would suggest that the way forward with these early poems is to examine them as narrative art, that art being conceived in terms of the relation of the narrator to a small audience, to whom the poet is a familiar entertainer, not a remote and unknown 'author' whose personality can emerge, if at all, only in the silent traffic of minds over the pages of a printed book. This art is unlike that of the novel or the drama. In the novel, since 'all must be told, for nothing can be shown' the artist's task goes beyond that of the dramatist, for he must 'describe the tone, the look, the gesture, with which [the characters'] speech was accompanied— telling, in short, all which, in the drama, it becomes the province of the actor to express'.[2] A poet who reads to a select audience can supply tone, look, and gesture at need; and these will serve as the readiest means to varying the perspectives of his telling, so that now he can come very close to his audience, addressing them directly, now mark his departure from them by growing absorption in his story or by stubborn clinging to a conviction (often with cheerful *naiveté*, as befits the actual status of the poet) which the course of his story may show to be ill-founded. This allows a subtle and highly variable range of effect, mixing grave and gay with a rapidity that may strike us as bewildering. It makes for a flexibility that knits together discontinuous and sometimes apparently discordant elements; and it can confer an entire simplicity to sustain the story at moments of crisis.

For developed instances we may draw on two passages in *Troilus and Criseyde*. First, there is a gently jocular effect when the

---

[1] See R. M. Lumiansky, *Of Sondry Folk, The Dramatic Principle in the Canterbury Tales*, Austin 1955, esp. pp. 15-28.

[2] Scott, quoted by Wayne C. Booth, *The Rhetoric of Fiction*, Chicago 1961, p. 2.

audience's potential distance from the standpoint of the hero must be humorously corrected:

> And forthi if it happe in any wyse,
> That here be any lovere in this place
> That herkneth, as the story wol devise,
> How Troilus com to his lady grace,
> And thenketh, 'so nold I nat love purchace',
> Or wondreth on his speche or his doynge,
> I noot; but it is me no wonderynge.
>
> II 29-35

The mimicry 'so nold *I* nat love purchace' draws its smile; and the audience is ready to accept the poet's lead, 'it is me no wonderynge'.[1] This mild shepherding of the audience into attention affords as good an instance as any of the tone and temper of the narrator as we ordinarily meet him throughout Chaucer's work. Greater emphasis can be gained at need—for example, in the companion-piece to this passage. This time the narrator must quite firmly head off the potential cynic in his audience, since now it is Criseyde who has begun to feel the onset of love, and any wisdom before the event must be stopped at the source. If anyone would murmur

> 'This was a sodeyn love; how myght it be
> That she so lightly loved Troilus,
> Right for the firste syghte, ye, parde?'—

then the poet must roundly reply

> Now whoso seith so, mote he nevere ythe!
> ibid. 667-70

If the capital problem of the novelist is to achieve and sustain an intimacy of effect with his solitary reader, the task of the oral narrator can be precisely the opposite—to win a measure of distance from the small, known audience, to express deepening

---

[1] Cf. Aage Brusendorff, *The Chaucer Tradition*, Copenhagen 1925, pp. 23-5, who suggests that MS Cambridge Corpus Christi College 61 was transcribed at the bidding of Joan, wife of Ralph Neville, earl of Westmorland, from a family copy of *Troilus and Criseyde* 'originally executed for her father, John of Gaunt, probably in the eighties, and sumptuously decorated with pictures of which the frontispiece showed the author reciting his poem at court'. Of these pictures, only the 'frontispiece' survives in the Corpus MS.

concern, troubled awareness of impending events, or final exaltation—as well as the more familiar gamut of cheerful haplessness, the varying fortunes of a bookish and woefully inexperienced servant of love whose predicaments will certainly amuse and, skilfully handled, may even surprise his benevolent audience. If we approach the earlier poems with this in mind we may see the groundwork of a narrative art which criticism has yet to assess adequately in Chaucer's career as a whole.

II

The usefulness of a dream-convention will be immediately apparent. It serves as a point of departure, and so gives room for manoeuvre; a chance, as it were, to open the range and therefore increase the scope of tactical opportunism, the narrator's freedom to move in on his audience in a variety of ways, some familiar, some totally surprising. *The Book of the Duchess* begins with the poet in an altogether accepted role.[1] He is sleepless, and this, being against Nature, can, if persisted in, end only in death (ll. 1-29). These opening lines sound, of course, as a gentle reminder to John of Gaunt to turn from unremitting mourning; at the same time, they are a covert plea for acceptance of this intrusion upon sorrow. The poet, being himself deep in grief, can become a substitute-figure for the real mourner.[2] What is beyond praise is that the story that follows is enacted by the narrator, Chaucer's skill supplying dialogue, tone, look, and gesture for both participants— the 'I' of the story and the mourner he meets, poet and patron each set in acceptable distance from actuality. It is the first foothold; once it is secure, Chaucer moves in to lighten the tension, and to plant the hint of something which will come to serve as a measure of all success and happiness. The narrator is —it is the accepted role—an unrequited lover; there is no prospect of his eight years' hopeless service being crowned with success. Only one can heal him; but her verdict is a foregone conclusion. Poor poet; not for him to know love's successes—

[1] On the dreamer in Chaucer and Gower, and a comparison with Langland, see my *Piers Plowman, an Essay in Criticism*, London 1962, pp. 286-91, 294, 297, 311.
[2] For the psychology of 'substitution', see Bertrand H. Bronson, 'The Book of the Duchess Re-opened', *PMLA*, LXVII (1952) 863-81, esp. 870-2.

so let us return to the story (ll. 30-43). For a moment there has been a glimpse of unattainable happiness; immediately we turn back to reality. The poet takes a book to 'drive the night away', and he rehearses the tale of 'Seys' and 'Alcyone'. It is appropriate that the poet should re-tell a familiar story; his dependence is upon *auctoritee*. But in the telling, and in the after-thoughts upon it, we begin to see a gap widening between the teller's understanding of his tale, and the significance the tale may plainly have for its present audience. In the tale, the longing to see again the dead one is fulfilled; but there is a direct implication in the departed husband's words to his wife:

> Awake! let be your sorwful lyf!
> For in your sorwe ther lyth no red.
> For, certes, swete, I nam but ded—

finishing with the brief but poignant truth:

> To lytel while oure blysse lasteth!
> ll. 44-211

Yet immediately the narrator counters this heartfelt counsel by giving his own understanding of the tale. We see him anxiously concerned not with the significance of Alcyone's vision, but with the powers that brought it about. He wishes he could propitiate any deity—Morpheus, Juno, 'Or som wight elles, I ne roghte who'—who could guarantee him sleep. The point is broadened into humorous desperation; he vows to give a featherbed and all the appurtenances of a bed-chamber. Behold! his wish is granted, and it leads to a dream of his own, more wonderful than any, and hardly capable of interpretation (ll. 212-90).

These are all, in a sense, the preliminaries of the story. The dreamer has been established as one whose concern is with the hopelessness of unrequited love; and that concern can make him curiously unaware of what is plain to all men else—as the simple moral of the story he has just told. In the long colloquy that follows, the dreamer draws out his woeful knight, by probing the nature of a love that is claimed as perfect. The matter is brought for judgment, as in the two poems of Machaut which are recalled, for some at least of the audience, by the *débat* between a poet-inquirer and the one who has experienced loss; and the tension is between loss by death and loss by infidelity.[1] The dreamer is satisfied at last upon the major point—no love is to be compared with the knight's, in its slow and beautiful development culminating in the lady's acceptance of the love-suit as an act of her free grace, 'The noble yifte of hir mercy' (no taint of merit hangs about this salvation), and the lady's taking the lover 'in hir governaunce'. Love is possible only to the gentle, and, manifestly, it makes them gentler yet.[2] The telling of past happiness has no doubt assuaged present grief; and the balance of nature, between a perfected happiness and the allotted time it has to run ('To lytel while oure blysse lasteth!'), has been nowhere stated but is everywhere implied. Now the poet pays his last tribute. The audience must return to the present, and to a time for endurance which, while it is not yet over, will be more bearable if it is frankly faced ('For in your sorwe there lyth no red'). Now the inquirer has forgotten all questions of greater or less in love. He asks only to be told where this wonderful lady is: and the reply, with its astonished counter-question, returns us to reality:

'She ys ded!' 'Nay!' 'Yis, be my trouthe!'
'Is that youre los? Be God, hyt ys routhe!'

The substitute-figure, absorbed first in his own grief, and then in testing, doctrinaire-fashion, the happiness claimed, serves the poet's last purpose by his entire forgetfulness. A dreamer who could see no future prospect of his own happiness learns—and in the learning makes plain to the poet's audience—that the knight's happiness is at once perfect, and wholly past. Immediately, the

---

[1] The poems are *Jugement dou Roy de Behaingne* and *Jugement dou Roy de Navarre*. Their significance in this context is discussed in my essay, 'The Pattern of Consolation in *The Book of the Duchess*', *Speculum*, XXXI (1956) 626-48, reprinted, with some abbreviation, in *Chaucer Criticism* Vol. II, *Troilus and Criseyde and The Minor Poems*, ed. Schoeck and Taylor, Notre Dame 1961, pp. 232-60.

[2] Love is 'from one point of view the flower, from another the seed, of all those noble usages which distinguish the gentle from the vilein' (C. S. Lewis, *The Allegory of Love*, Oxford 1936, p.2). In this instance, however, there is no question of 'what the nineteenth century called "dishonourable" love' (ibid.); see my article referred to at note 1 above, esp. pp. 628-33.

dream is over, and the striking of the clock[1] marks the transition to a world which re-assembles itself under familiar names (Richmond, Lancaster and John, Blanche)—a world in which time bears all away:

> This was my sweven; now hit ys doon.

III

The poet of *The House of Fame* is, again, a dreamer; and the audience is first attuned to what is to follow by a reminder that dreams are mysterious in their origins and in their significances. Who can say for certainty, where there is so much debate? Not the poet:

> For I of noon opinion
> Nyl as now make mensyon.

It is a special standpoint, as the audience is later to discover. The dream eventually to be told will release the poet from his ordinary position of dependence upon authority, the stories that have all been told by his predecessors, and which, since his role is that of merely the latest teller from common stock, require in him dutiful obedience in the telling and a proper veneration for the great masters. However, the dream that is first told promises to be faithfully of that very kind, an ample re-telling of Virgil's *Aeneid*; and there are two notable devices that help towards this traditional end. Firstly, there is an invocation which by its sing-song, spell-making character lulls the audience into habitual acceptance:

> And he that mover ys of al
> That is and was and ever shal . . .

This patters its way to:

> pray I Jesus God
> That (dreme he barefot, dreme he shod)
> That every harm that any man
> Hath had, syth the world began,
> Befalle hym thereof, or he sterve,
> And graunte he mote hit ful deserve!

[1] Cf. Bronson, 'Concerning Houres Twelve', *MLN*, LXVIII (1953) 515-21.

The mood is broken by an immediate change of rhythm and construction:

> Lo, with such a conclusion
> As had of his avision
> Cresus, that was kyng of Lyde . . .

But the spell has done its work: an obedient re-telling of familiar story is awaited. It is the reaction of those who, as Eliot said of a somewhat different audience, 'expect to be patiently bored' and who will be satisfied 'with the feeling that they have done something meritorious'.[1] This effect is reinforced in the telling itself. Everywhere the poet is external to his material; he is the spectator of the 'table of bras' recording Virgil's proem:

> I wol now singen, yif I kan,
> The armes, and also the man . . .

and each successive episode is introduced by the phrase 'I saw'. ('First sawgh I', 'I saugh next', 'Ther saugh I', 'Ther sawgh I grave', etc.) What the dreamer beholds is fixed, unchangeable, enshrined in 'a temple ymad of glas'.

It is understandable that there is a sense of relief and of enlargement when the dreamer leaves the temple. Now he can look around:

> I faste aboute me beheld . . .

But if the prospect is unlimited, it is featureless:

> a large feld
> As fer as that I myghte see,
> Withouten toun, or hous, or tree,
> Or bush, or grass, or eryd lond.

This barren landscape is indeed a halting-point for the audience. What comes next? They are used to a tradition of dream-poetry in which the transition from awaking within the dream to the beginning of major action is covered by the advent of a Friendly Animal. But here nothing lives or moves:

> Ne no maner creature
> That ys yformed by Nature
> Ne sawgh I, me to rede or wisse.

[1] *Poetry and Drama*, London 1951, p. 23.

The situation is arresting. All is ready for a strange and new thing: and down from the heavens it comes, as strange a Friendly Animal as any that Chaucer's audience had ever heard of—a golden eagle, of dazzling brightness and immense size.[1]

With the descent of the eagle, one established order of poetry is changed as only a master can change it. The expectations of the audience are simple enough—and they may appear to us less as expectations than as exactions. The audience wants (or has been trained to want) the re-telling of a familiar story; and they have a comfortable preference for length and miscellaneity. The poet must be encyclopaedic; he will not easily bore his audience, but he must be properly reverential before them and their established gods. His role is that of a dependant—upon his 'bokes', the pre-existing stories, and, in actuality, upon his audience's favour. However often the tables may be turned as the story reaches unexpected climaxes or steers to unusual ends, the relation between audience and narrator is, unalterably, *de haut en bas*, tolerance (with, we need not doubt, proper affection) towards a licensed entertainer. Chaucer's art can be epitomised as his resourcefulness in not altering or minimising this relationship, but turning it unfailingly to good account. He is an artist who has found in the necessary standpoint and the ordinary expectations of his audience a region of challenge; exhilaration and humour are the marks of his response. In *The House of Fame* the weights of convention—the encyclopaedic-didactic demand; the dutiful posture of the poet re-telling from common stock; and the self-ridicule which is the established form of grotesque relief in this monumental architecture—all are lifted with marvellous ease. For it is the eagle who is determinedly loquacious; 'Geoffrey Chaucer' is veritably his pupil, and so backward a pupil that the argument must go beyond instruction to demonstration. The plight first of a helpless listener, in peril of his own skin during

---

[1] J. L. Lowes comments on the metamorphosis of Machaut's lion (resembling, in his docility, *un petit chiennet*) into the fawning puppy of *The Book of The Duchess* (*Geoffrey Chaucer*, London 1934, pp. 98-9). The eagle of *The House of Fame* illustrates a comparable transformation—though this time from awe-inspiring outward appearance (an impression shared by both Chaucer and Dante, whose wheeling eagle is *terribil come folgor, Purg.* IX 29) to a comically insistent loquacity which is all Chaucer's own.

the flight, and then of a frustrated and finally irritated seeker, releases the narrator from tight control over the story. Now the dreamer is the patient of events all can follow without prompting from the 'I' of the story.

The content of Books II and III, considered as science-fiction, deserves a word to itself. When I first read Chaucer's poem I recognised the essential principle of a magazine story I had read and forgotten a good many years ago. In the magazine version (written long before supersonic flight was seriously envisaged) two inventive young men had come to the conclusion that if a vehicle could be designed capable of travelling faster than sound it should be possible to recover past speech. Beginning in a modest way with the Gettysburg Address, they were soon able to pick up Queen Elizabeth's oration to her troops at Tilbury; and, I think, got fairly quickly on to King John addressing the assembly at Runnymede. The reader left them, I believe, tuning in to the Sermon on The Mount. I still don't remember how it ended. Clearly, the ending of any story in which 'invention', in this sense, plays the largest part, is the great difficulty. After so exciting a start (the promise of the marvel to come, if only it can be managed), and a satisfying middle (the marvel in action), the end is likely to be unmemorable anti-climax. Chaucer, at any rate, one feels, is not finding it easy to manoeuvre his poem to a satisfactory conclusion. His beginning is brilliant. The poet has served love after his fashion—a bookish service,

> To make bookys, songes, dytees,
> In ryme, or elles in cadence—

so it will receive an appropriate *guerdon*—not the yielding of any lady, but the true, the only, 'copy' for a writer, the actual sounds as they are finally lodged in the place of their 'kyndely enclynyng'. The poet will, for once, be freed from dependence upon the authorities, the books which he must pore over in Aldgate. Now he may know by experience, rarest of opportunities. It is indeed 'a wonder thyng', and after his instruction by the affably condescending eagle in Book II, the dreamer is all agog. But the cataloguing of wonders begins to tail off, and the unconvincing *occupatio* begins to multiply—from

> What shuld I make lenger tale
> Of alle the pepil y ther say,
> Fro hennes into domes day?

through

> Men myghte make of hem a bible
> Twenty foot thykke, as I trowe,

to

> Loo! how shulde I now telle al thys?

which leads to the comic 'alienation-effect' of contrasting imagined gold with the speaker's actual empty purse:

> As fyn as ducat in Venyse,
> Of which to lite al in my pouche is.

The narrator is here external to his material, for the dreamer has become a spectator who now dutifully peers (as he did in Book I) at the 'pilers' crowned by the major poets. This is followed by action around the throne of Fame as successive companies of petitioners seek her favour. The clamour dissolves after a final petitioner, 'that ylke shrewe'

> That brende the temple of Ysidis
> In Athenes,

has been granted his boon. Fame, we see, is even-handed in her justice:

> as gret a fame han shrewes
> Though hit be for shrewednesse,
> As goode folk han for godnesse.

What next? A friendly, or at least an authoritative, guide is clearly needed. But when he appears he is slow in understanding the dreamer's predicament; and the energy of the dreamer's protest overflows into comedy. He came, he says,

> Somme newe tydynges for to lere—

But now he would be content with anything at all—only let it be 'newe thinges'. All he has seen so far has only confirmed what he already knew. His guide takes him to 'Domus Dedaly, That Loboryntus cleped ys'; and with the help of the eagle, now returned and magniloquent as ever, the dreamer is deposited within its spinning structure, where rumour spreads with lightning speed. There at last, in a far corner, is the 'gret noyse' and pell-mell confusion, each treading the other down, of those who tell 'love-tydynges'. Here is the centre of the narrator's own labyrinth. How to carry the story forward—and homeward? Enter 'A man of gret auctorite . . .'; and the poem breaks off.

In it, Chaucer has shown his first considerable powers in writing accurate dialogue, ranging from the eagle's jocular condescension and self-delighting orotundity to varying notes of direct speech, whether monosyllabically fearful, dutifully inquiring, or comically petulant. These characteristics of his poetic art will be discussed below (Section V) along with *Anelida* and *Mars*. In terms of narrative art, a way forward has been found to characterise the dreamer in some detail, by vividly humorous emphasis upon his role as patient or victim, and, in due course, a transition from hapless acquiescence, through renewed curiosity, to growing irritation. By these means the author is enabled to vary tempo and interest, mediating the content of an 'aerial ascent' story through a dreamer whose anxieties and doubts are skilfully used to counter any flagging interest on the part of the audience. The dreamer here, as in *The Book of the Duchess*, is a figure touched with gentle ridicule. But there is a reversal of roles. This time it is the dreamer who must encounter both comfortable self-possession and well-meant but inadequate kindness in his interlocutors.

III

In *The Parliament of Fowls* there is no incompleteness, no final confusion, no manifest disproportion between the dreamer's needs and his guide's capacity. The opening stanza is miraculously poised. Here is that quiet exaltation, an open-handed acceptance of life as it unalterably is, which is the individual and unmatched mark of Chaucer's workmanship:

> The lyf so short, the craft so long to lerne,
> Th'assay so hard, so sharp the conquerynge,
> The dredful joye, alwey that slit so yerne:
> Al this mene I by Love . . .

The note modulates at once into the familiar tone of poet-not-lover, the bookish servant not the experienced practitioner, a role that had served very different ends in *The Book of the Duchess* and *The House of Fame*—

> For all be that *I* knowe not Love in dede,
> Ne wot how that he quiteth folk here hyre,
> Yit happeth me ful ofte in bokes reede . . .

The audience is at once attuned; the court *jongleur* has taken up his familiar stance. Now there is room for both graceful allusion and broad humour, learned disquisition and tender sentiment, detached observation and playful absurdity. The standpoint is familiar; but a particular kind of delicate gravity, heard in the first stanza, is repeated in the fourth:

> For out of olde feldes, as men seyth,
> Cometh al this newe corn from yer to yere,
> And out of olde bokes, in good feyth,
> Cometh al this newe science that men lere.

Past and present are linked, not as progression, but as cyclic rebirth. The transition is made from old tales and the matter of love, to a Nature who presides over all.[1] The narrator takes up *The Dream of Scipio*, that most seminal of all works surviving from the classical past into the Middle Ages,[2] and the perspectives hinted at in the poem's opening are now developed. Life, we heard, is short; there is much to be learned—too much for one life's brief span: so man's spirit was to be nourished from 'olde bokes', as his body from 'olde feldes'. Now we see more precisely. Firstly,

> oure present worldes lyves space
> Nis but a maner deth—

and this mental enlargement has its counterpart in the proportion of

> the lytel erthe that here is,
> At regard of the hevenes quantite.

---

[1] For a detailed consideration of Nature, and her relationship to Venus, see J. A. W. Bennett, *The Parlement of Foules: an Interpretation*, Oxford 1957, pp. 107-32; and on Nature and 'Kind', ibid., pp. 194-212.

[2] A literal translation is conveniently accessible in *The Parlement of Foulys*, ed. D. S. Brewer, London 1960, pp. 133-7.

Secondly, the cyclic repetition of the Seasons ('from yer to yere') is placed in a wider background, and the argument deepens; for the grand climax will be a passing-away of all we know:

> al shulde out of mynde
> That in this world is don of al mankynde.

Man, however, is not made for death. Scipio must learn

> Know thyself first immortal.

The significance of the harmony he had heard at the outset lies in human conformity to divine order; and this is expressed in terms of law. But those who offend against that order are not merely 'breakers of the lawe'; they include 'likerous folk'. Love, we begin to see, is a fundamental principle of the universe, and its attributes are stability, steadiness of motion, over against that sickeningly purposeless rotation (to 'whirle aboute th'erthe alwey in peyne') which Dante took as epitomising the purgatorial torment of carnal sinners.[1]

The poet's work of preparation is almost done. Love is his theme, and it is love in its most solemn aspect—'an ever-fixed mark That looks on tempests and is never shaken'—conforming in its steadfastness to the order and harmony of an uncorrupted universe. Characteristically, this august note is at once modulated. In a poem which touches (however lightly, as befits St Valentine's Day) on the happiness of great ones in his audience,[2] the poet humbly makes of himself, as he did in *The Book of the Duchess*, a surrogate figure—one who, having his share of unhappiness, is best placed to voice the wonder of perfected union between others. He is

> Fulfyld of thought and busy hevynesse;
> For both I hadde thyng which that I nolde,
> And ek I nadde that thyng that I wolde.

This sentiment from Boethius has, in Chaucer's use of it elsewhere,

---

[1] *La bufera infernal, che mai non resta*, 'The hellish storm which never ceases' (*Inf.* V 31ff.). For other references to Dante, see Brewer, op. cit., pp. 45-6.
[2] If we date the poem (from the astronomical reference at ll. 117-18) as begun in May 1382, and completed in time for St Valentine's Day, 14 February, 1383, it is pleasant to suppose that King Richard and his young bride presided at its first reading (cf. Brewer, op. cit., p. 7).

only one application—to the woes of the unrequited lover, who, lacking the gift of his lady's mercy, has all that would make him wretched.[1] It is a fitting standpoint for the mere poet. With a similar lightness of touch, away from the exalted to the disarmingly unpretentious, the dream now to be told is given its true place in the Macrobian system. Preoccupation and weariness lead to a dream which repeats what was in the forefront of consciousness at the time of falling asleep. The borrowed majesty of the *oraculum* recorded by Cicero is blended, on this holiday occasion, with the amusing turns of an *insomnium*,[2] where the dreamer is victim rather than lofty observer. Once again, a bookish poet receives a bookish reward. It is a pleasantly, even deceptively, easy point of departure; and, as before, outright comedy occurs at the moment of transition. Africanus, like the eagle, shows a genial condescension; and the dreamer here, as on that other occasion, humorously despairs of setting down his strange adventures. The appeal, as before, is to the goddess of love; but now she alone, not the Muses nor Thought itself (*The House of Fame* ll. 518-28), can help the poor poet:

> Cytherea! thow blysful lady swete,
> That with thy fyrbrond dauntest whom the lest,
> And madest me this sweven for to mete,
> Be thow myn helpe in this, for thow mayst best![3]

As befits love's neophyte, the dreamer has to be encouraged ('Affrican me hente anon'), and this leads to an even more direct measure when he hovers timorously on the brink of new knowledge:

> Affrycan, my gide,
> Me hente, and *shof* in at the gates wide.

The dreamer is one who has to be brought face to face with the

---

[1] Cf. *Pity* ll. 99-104; *Complaint to his Lady*, ll. 43-5.
[2] For a convenient account of the Macrobian classification of dreams, see W. C. Curry, *Chaucer and the Medieval Sciences*, 2nd ed. New York 1960, pp. 199-202.
[3] The simplicity and clarity of this prayer to Venus, as compared with the Proem of *HF* Book II, may best be understood if we see it as giving to the mere *somnium animale* 'a touch of the *somnium coeleste*' (Curry, op. cit., p. 235). (The classification is that in common use by physicians; cf. ibid., pp. 207-8.)

true matter of love—for there can be no question of his exper-
iencing it in his own person. The point, again, is put with
humorous condescension:

> although that thow be dul,
> Yit that thow canst not do, yit mayst thow se . . .

and he is helped over the threshold:

> With that myn hand in his he tok anon,
> Of which I confort caughte, and wente in faste.

In this poem, as in those that have preceded it, a period of external
observation gives way to the direct speech of debate. But this
time it is a debate in which the dreamer takes no part; so the
setting of the 'Parliament' to come is carefully established. All the
attributes of courtly love are present, including 'Venus and hire
porter Richesse'. But 'fayrer . . . than any creature' is Nature
herself; and it is she who presides over all, the supreme representative of omnipotent order:

> the vicaire of the almyghty Lord,
> That hot, cold, hevy, lyght, moyst, and dreye
> Hath knyt by evene noumbres of acord.

The debate that follows begins on a plane of high orthodoxy.
The aristocratic birds naturally speak first; and in the noble
declaration of the first 'tersel' eagle we have the very heart of
passionate ardour as courtly love conceived it. No merit can be
claimed by the suitor; the lady is 'sovereyne', and the only plea
is one for 'merci' and 'grace' upon the predestined lover:

> syn that non loveth hire so wel as I,
> All be she nevere of love me behette,
> Thanne oughte she be myn thourgh hire mercy,
> For other bond can I non on hire knette.

It is, apparently, unanswerable. But a second 'tersel' (one 'Of
lower kynde') immediately puts his claim. As before, there can
be no appeal to merit; but this time duration of service is called
in as proof of constancy:

> at the leste I love hire as wel as ye,
> And lenger have served hire in my degre.

The simplicity of ideal love begins to disappear; and on the advent of a third claimant we begin to hear the rising clamour of impatience with any high-flown sentiment that threatens to go beyond elegant declaration:

> Now, sires, ye seen the lytel leyser heere;
> For every foul cryeth out to ben ago
> Forth with his make, or with his lady deere . . .

The distinction between 'sweetheart' and 'lady' reminds us that not all lovers have feelings as finely drawn as those we have so far heard. Time is pressing; and this suitor is not slow to turn the fact to his own account. He makes a neat application of a principle which would cut across any conceptions of proportionate reward. Courtly love can quote Scripture for its own ends; and here it is the parable 'Unto this last'[1] which underlies the proud claim:

> Of long servyse avaunte I me nothing.

The plea is, on its own level, unanswerable:

> A man may serven bet and more to pay
> In half a yer, although it were no moore,
> Than som man doth that hath served ful yoore.

It is the beginning of long debate:

> from the morwe gan this speche laste
> Tyl dounward drow the sonne wonder faste.

Now the humour broadens into outright comedy. Raucous impatience is heard, putting the plain man's case:

> 'Com of!' they criede, 'allas, ye wol us shende!
> Whan shal youre cursede pletynge have an ende?'

The sting is in the rhetorical question:

> How sholde a juge eyther parti leve
> For ye or nay, *withouten any preve*?

'Proof', the test of experience, is the other side of the medal engraved with the sovereign's head of *Auctoritee*. Now cacophony usurps on the measured tones of forensic appeal:

---

[1] 'I will give unto this last even as unto thee' (Matt. 20:14).

> The goos, the cokkow, and the doke also
> So cryede, 'Kek kek! kokkow! quek quek!' hye,
> That thourgh myne eres the noyse wente tho.

Order may be restored, but the voice of popular sentiment is all for realism and expediency. The goose's verdict is simple:

> But she wole love hym, lat hym love another!

The 'turtel trewe', that genteel little creature, may side with the high romantic line that the noble birds had taken:

> 'Nay, God forbede a lovere shulde chaunge!'
> The turtle seyde, and wex for shame al red,
> 'Though that his lady everemore be straunge,
> Yit lat hym serve hire ever, til he be ded.'

But the duck has an answer to that kind of high-mindedness:

> 'Ye quek!' yit seyde the doke, ful wel and fayre,
> 'There been mo sterres, God wot, than a payre!'

In the end, the debate must be adjourned. Let the courtly suitors serve for a further year; and, as for the rest,

> To every foul Nature yaf his make,
> By evene acord . . .

The phrase returns us to the order and symmetry revealed to Scipio; and the harmony of a stable universe is suitably echoed in song, a 'roundel' 'To don to Nature honour and plesaunce'. All ends, as it had begun, with the poet at his task of reading the 'bokes', the source of all his knowledge about love.

The Parliament is a singularly complete poem—in structure and range of effect, but, before all else, in its acceptance of a world in which *auctoritee* and *pref* have each a distinct and unchanging part. This is a holiday poem, whose audience can accept at one and the same time the filigree-work of tender sentiment, the subtleties of forensic pleading, and the comic self-composure of the unabashed realist. The poet as narrator sets down all he reads, and all he sees; and in the conclusion he returns to the fount of knowledge, his books. In the course of his *tragedie* of *Troilus* and *Criseyde*, as we saw earlier, the case is somewhat similar. When the growth of love in Criseyde's timorous heart is to be established, then the poet shows a lively awareness of the duck and goose in his own audience:

'This was a sodeyn love; how myght it be
That she so lightly loved Troilus,
Right for the firste syghte, *ye, parde?*'

It is the politer echo of 'Ye quek!' But in the *tragedie* conflict begins to grow between what the books maintain and what the narrator can see, and feel, for himself. At the climax of betrayal, what is reported, and what the narrator can *know* for himself, are poignantly but firmly disjoined—

Men seyn—I not—that she yaf hym hire herte.

In *The Parliament* we see untroubled and delighting acceptance of a world centred upon 'Nature', 'knyt by even noumbres of acord'. In *Troilus and Criseyde*

Things fall apart; the centre cannot hold;
Mere anarchy is loosed upon the world.

But the dream of *The Parliament of Fowls* was no lie; in the end of the *tragedie* no illusion remains:

Al nys but a faire,
This world, that passeth soone, as floures faire.

In the close of *The Parliament* the poet rightly returns us to the 'bokes' which have nourished his dream; for the dream is not of the world we know, but of a region where flowers are forever fair, unshadowed by any approach of night:

Th'air of that place so attempre was
That nevere was ther grevaunce of hot ne cold;
There wex ek every holsom spice and gras;
No man may there waxe sek ne old;
Yit was there joye more a thousandfold
Than man can telle; ne nevere wolde it nyghte,
But ay cler day to any manes syghte.

In such 'cler day' the poet, like any other man, has an uninterrupted and all-embracing vista of happiness.

V

The range of Chaucer's poetic skill in these poems is striking. The octosyllabics of *The Book of the Duchess* sometimes verge on that stop-and-go monotony which is the peculiar peril of an even number of syllables:

> This was the tale: There was a king . . .
>
> And byd hym that, on alle thynge,
> He take up Seys body the kyng . . .
>
> Out of hys slep, and gan to goon . . .

But more noticeable is a skill in avoiding this, by constructing the run-on line:

> And as I wente, ther cam by mee
> A whelp, that fauned me as I stood,
> That hadde yfolowed, and koude no good—

and, more impressive yet, the brisk exchanges of direct speech,

> 'Syr, th' emperour Octovyen',
> Quod he, 'and ys here faste by'.
> 'A Goddes half, in good tyme!' quod I,
> 'Go we faste!' and gan to ryde.

The first of these lines is mouth-filling, if finally under control. An ability to place the polysyllable without wrecking the line is clearly evident in the antithetical balance of the Knight's lament—

> My song ys turned to pleynynge,
> And all my laughtre to wepynge—

and here the possibilities of double rime are explored, with some effects that are not always happy:

> trewly she
> Had as moche debonairte
> As ever had Hester in the Bible,
> And more, yif more were possyble—

where bathos is almost predetermined by the struggle to match the rime-word.

A fuller effect (holding the promise of that 'aureation' which

was to mesmerise Chaucer's fifteenth-century admirers) is to be
heard in the recital of the Lady's virtues:

> To have stedefast perseveraunce,
> And esy, atempre governaunce . . .
> To holde no wyght in balaunce
> By half word ne by countenaunce . . .

This, in Chaucer's hands (though alas ! not his disciples') becomes
a highly effective mode of characterisation:

> . . . herkene wel, for-why I wille
> Tellen the a propre skille
> And a worthy demonstracion
> In myn ymagynacion.

Who can miss the eagle's satisfaction in this mouth-filling
loquacity?

> Telle me this now feythfully,
> Have I not preved thus symply,
> Withoute any subtilite
> Of speche, or gret prolixite
> Of termes of philosophie,
> Of figures of poetrie,
> Or colours of rethorike?

It is the first virtuoso-piece of its kind, drawing upon the mixed
resources of our language to establish unmistakable characterisation, and stamped with this poet's individual trick of immediate
anti-climax as the breathless recitative comes to a halt—

> Pardee, hit oughte the to lyke !

The last line neatly rounds off brilliant mimicry of the eagle, a
tour de force for any narrator, by playing directly to the poet's
actual audience the eagle's preening himself for applause. For the
moment, the audience becomes the hapless pupil and the poet his
own complacently loquacious eagle. Who can doubt that it won
a murmur of amused approval? The marvel is the ease of the thing.
Humour and tact broaden into comedy but are not submerged
by it; for the joke is, as always, on the narrator.

Skill in dialogue moves a step towards perfection when the
patient dreamer is goaded into protest:

> 'That wyl y tellen the,
> The cause why y stonde here:
> Somme newe tydynges for to lere,
> Somme newe thinges, y not what,
> Tydynges, other this or that,
> . . . wonder thynges;
> But these be so suche tydynges
> As I mene of—'

the speaker pauses: surely his questioner has grasped the point? But

> —'Noo?' quod he.
> And I answered, 'Noo, parde !'

The repetition of 'Somme' is paralleled in the long catalogue of the wonders of 'Laboryntus', each introduced by 'Of'—

> Of werres, of pes, of mariages,
> Of reste, of labour, of viages, etc.

In *Anelida and Arcite* a decasyllabic line and stately stanzaic pattern give full scope for the use of high-sounding polysyllables, placed finally (with all the obvious and exciting possibilities of multiple rime) and also medially, where the august word can act as cantilever for the whole line:

> thou Polymya,
> On *Parnaso* that with thy sustres glade,
> By *Elycon*, not far from Cirrea . . .

The line that follows—

> Singest with vois memorial in the shade—

'seems to contain within itself the germ of the whole central tradition of high poetical language in England'.[1] The other half of our tradition, a language which is (designedly) not 'high' or 'poetical', is perhaps equally evident in the pleasing simplicities of the story proper:

> Yong was this quene, of twenty yer of elde,
> Of mydel stature, and of such fairenesse
> That Nature had a joye her to behelde.

Anelida is, as Robinson observes, 'conspicuous among Chaucer's

---

[1] *The Allegory of Love*, p. 201.

writings for a tendency to poetic diction'[1]; but it is not, in its essential nature, a piece of fine writing. Rather, we may see it as a poem standing at the meeting of the ways, before the divorce between 'heigh style' and plainness threatens to be final. Here is a vein of language which allows the writer, in composing Anelida's 'compleynt', an equal ease of treatment, whether he attempts complex syntax and multiple rime—

> So thirleth with the poynt of remembraunce
> The swerd of sorowe, ywhet with fals plesaunce,
> Myn herte, bare of blis and blak of hewe,
> That turned is in quakyng all my daunce,
> My surete in awhaped countenaunce,
> Sith hit availeth not for to ben trewe

(where the funereal note is sustained by alliteration and the gauntly strange words 'thirleth', 'awhaped')—or the plangent simplicity of

> I wot myself as wel as any wight;
> For I loved oon with al myn herte and myght,
> More then myself an hundred thousand sithe.

Such a language can equally encompass the recitative-pattern of

> Now, certis, swete, thogh that ye
> Thus causeles the cause be
> Of my dedly adversyte . . .

Anelida is highly-skilled work; here is a poet whose control over his medium is virtually complete. The easy transitions which we have seen in The Parliament, from plain and at times comic assertion to exalted speech, are evidence of the same order of poetic skill.

In both The Parliament and Anelida, the presence of a narrator, a poet who comes before his audience either as participant in the action or as teller of the story, contributes to our understanding and delight. But in The Complaint of Mars we have an extended example of dramatic writing. The 'I' of the narrator plays a negligible part; he is the objective recorder. After a short and decidedly brisk proem, we settle to reported action (ll. 29-154), followed by the 'compleynt' which he overhears and sets down. This is Chaucer without the innumerable touches of a dramatised narrator, especially that dexterity of appearing and disappearing

[1] Op. cit., p. 304.

within and around the margin of the story, which have constituted
the specific and skilfully varied appeal of his work so far. Again,
Mars attempts a consistently sad, not to say lugubrious, tone.
This makes for a certain overt labour in attuning the audience's
attention:

> The ordre of compleynt requireth skylfully,
> That yf a wight shal pleyne pitously,
> There mot be cause wherfore that men pleyne—

which is unexceptionable doctrine, but sadly dull execution. This
tragic manner requires both an exclamatory mode—

> To whom shal I than pleyne of my distresse?
> Who may me helpe? Who may my harm redresse?—

and some experiment with that most dangerous of devices in
reported speech, the inset sententious reflection:

> For evermore—how dere I have hit boght! . . .
> Of riche aray—how dere men hit selle! . . .

The modern reader may ask, with Mars,

> What meneth this? What is this mystihed?

and attempts have not been lacking to find an ulterior significance
for this poem.[1] But the truth about its poetic nature is simple
enough. Chaucer is here, for once, adorning an admired species
of poetry 'with ful devout corage'. The subtle, ingenious Chaucer,
ever alert to the possibilities of inherent absurdity in the tale or
his telling of it, is no figment of latter-day imagination, however
unsuitable he may be as a father-figure of English poetry. I have
suggested that Chaucer's is an art which springs from direct
confrontation of a small audience, with whom his relationship is
that of licensed entertainer. His gifts are those proper to a training
in courts—an unerring eye for pretence, for that attempt 'to been

---

[1] John Shirley in the fifteenth century recorded the view that *Mars* alluded to a
liaison between Isabel, duchess of York and John Holland, Earl of Huntingdon.
For a recent conjecture which would link the poem with John of Gaunt and
Katherine Swynford, see George Williams, 'What is the meaning of Chaucer's
Complaint of Mars?' *JEGP*, LVII (1958) 167-76. It should be added that Mr Williams
would see *Troilus and Criseyde* as an allegorisation of the same love-affair ('Who
were Troilus, Criseyde, and Pandarus?' *Rice Institute Pamphlet*, 1957).

estatlich of manere' which, whether in actual dress and deport-
ment, or in the attempt to don the singing-robe of master-poet,
must bring disaster, if, aspiring above its station, it aims merely
'to contrefeete cheere of court'. This, the matrix of his art, is
wholly evident in the early poems; but at its highest development
that art keeps touch with its origins. Whatever his tragic work is
to be, it will not be dolefully fine writing; and with the story of
Troilus and Criseyde he succeeds beyond all expectancy or imitat-
ation. For there, in the end, is no attempt to retreat from his
audience into unsearchable authority. Towards his woeful lovers,
and more particularly to the 'sely' Criseyde, he makes what was
the first and last offering to his patron in *The Book of the Duchess*,
the gift of an entire pity through gentle ridicule of a narrator who
was wise before the event.

Mars, then, is an experiment in one mode of tragic utterance, and
that not the greatest; yet it most certainly is not all labour and
stiltedness. It comes to rest in an appeal for compassion, made in
a stanza that is among at once the most complex and the most
moving of any Chaucer ever wrote. We advance from the
simplicity of the opening address—

> And ye, my ladyes, that ben true and stable,
> Be wey of kynde, ye oughten to be able
> To have pite of folk that be in peyne—

to the reiterated and cumulative appeal of 'compleynt'—

> Compleyneth eke, ye lovers, al in-fere . . .
> Compleyneth her that evere hath had yow dere;
> Compleyneth beaute, fredom, and manere;
> Compleyneth her that endeth your labour;
> Compleyneth thilke ensample of al honour—

which modulates in the close to an unswerving simplicity:

> That never dide but al gentilesse;
> Kytheth therfore on her sum kyndenesse.

The poet's range and assurance of execution are complete. If we
wish to assess his characteristic bent, the formal beauties of *Mars*
are to be contrasted with the skilfully laboured heroics of *The
Legend of Good Women*, where a narrator under sentence by the
God of Love is dutifully obedient to the prescription to look not

at the world but into his books. There once again the narrator peeps around the margin of his penitential story to move our amusement at the uncrossable differences between *auctoritee* and *pref*. The Chaucer we come to know in the early poems is in all respects an individual and elusive poet, one whose service to the God of Love preserves a perfect, if highly unorthodox, freedom. Professor Frye has perceptively observed the Renaissance poet's preoccupation with love as with a kind of 'creative yoga'.[1] Since the Renaissance poet speaks with the voice of pretended experience, latter-day criticism has sometimes been perplexed, more particularly if it would take a 'bioliterary'[2] line, relating 'literature' to 'life' without overmuch reflection on either. The fourteenth-century poet, like his sixteenth-century descendant, takes love's anatomy as the map of the known world, the guide to his voyaging in all that is not divine. But the medieval poet's standpoint, as we see it in Chaucer, is not that of an intense explorer. Rather, it is that of the innocent abroad, a hapless figure who must be love's doctrinaire since he lives forever on the hither side of experience. This makes for a cheerful *naiveté*, and for a disarming candour which sometimes serves to divert the audience's attention from the trap which is to be sprung. But it also makes for an utter simplicity of reference to the actual situation of men and women when all illusion, whether noble or pathetic, must be laid aside; and then a narrator whose inadequacy is no secret can not only evoke but can himself enact the compassion or genial comprehension which the story, faithfully followed, may in the end require.

[1] See his contribution, 'How True a Twain', to *The Riddle of Shakespeare's Sonnets*, London 1962, pp. 25-53.
[2] The term is Professor B. A. Wright's. See his *Milton's Paradise Lost*, London 1962, especially pp. 13-40.

Troilus and Criseyde

G. T. SHEPHERD

Troilus and Criseyde is a story of love and war—a story about sex in an aggressive society. It is well to see the story plain. It is the stuff of romance in every sense of the word. When we begin the poem, we are immediately aware of the type of treatment to expect. Quickly too we become conscious of the weight and scale of the poem and of the grand ambition of the poet. We know that this was intended to be, that it was and remains a major piece of European writing. We can recall that this is the work which for three centuries at least was Chaucer's best known work, the work most closely associated with a recognition of his genius.

Yet nowadays it is easy to feel a sense of inadequacy in the reading and in a re-reading of the poem. We are like modern visitors in an old cathedral, aware in a general way of what cathedrals of this sort are about, and immediately sensible of the size, majesty and complexity of the structure, but troubled by a sense that what we see is the product of a piety different from our own, and by the suspicion that there are coherences and intentions which are no longer obvious. Frequently our notions of an antique grandeur are focused by memorable images of trivia. Rather mournfully we have to admit that a baffled astonishment and a superficial analysis may have furnished us with respectfully patronising phrases to last us all our lives.

Entry to poems, as to English cathedrals, is free. Anyone can look at what he likes and linger by what he pleases. Life is short and this poem is long. We can come and go and make all sorts of abstractions from it. And we can usually go back once more to the poem and show by book and verse that most of these abstractions are incomplete or wrong. We might, for instance, sharpen our modernity on the poem and read it as if it were a tale of

inverted sentimentality about a tearful bullyboy who could sit
and watch Pandarus laying the long string of traps to catch a
provocative Criseyde as deftly as poachers catch rabbits, and yet
himself lacked the resolution to make a clean appropriation of
the victim: and yet if we submit to the poem, we are bound to
acknowledge eventually that however unattractive Troilus may
appear, however little we approve of his role in the action, the
poem presents him unequivocally as the dominant figure, quite
wholeheartedly and admiringly as its hero. And similarly we shall
subdue at length any tendency to read Pandarus into prominence
as the one figure of sense and sanity in what, were the story a
mere scheme of incidents, might be taken as an ironic exposure
of social hypocrisy. For in the poem itself, in the Fifth Book
Pandarus shrivels to complete insignificance.

The readiest temptation perhaps is to read the whole as another
Romeo and Juliet story, as if the two young lovers stood out
stereoscopically against a hostile world. But here again we shall
observe that the ethic of the lovers is never at odds with the ethic
of their society, that neither Troilus nor Criseyde fundamentally
opposes the moral decisions towards which society drives them.
Troilus falling in love as a young man should, becomes thereby,
so we are told explicitly, more militarily useful, more socially
acceptable. The pair of lovers discussing the line of action to be
taken when Criseyde must leave Troy, reject all but the obvious
course of separation, obedient to their social duties. Criseyde's
conventional behaviour is never meant to trouble us. Rather it is
her one act of apparent spontaneity, her one lapse in decorum—
the giving of Troilus's brooch to Diomed—that is received as the
confirmation, almost as a sacramental sign of her treachery.

If we emphasise the determinism of the story and see human
endeavour completely blocked and thwarted by a Fate enforcing
a pattern of its own on to the sequence of events, the text obliges
us to acknowledge that much of the narrative is given up to
describing the ingenious contrivances by its actors which
presumably bring about events exactly as the course of Fate
requires. Crises may be ordained by the stars in their courses, as the
poet allows; the rain-storm which brings the lovers together was
marked for this purpose by the conjunction of the planets. But

Pandarus had already noted that the night was likely to be wet and planned accordingly. In a careful and engrossed reading Pandarus must appear quite as active as Fate in the development of the affair.

When the end is reached, could we really think of the story primarily as a cautionary tale for these young folk, who allow themselves to be seduced by false goods and transient pleasures? But in casting backwards from the final dazzlement of the poem, it is plain that in the Third Book the love of Troilus and Criseyde was treated as a real good, and that throughout the poem Troilus again is a figure not merely of potential, but of realised worth and *trouthe*. What was done earlier was done gloriously, and is not undone by a nobler end.

Interpretations multiply. Maybe one or other reading of the poem can satisfy at some time or other: but not all the time. A sense of inadequacy will reassert itself, and it is not simply that virtuous sense of inadequacy in response that afflicts any sensible person confronting a masterpiece, but in the case of this medieval poem a suspicion of miscomprehension.

Most of our ready abstractions indeed rest quietly upon the assumption that the poem is a lengthy working out in words of one or other of our own moral prejudices in situations and action like those we believe we observe directly in life. This is a situation, affecting the critical judgment, which it is difficult for a modern reader, especially a modern English reader fed on novels, to escape from, for several reasons. In the first place and obviously enough, because *Troilus and Criseyde* was written in the fourteenth century, the conventions that control the moral values in the poem are sufficiently different from our own to invalidate some of our tacit requirements.

The poem is about love and war but not about modern love and war. No doubt every age struggles consciously or unconsciously to set the instincts of sex and aggression loose from old outworn convention and to discover new patterns into which current expressions of sex and aggression can be worked so that they seem tolerable and socially decent. There is plenty of evidence that fourteenth-century English society sought to emancipate itself from some earlier medieval conventions by which sex and aggression had been socialised. But in the outcome, men at this time managed these things in a fashion very different from our own, and their writing (which is one of the most powerful ways of establishing and of expressing these social conventions) embodies their different attitudes.

Nowadays we usually assume that we have excluded sex and war from the approved routine of patterned behaviour and have relegated them to the unconventionalised areas of social life. War remains perhaps an intermittent dread but it is dreaded as alien to our life, an extra-human event, something that breaks in from outside. Ordinary life is not controlled by unquestioned assumptions that business as usual means war. But in fourteenth-century England war was a normal state of affairs. Mars ruled and men kissed the rod. Year after year they shipped out to France the armies, the elaborate munitions and provisions of war. War was strenuous day-to-day drudgery for kings and courts and commons.

Troilus and Criseyde reflects and accepts this tedious insistence. The background of war is much more prominent in Chaucer's telling of the story than in Boccaccio's. The confrontation of the nations, the everlasting state of siege, the daily skirmishes and the truces, the counsels of state and the debates on policy, these constitute a great stable pattern to the life imaged in the story. It is the world of the commissariat and general headquarters, where war is routine business. There is no real and lasting escape possible for the lovers out of this grim world to some soft paradise of love. Exchanging Criseyde for Antenor is plain political good sense on both sides. Criseyde indeed throughout the story is vulnerable, because she is always politically expendable. The story of the lovers is not a private story: its occasions and crises rise from the public war. Their struggle for secrecy emphasises rather than obliterates the intrusiveness of the society.

We do not take war like this and refuse to let our storytellers present it with these conventions, except perhaps in cowboy stories, part of whose charm no doubt resides in the recall of ancient behaviour patterns of European aggressiveness. But normally we reject an image of life enclosed in conventions of war. Even the modern cult of violence in fiction is, somewhat paradoxically, part of this rejection, for violence offers opportunities for exciting incursions by the extraordinary into the accepted normality of life which is now essentially pacifist. There is no interest at all in violence in *Troilus and Criseyde*. Permanent war swallows Troilus very quietly in the end. In fourteenth-century England war was too ordinary for noisy demonstrations.

We also struggle nowadays less successfully to deconvention-alise sex, by alleging in our fictions that sexual relations are most ideal when all formal bonds, whether exercised by society, inheritance, or rationality, are as loose as possible. Sex is treated as an exercise in freedom, in which the spark of personality should be least restrained, most emergent and most sensitive. There is of course a subtle continuity and modification over generations in ideas of this sort, but there is little evidence to suggest that men and women of the fourteenth century regarded love in this way. In its most developed manifestations love between the sexes was concerned with conquest and service, not with freedom. Love was treated as a state of dependence existing between unequals. In some aspects the man was the inferior; in others, the woman. Always many social obligations and questions of honour were directly involved—and honour has always a public face. Indeed what we may tend to think of as barriers to union or the external superfluities of true love, these earlier people regarded as the prerequisites of a love that could be esteemed. The observance of convention was what made love human and noble and distinguished it from careless instinctive sexuality—with which the Middle Ages were very familiar. No doubt hypocrites could flourish as well in the fourteenth century as in our own times. No doubt also that our own assumptions about sexual love will look as queer and arbitrary and inconsistent after a few centuries as fourteenth-century attitudes look to us.

That age then did not think of war as an avoidable evil, or of sex as an unmitigated good. Often enough it seems scarcely to have distinguished the underlying instincts at all and to have acted as if it regarded the manifestations of sex and war as the indifferent marks of general personal assertiveness. This is one reason why chivalry often strikes us as such an amorphous, inconsistent ideal. In the history of the time war often has the appearance of an extension of sexuality by other means. This was the very character of the Trojan War:

And in diverse wise and oon entente,
The ravysshyng to wreken of Eleyne,
By Paris don, they wroughten al hir peyne.
                                    I 61-3

A singularly squalid and dishonourable occasion we may think for a great war. Yet Troilus uses the same precedent (IV, 547-50) as a compelling reason for preserving Criseyde's honour. Hector and Deiphebus too are willing to accept Criseyde as part of the cause for which they fight. The appreciation of the values of sex may be noble, it is certainly not tender. Troilus and Criseyde are not two gentle hearts bound in an equal love. Love stirs in Criseyde as she sees Troilus when

His helm to-hewen was in twenty places:
                                    II 638

she has a keen prevision of what her surrender will be like:

How that an egle, fethered whyt as boon,
Under hir brest his longe clawes sette
And out hir herte he rente.
                                    II 926-8

These are both victor-victims. Their careers focus the values which the story assumes.

With some effort it is perhaps possible even at this distance of time to discern a configuration of these values. But there is a more subtle difficulty in reading *Troilus and Criseyde*. Normally, a modern novel exemplifies and embodies certain moral prejudices as well as a certain view of them. This may be some traditional European view of unembarrassed acceptance, or more likely now it will be an avowedly progressive, or plain anarchic view of social behaviour. Whatever it is, it will be implicit, recognisable and in a successful novel sufficiently consistent. Once we have made the backward leap through conventions this is also what we should find in reading most medieval romances. Usually a romance writer takes over his matter from some other story and then gives it his own *sens*, the particular colouring of sentiment and moral appeal which unconsciously and consciously he has decided is appropriate to the story. With a moderately practised storyteller each telling will have its own consistency, and once the story is under way the audience will have selected and fitted for reception the right emotional filter and can respond to the story directly without constant reference to this distinction between matter and *sens*.

But this is not possible with *Troilus and Criseyde*. Although the story is told in terms of historical conventions about love and war which can perhaps be broadly identified, the *sens* of this poem was never simple and consistent, to be absorbed unconsciously in large measure. The view we are required to take of the *sens* as well as of the matter is being constantly altered and manipulated. The telling demands that we change our filter repeatedly and the changes seem to be quite deliberately devised. In the poem the signals of change are given by the Narrator. In the original telling of the poem they were probably actually worked by the reciter of the poem.

It could be claimed that the Narrator is the only fully-developed character in the poem—he is certainly the only figure who reacts and changes with the sequence of the events narrated. The Narrator is an I, a mask worn by the person who speaks the script. This public apparition of an I is not, of course, Chaucer the man, not even Chaucer the poet: it is the mask made by Chaucer, originally perhaps, as the frontispiece to the Corpus *Troilus* Manuscript suggests, for Chaucer the performer to wear as he delivered the poem to a court audience. The I is not then the voice of the 'second author', as this apparition is sometimes called in dealing with a modern novel: it is rather the voice of a 'third speaker'. As long as a printed text is thought of as the standard form of a story, the recession of speakers is difficult to grasp. Chaucer certainly aspired to give *Troilus and Criseyde* a fixed text and said so quite plainly at the end of the poem. But the norm of composition for a vernacular poet was still the actual speaking of the story, the *narratio*. In composing *Troilus and Criseyde* before delivery, Chaucer was doing what an established comedian of stage or screen who is his own script-writer does in preparing one of his entertainments. He has to subdue his selected matter to his own technique of delivery, to exploit the reputation he has already acquired and the responses he should be able to anticipate from a particular and fairly familiar audience. He has to make a script which shall suit his story, his public appearance and the audience. He knows that the recognised features of the mask he is to wear will modify and be modified by the story. For the mask mediates the story. The entertainer is the manipulator and also part of the story he is presenting.

Similarly, the Narrator in *Troilus and Criseyde* is both inside and outside the story. Introducing the poem the Narrator speaks about himself. Later, at points of the story he will act the part of Troilus or Pandarus or Criseyde, and project to his audience a degree of identification. Sometimes he will speak as if he were the unobtrusive and rapid recorder of events. Sometimes, the Narrator delivers, in his own assumed first person as *auctor*, appropriate didactic comment. Sometimes he is on intimate and knowledgeable terms with the audience, and distances his story material. He exhibits a whole range of devices by which he guides or participates in the audience's reactions, devices familiar to medieval storytellers, but rarely given the artistic coherence in a finished text independent of actual performance. In *Troilus and Criseyde* Chaucer has convincingly stylised in permanent form the ephemeralness of a living entertainment and the mobility of actual delivery.

Yet the purpose of Chaucer as 'second author', if we may judge it from the development of the poem, as well as from its total effect, is surprisingly serious. He is handling a venerable story with dignity and with strong and deep moral and philosophical implications. His original audience we may assume was not expecting to take the performance quite so seriously as on reflection afterwards they would discover Chaucer had intended them to. The depth and range of the poem, announced with a disingenuous simplicity at the beginning, hinted at more confidently in the openings of the successive books, is only gradually disclosed in the narration, and only fully revealed at the very end. Chaucer is not competing with his contemporaries, the 'makers' of vernacular romance:

> But litel book, no makyng thow n'envie,
> But subgit be to alle poesye;
> And kis the steppes, where as thow seest pace
> Virgile, Ovide, Omer, Lucan, and Stace.
>
> V 1789-92

And *poesye* is the title of honour Chaucer reserved for the work of the great poets of antiquity and Italy, whose achievements in this poem he emulates.

Thus as a composition the poem moves along two distinct lines. The *narratio* is visible enough. It is concerned with the story-material Chaucer took out of Boccaccio. It is with the telling of this story that the Narrator is kept busy. But there is in the poem a concern to describe a line of causality and destiny, which shall show the events of the story at a higher degree of generality. To recognise this line is not to abstract from the poem, not to disentangle a meaning or a message, for the line runs throughout the poem. The poet himself, not the Narrator, is in charge of this line. This is what the old rhetoricians called the *argumentum* of a piece of writing. Commentators on Boethius' *Topics* called it the *vis sententiae*. It is the theme of a work in the actual process of evolving, the line of force along which the *narratio* is directed.

From the beginning of the poem we are conscious that the whole action is under the grip of a larger control. On the surface the Narrator presents it as 'the lawe of kynde' we are advised to follow. But the counterweight comes early, 'O blinde world, O blynde entencioun', a sombre murmur which gathers strength. The naive Narrator is another blind man leading blind men to their fates. We are acknowledging the *argumentum* when we realise the illusion implicit in the *narratio*. All the ways of the world, all the solemn dealings with sex and war which seem so compulsive and yet so uncontrollable, are neither one nor the other. As guides by themselves they work confusion, as values they are a vanity. The fixed and familiar courses down which men seek to outrun and outwit their fellows lead nowhere any man wishes to be. The world with its seemingly hard and inescapable conventions imaged in the poem is illusion, a necessary illusion, which exacts from us a disillusionment. Hope lies in another realm, scarcely related to the iron necessities of human society. The *argumentum* of the poem depends upon a melancholy, unsensationalised view of life, compounded out of a Christian quietism and a faintly sentimental stoicism. It reflects a mood of many Englishmen in the late fourteenth century.

In public Chaucer was no more than a minor functionary and

his appearance in court would depend upon a reputation as a sophisticated entertainer, not as a speculative moralist or an interpreter of his times. The *narratio* must carry the *argumentum* very lightly. To the secret hearts and thoughts of men in high places he remained a stranger. What went on in public he could learn only by humble and deferential observation. He could earn a little licence for solemnity as well as for jest if he were sufficiently entertaining.

The poet's intention and the anticipated responses of this court audience control the strategy: which in brief was to introduce the story with a touch of disengaging flippancy, to develop it swiftly, brightly but elaborately, to let the passions and the responses of the audience run and gather head, and then to make his purpose plain when the emotional effects are irresistible. There is much jocularity and irony in the detail of the telling. But it is often mock-jocularity and the irony of enhancement. Chaucer talks a thing down in order to build it up.

The use of this sort of device indicates the delicacy of the whole task. Perhaps we can assume that a medieval audience, even the most sophisticated, was pretty inflammable. Most of the way the poet cannot go too far or too fast in evoking participation with the story and identification with its characters. The audience must not find its conventional values openly mocked by unrelieved catastrophe. So the Narrator must maintain throughout something of that initial *naiveté*, lest he be held responsible for the calamity. The poet cannot make a moral too emphatically, so the Narrator cannot be seen to identify himself too steadily with the logic of the destinies involved, or pass too magisterial a judgment on the actors who suffer them. The poet has to satisfy a whole range of worldliness which appreciates display, luxury, leisure and the solid reassurance of wealth and power and rank. So the Narrator presents, quite simplemindedly, sequences of fashionable behaviour, moments of worldly triumph and success, counsels of conventional wisdom. Throughout the poem there is sufficient humour to placate the unsentimental, enough undiscussed absolutes to win the idealist, some unwounding cynicism to disarm the disillusioned. By using the Narrator the poet can recall the audience from an excessive engrossment in certain aspects of the story. The Narrator can be used to lighten the ominous, to anticipate and therefore blunt the distracting keenness of the miseries, and still, by exhibiting the degree of his own involvement, inject expectancy into a story of what is already foreseen.

In the practical management of his Narrator Chaucer had of course a duty towards himself. He had to write—probably this came easily enough to a writer of his experience—a part which would suit his own delivery, his own powers of expressiveness of voice, gesture and elocution. More important, the poet in putting he poem together had to maintain his own morale, to remain confident that what he was doing was worth doing, to refuse to lose his own way in the story, and to ensure that in working out his intention he should achieve what every author aims at in a major work, a continuing fall-out of meaning, which should sift slowly down into the memory and modify understanding. The *argumentum* must shine clear even though it may seem to annul in part the *narratio* that carries it forward.

Problems of narration at this degree of complexity and skill fascinated Chaucer. He was to devise new and more complicated problems for himself in *The Canterbury Tales*, which represent the ultimate achievement in medieval storytelling, when the mobile recession of the narrating voices is often as puzzling and ingenious as the construction of a Chinese box. Fortunately *Troilus and Criseyde* is easier to follow. It is all one story and its narrative advancing through the complexities of presentation is strong and clear.

Perhaps we marvel more at the construction of the poem than Chaucer's contemporaries would have done. For he was practising, albeit with the greatest skill and success, what the schools and handbooks had taught Europeans about composition for nearly two millenia. Usually in the arts of rhetoric, instruction on how to develop a *narratio* is included in the teaching on the presentation of a case in a court of law, but even in the earlier handbooks some attention is given to the presentation of fictional material, whether drawn from legend or history or the contemporary scene. It was recognised that such fictions required a highly flexible method of treatment. Style and delivery was expected to follow the variety of incident and the reactions of the persons involved, so that the audience should become directly concerned in affairs as they were being presented. Even a perfunctory reading of, for instance, the pseudo-Ciceronian treatise *Ad Herennium* will illuminate Chaucer's methods in composition and elocution in *Troilus and Criseyde*.

But the practical and slightly mechanical exposition of rhetorical teaching in *Ad Herennium* does not deal with the subtler but overriding need in all effective discourse for a narrator to carry his audience with him all the time. This is what more sophisticated theory knew as *ethos*. It is the witness a speaker bears, in telling his tale, to his own integrity and to the credibility of his matter, thereby exhibiting these qualities to the audience as instruments of persuasion. It creates a milieu satisfactory and attractive to the audience and propitious to the speaker's cause. *Ethos* is properly employed, Quintilian observed, when it is applied throughout the whole discourse and thus builds up a slow but ineradicable conviction in the audience.

Ethos then will assume the employment of certain artistic principles. It is never easy to discern the standards of taste and the canons of excellence that a poet is implicitly accepting in his composition. If we judge a work successful then we rationalise our judgment, usually by invoking criteria taken over from our own critical inheritance and training. These have no absolute value, and most of our attempts to make them more precise even to ourselves will distort them. To seek for the artistic principles behind the composition of *Troilus and Criseyde* is as difficult as to evaluate the moral world of its story. But once again we can be comforted that Chaucer's own professions of faith in art are likely to have been nearly as ill-defined, semi-consciously indeterminate and arbitrarily traditional as our own but, quite certainly, different. If we are to assess his ideas about his art, and his works of art, these differences require very delicate and modest exploration which must always remain mindful that every clear discrimination carries with it the seed of an exaggeration.

In modern poetry, as was pointed out by Cecil Day Lewis, we look for marks of originality of thought and expression, intensity in emotional effect and evocative power in the use of words. No medieval poet sought to display these virtues. It is true that in

some medieval poems (including *Troilus and Criseyde*) we sometimes think that we can observe them, but no medieval poet and
no medieval audience seems to have attached any particular value
to these instances, and as often as not, it may be suspected that we
deceive ourselves when we believe we have observed them
displayed. It is wiser to turn to another triad of artistic virtues, to
the Dionysian triad of integrity, harmony and clarity, for guidance
in assessing the aspirations of a medieval artist. And although in
formulations of medieval thought this triad was associated with
the contemplation of the Divine Beauty itself, there can be little
doubt that, over centuries, secularised versions of these ideals
conditioned and qualified the construction and the assessment of
human artefacts. In some such terms as integrity, harmony and
clarity we can best sum up Chaucer's aesthetic.

Integrity expounded in literary terms implies full and complete
development—the wholeness of perfection, grandeur and size.
The *formosus*, the pretty, is beautiful, but with an impairment in
magnitude. Perfection suggests a controlled prodigality, a
plentitude in utterance. Thus we can appreciate in part the
medieval poet's quest for *amplificatio*. *Troilus and Criseyde* has this
fullness.

Every story has to be given adequate setting and sufficient
motivation. Most modern storytellers, however, select from a
much narrower field than Chaucer thought necessary. There is a
mass of particularity in the poem far in excess of what Chaucer
found in his source. His method of narration in this poem requires
that he should maintain throughout a total relevance. All
Pandarus's guileful persuasions, Criseyde's wavering calculations
and Troilus's Boethian speeches are needed. Though he abhorred
prolixity and condemned it as the vice of his age in its writing,
he did not mark the boundaries of relevance where later writers
would. In Book Five, for example, when Troilus wishes to know
the truth about Criseyde's delay among the Greeks and to learn
the meaning of his dreams of the boar, he consults his sister, the
prophetess Cassandra (V 1450-1533):

> She gan first smyle and seyde 'O brother deere
> If thow a soth of this desirest knowe
> Thow most a fewe of olde stories heere . . .'

And she begins far back with the story of Diana's punishment of Greeks and how the war of Thebes began and summarises all twelve books of Statius's epic:

> And so descendeth down from gestes olde
> To Diomede and thus spak and tolde.

coming at length to an exposition of the dream. In such a proceeding sudden intensity is never achieved and evocation is dispersed. But there is another power to replace the delightful mysteriousness of supposing more than one is told. We are exposed to more than we want to comprehend, and excess squeezed into a narrow space can have a genuine artistic function. Again the comparison with the multitudinous decorative effect of a great cathedral can be invoked. Prodigality is impressive, so is the open suggestion of endless involution of destiny.

The same principles are at work in Chaucer's presentation of character. The plot is central. But the story, as Chaucer tells it in its wholeness and fullness, generates the characters it needs. If we insist on assessing the individuality and psychology of these characters we do it from outside the poem. They needed not to be psychologically coherent as long as their presentation sustains and gives substance to the *narratio*. That we can reassemble them and interpret them as portraits of potentially real people is an astonishing testimony to the integrity and consonance of Chaucer's art, but should not be taken as a guide to his method.

This method is seen most simply in the treatment of Troilus. If we read his character from the action in which he is involved we see him as a prince, as a hopeful, successful, then despairing lover, as a bitter fighter. We are told he is handsome, young, fresh, strong, resolute in action and successful in war. We watch him behave in love as a pattern of amorous gallantry should behave. He suffers 'this wondrous maladie' to perfection. He swoons, he weeps, he languishes. He is properly passionate, both masterful and humble in the consummation of his love. He becomes jealous and desperate and angry. He is indeed the ideal young male character, quick, proud, active, passionate, easily cast down, resolute when his course is clear, delighted by success, impatient of delay—psycho-biologically, the perfect specimen, or as Chaucer puts it,

> Oon of the beste entecched creature
> That is, or shal, whil that the world may dure.
> V 832-3

Accordingly, readers find him the least satisfying of the major characters of the poem, somewhat flat and characterless; and properly so. He refuses to come out of the poem. There, he serves as one of the poles where the forces converge in this story about sex and war. He is what the story needs him to be. His function is obvious, simple and directly comprehensible.

Criseyde's function is not much more elaborate. Though her appearances in the poem are covered with a continuous sheen of sentiment and charm so that at the slightest encouragement we are willing to lead her out of the poem as if she were a particular woman whom we delight to know, yet she is the familiar, if never commonplace figure of every English romance, of every woman's magazine, another Emily or Felice, the passive pole in this story of a struggle for possession. She is presented as the type of the unlucky beloved. When she is described in Book Five, the Narrator speaks of her, as he speaks of Troilus, as an example of the general. She is set alongside Nature's mean, she embodies the virtues that all heroines of romance exemplify, the beauty of figure, face and hair; discretion, fairspokenness, kindness in word and thought, a dignity, liveliness and gentility, sentimentality and fearlessness. These are characteristics that had been tabulated centuries before Chaucer's time, for example by Hugh of St Victor in his *Summa Sententiarum*, VII, 1, as the moral and social gifts in a woman that draw men's love. Even in describing her, the Narrator disassociates himself from any knowledge of Criseyde as a person. He knows her only in the story. He can do no more than report of her what 'they writen that hir syen'. 'Trewely I can not telle hir age', nor whether she had any children.

The effect of this last device is, it must be allowed, equivocal. Chaucer's refusal to let the Narrator know these things can indeed reinforce the sense of verisimilitude by inviting the imagination to supply the illimitable reality of a completely individuated character. No doubt Chaucer knew as well as we do what was won by withholding. But it is an aspect of his management of the Narrator, not of his characterisation. He is controlling the audience's responses of pity and moral bewilderment. Criseyde is only the part she plays. She is presented whole and without development. Her faithlessness is imprinted on 'hir browes joyneden y-fere'. She is throughout her final reputation. Again and again in the last book the Narrator tells us that these things fall and can fall no otherwise than as 'the story telleth us'. Criseyde, like Troilus, is a function of the plot.

Pandarus may make a somewhat different impression from the two main characters but the method of presentation is similar. He is established in an extraordinarily rich and complex fashion through word and deed; so much is given that we are willing to take more, and ensconce him beside Falstaff or Polonius, Pickwick or Micawber. Let no-one deny Chaucer the achievement and the triumph. Yet Chaucer uses him as a trigger mechanism to the action, as a support to the main figures, and is as merciless in despatching him when he is superfluous to the action as ever King Henry was to Falstaff. In the story he is the fluid element between the two static presentations of the exemplary figures, the princely lover and the unlucky beloved. He appears rich and complex because, in himself less important, he promotes and takes part in their interaction.

To incorporate a static exemplary figure into an action, especially to show reciprocal interaction between two figures of this kind, is a difficult task. It was a difficulty encountered by many medieval storytellers and certainly rarely solved by them to our satisfaction. Often the difficulty is by-passed by the use of arbitrary incidents such as the giving of love-potions, or magic girdles, by casual hunts, or dreams, by supernatural events, or by the use of the equally arbitrary but formal device of allegory. In such ways the narrative can be jerked forward in the desired direction. For though *Troilus and Criseyde* is a much more complicated piece of writing than the ordinary romance or saint's life, it does not escape from similar problems in narration. Troilus is so completely a prince in love, constrained by honour and truth, Criseyde so plainly a desirable young woman, protected by 'danger', that they cannot so transform themselves out of character to take part in the story without an intermediary.

Pandarus's role then is what by the sixteenth century all readers knew it to be, that of pander. He embodies society's acceptance of the ways in which lust and aggressiveness can get to work, the element in which the lovers move towards each other, the means by which the two predetermined characters are interlocked in the action of the poem. Once again characterisation is dependent upon the story. In Book Three (ll. 241ff.) the Narrator indulging the irony has Pandarus confessing to be exactly what the action of the story will make of him.

A realisation of the wholeness and integrity of a poem of this size comes slowly. But we can often on reflection discern aspects of it as we proceed. For example, we might take note of a response we make to the last book. The book seems to go on for a very long time. It is certainly not that the story loses its power here, nor that the telling of it flags. This last book is perhaps the most compelling part of the whole poem. But this is the book of Troilus's woe, a record of the interminable ache. I suppose that it offends our modern moral sense. We know from the beginning of the poem that the end is Criseyde's unfaithfulness. But Chaucer has his Narrator disclose it as steadily and carefully as he began the story of Troilus's joy, omitting nothing, no single anguish, conducting his hero through ever-diminishing circles of hope to the central black despair. The unprotesting objectivity about this even-paced narration is almost inhuman. It has an integrity which we sentimental moderns find difficult to face.

Our response to the last book and its effectiveness in preparing for the end serve as indications of the careful structural composition of the poem and the harmony and consonance of its parts. The five books of *Troilus and Criseyde* recall the five-act structure of the Elizabethan play. But Chaucer employs the structure differently. Though *Troilus and Criseyde* is 'litel myn tragedye', he does not produce in it the line of the Shakespearian tragic plot, where we expect and usually find a rise in emotional tension through the first four acts to a climax towards the end of the fifth: a line of asymmetrical development. *Troilus and Criseyde* shows nothing of this unidirectional development in mounting intensity.

The feeling that the Fifth Book goes on for a very long time is in part prompted by finding the conventional expectancy disappointed. The narrative climax of the poem occurs undoubtedly in the Third Book, where the lovers come to their felicity. This is the pivot about which the poem swings. The end is announced at the beginning. The climax of the action stands almost plump, even by arithmetic, in the middle of the whole. It is the story of double woe, the misery of longing leading through joy to the anguish of losing. The trajectory is circular rather than ballistic. The end of the poem is a deliberate anticlimax.

The effect of the whole construction is curious. Whereas in modern writing the structure seems usually to be related to a psychological development, many medieval works seem to rely upon purely formal or mathematical relationships. We expect the form of a work to follow and to imitate and to reinforce the psychological curve of the narration. And perhaps insofar as this identification of form and content has been mastered as a technique of composition, modern literary practice has effected a real advance on that of earlier times. It is difficult to see how at any time the simple cyclical effects of some of the alliterative poems or even the formal triptych arrangement of seduction and hunting scenes in *Sir Gawain and the Green Knight*, or the careful numerical arithmetic in compositions of some French and German poets can have contributed to the strictly literary power of these works. These formal devices are usually neither audible, nor visible nor legible. They require a spatial apprehension and suggest that a poem was assumed to be a flat material object, an inscription on some extended surface. We can allow that *Troilus and Criseyde* has a hard, marmoreal elegance and symmetry. But Chaucer turns all things to advantage. The actual form of the poem encompasses the intention of the story. The circular and spatially symmetrical arrangement of his *narratio* is perfectly suited to his *argumentum* of the disillusioning power of necessity. The narrative line by the end has described the wheel of fortune. In this medieval poem at least, a curious spatial form is used to identify the psychological curve of the story.

Many details in the poem reveal this consonance and harmony

of construction. Songs and letters and dreams are introduced symmetrically and significantly. Recurrent themes such as the Procne legend, and images such as that of blindness and fire knot strands of the narrative together. Incident after incident ironically answers back one to another. The twelfth-century *Arts of Poetry* had compared a poem with the human body, beautifully proportioned and articulated, designed in detail for complex activity directed to a single end. Chaucer had learned his lesson well.

But the greatest lesson English poets in the last medieval centuries learned from the *Arts of Poetry* was elegance—a graceful clarity comparable with that which shines in stone from the sculptures of the Northern cathedrals. They taught English writers a New Poetry. The poetry of the Anglo-Saxons had great resources of force, economy, allusiveness, and resonance—a concrete splendour which we readily appreciate nowadays. In the progress of English poesy the first poem that can be put beside *Beowulf* for artistic achievement is *Troilus and Criseyde*, and it marks in English the triumphant fulfilment of those ideals of clarity, brightness and sequaciousness which the twelfth-century *Arts of Poetry* promulgated and which were extraordinarily difficult for English vernacular poets to make their own. In *Troilus and Criseyde* elegance, brightness and clarity are at once functional and decorative. In verbal style the poem is rich, varied, highly ornamented, making use of all those devices recommended by the rhetoricians and named appropriately enough colours.

Imagery of light carries much of the meaning of the poem, most obviously in Book Three, which opens with the invocation drawn from Dante. With our modern training in symbol reading we can readily submit to the power of the recurring opposition of light and dark, day and night, which often marks changes in gradient of the narration. The accounts of vigils and daybreaks, of Pandarus first setting out on his mission while the small birds sing in a May sunrise, of the midnight darkness when the lovers come together and Pandarus withdraws the little lamp, of Troilus watching at the city-gate till daylight has completely gone, owe a great part of their effectiveness to the unobtrusive use of highly affective symbols. Criseyde's grace and beauty are invariably presented in terms of light.

But the clarity Chaucer achieves in the poem is more than decorative and more than symbolic. There is a light which gives form and definition to the whole, casting on the *narratio* and the *argumentum* the illumination of an intellectual light which sharpens indeed the complexity, but banishes obscurity. And this is perhaps part of the abiding impression of the poem as a whole. It is hard and vast and also luminous. It is this *lumen siccum* which penetrates through the story to the mind and then to the conscience of the reader. It has made the whole complicated story as plain as daylight and yet is able to reveal it as a fiction. The clear-eyed detachment in the telling should have prepared us against the moral weariness we encounter in the last book if we were reading it too simply and too sentimentally. In the foreknowledge indicated throughout, in the premonitions, in the melancholy infused into the joy, in the constantly flickering ironies, in the comic and tender handling of detail, in the juxtaposition and succession of incommensurate standards, the Narrator has warned the audience throughout. The end has been prepared for. It is, after all, only a made-up story, just pretence.

Nowadays we want novels to claim something more, to claim to be an illusion of life complete and unbroken. Yet here in *Troilus and Criseyde* we find Chaucer constructing a whole long complex narration of human behaviour, presenting, albeit in poetic mode, a realistic account of life, holding the outcome firmly in mind throughout, and yet when he comes to the end admitting that it is only a tale. As a general rule most modern readers, following Flaubert, would deny that any author could get away with this somersault. It is of course a device of alienation, but a device available only to writers of fairy stories. And yet this conclusion which at first sight, and perhaps always to a thoroughly secularised eye, looks like a petering out of purpose is a product of the illumination that shines through the poem, the manifestation of the *argumentum* which the *narratio* has been secretly harbouring. It gives an image of truth and order to the poem which the fictional story itself does not possess.

In the epilogue to the poem the variable accents of the Narrator seem to be lost in the voice of Chaucer the poet (still not of Chaucer the man). How often does an entertainer at the end of his piece add, 'But all you people here, seriously now, I want to say a few special words in conclusion . . .' The device itself is not puzzling. It is the direct appeal recommended for the peroration. We can, if we choose, believe that Chaucer the man believed his own words here. Indeed he would have been a very peculiar medieval person if he had not. But the technique of detachment that the Narrator has employed in the last book, the quiet and unemphatic dismissal of the characters, allows him to take up this new posture from which he makes a final withdrawal from his audience with no sense of discontinuity or surprise. It is the most affecting, the most beautiful ending to any work in English. It is holy and mysterious, repelling tumult and applause. It retrospectively realigns the whole work it concludes.

Yet it cannot be denied that taken as a statement of substance this epilogue contradicts and annuls what the story was about. The Narrator has at many stages cast a glow of joy and glory upon sex and war. Troilus is a figure of manly virtue, of honour and good faith; Criseyde is eternally desirable; their love is a human good. Their parting, Troilus's misery and Criseyde's weakness, these are evil. Artistically the poem is triumphantly successful, but at the level of moral abstraction the story falls apart.

Behind the story is the double standard of the times. It is difficult to recognise that the secular culture of Plantagenet England with all its brilliance, wit and elegance, and its social and administrative complexity, its achievements in peace and war, was only a sub-culture. It rested on no firm, comprehensive frame of its own, but relied for its intellectual cohesion upon the postulates of ecclesiastical thinking and the standards of monastic morality. These were still so powerful and ingrained in the habits of thought and expression that they were able to control the wills of men and the habits of a society which could be embarrassed by them. New paths to virtue, new forms of moral perfection, had still no firm identity. Even glimpses of them could look too readily to be no more than illusions produced by feebleness of will or ignorance of truth or perversity of judgment. In the fourteenth century any rival morality still lacked the intellectual substructures needed to give it plausibility and conviction. Men of that time extracted the sting out of crises of faith and reason by an honest acceptance of a complete divorce between them. They lived as awkwardly or easily with fundamental inconsistencies as we do now. Late medieval society had to wait another century or so before their old problems of faith and morality were stabilised again. Literature in England waited still longer, before another amorous prince, Spenser's Red-Cross Knight, could seek and find his love and heaven together in the pursuit of Holiness. But from the inherent contradictions in his own society Chaucer in *Troilus and Criseyde* makes a huge coherent success. Indeed Chaucer's work can always serve as a triumphant denial of that idle and fashionable truism that a chaotic and muddled age deserves a chaotic and fragmentary art.

But *Troilus and Criseyde* is not an heroic poem exemplifying ideal conduct. It is a romance in a tragic mode, the fullest and most explicit working out in English of the mood of doom and fatality which overhangs the best of the medieval stories. No explanation of Beowulf's death satisfies. It is not easy to accept that Roland died at Roncesvalles simply because he broke a blood vessel. We cannot readily discern what brings about the disaster that overlays all the second part of the alliterative *Morte d'Arthur*. All that lies between the actions of such heroes and their lamentable deaths is an impenetrable and gathering gloom. We sense in these tragic stories an inexorable process, we cannot see it at work. This would be true also of *Troilus and Criseyde*, if the conclusion of the poem with its backward extension in significance did not illuminate the process. The leap into transcendence here shows this medieval manner of tragic storytelling aware at last of its own law and intention and purpose. All these medieval stories involve in their telling an encounter with the limits beyond which human will or human passion or human virtue cannot pass. But these stories are told so that the audience is aware, vaguely perhaps, that at these boundaries there *is* something beyond. The fiery breath of the dragon is not the only cause of the tragic death. What else it is, we cannot see; the story points to the unexpressed, to what we may often conveniently but inexpressively call Fate, but it is unconditioned even by a name, for it exists at the limits of interpretation even, a featureless, unimaginable power which is felt to encompass the whole life of man and society. This is indeed the *apeiron*, the unlimited, of the old Greek philosopher Anaximander. Out of the *apeiron* a cosmos is built up by the mingling of opposites. Back into the *apeiron* the cosmos crumbles at length by the unavoidable conflict of these opposites. This is the world of medieval tragic action. The forces that begin life are the forces that destroy life. They are the forces of self-assertion working in the forms of love or war or both. The tragedy itself, the pitiful event, is not very significant. A fall from prosperity to adversity is ordinary enough. What is significant is the illumination that tragedy should bring of another order. What Troilus sees looking down from beyond the seventh sphere is the truth of this sort of tragedy, an apprehension of what is 'Uncircumscript, and al maist circumscrive'.

This is not the mode of Shakespearian tragedy, nor of the Greek, nor of Romantic tragedy. It is not a kind of tragedy that justifies or enhances the moral statures of its actors, or works a moral purification in the consciences of its audience. In this more intellectual mode the actors are absorbed into the tragic story, and it is the full and completed story that instructs the audience of the inadequacy of the action displayed.

The Canterbury Tales: style of the man and style of the work

CHARLES MUSCATINE

I F the whole of *The Canterbury Tales* can be said to have a
single style, that style has within it an extraordinary variety,
which derives from the great range of Chaucer's themes and
the way in which his style supports or expresses them. The tales
were long in the writing, but nothing suggests that their styles are
in any way related to their chronology. Chaucer's mature style
(like Shakespeare's) was a protean one. Medieval rhetorical theory
described three styles, the high, the middle, and the low, corresponding to the social dignity of the subject matter. But the study
of literature taught Chaucer much finer discriminations, and his
mature works show a quite independent sense of style, trans-
gressing decorum and even genre in the interest of meaning. *The
Canterbury Tales* fulfil in a particularly satisfying way the familiar
dictum that style and meaning in art are interdependent.

Though we shall be finally concerned with this aspect of
Chaucer's style, with style as differing from tale to tale as it is
deployed for literary effect, we should be aware that Chaucer's
range is not limitless. In the very widest sense, his style is 'late-
medieval', inevitably rough-hewn by the traditions, issues,
attitudes and forms of apprehension that belong to his epoch. On
the other side, if the style of the work is shaped by Chaucer's
immediate literary strategy, that strategy may be in turn influenced, limited, partly determined by his natural literary gifts,
habits and propensities. The reader who attends patiently to the
whole work will find beneath the local variations some constant
traits, a peculiarly Chaucerian personality in style and language,
an array of favourite stylistic devices. In the ensuing remarks I
shall first attempt to describe some of the principal traits of this
'style of the man', hoping thus to set the 'style of the work' in

relief and also to suggest how the nature of the one may be related
to the formation of the other.

I

Perhaps the most common denominator of Chaucer's literary
personality is a certain air of insouciance. His manner is indeed so
relaxed that new readers have to be reminded that he was a
highly sophisticated literary artist. But most critics are likely to
err in the other direction. If we believe, with Kittredge, that
Chaucer always knew what he was about, we must not forget
that his sophistication includes a casualness and playfulness that
we rarely associate with our greatest poets. Chaucer has none of
the apartness and sense of the poet's special status that we feel in
Milton or Wordsworth, little of the artistic self-consciousness of
a Spenser or a Pope. Like all of these an artist to the bone, he
seems nevertheless always to have prized his amateur status. He
seems perpetually to be conducting a conversation with friends,
and he cannot for long stand on ceremony with them. By inviting
us at least once to 'turne over the leef and chese another tale' he
shows that he thinks of his poetry as something written down; yet
it retains many of the qualities of the oral tradition, of poetry
recited aloud, as no doubt it often was.[1] It is only occasionally a
poetry of high compression or of jewel-like polish. Though one
could cite scores of 'great' single lines in The Canterbury Tales,
Chaucer's characteristic triumphs are based more often on
cumulation and sequence. We must always be prepared to tolerate,
if not enjoy in him, a certain amiable inconsistency of tone, or of
perspective, or of detail, as his narrative goes along. The fact is,
Chaucer does not seem to have worried about consistency beyond
a certain point.

No doubt the unfinished state of The Canterbury Tales exag-
gerates this quality. But by the same token, the rough edges and
unmatched joints give us a sense of how he worked. Although
we know that he revised some of The Canterbury Tales, one cannot

[1] Miller's Prologue, l. 3177; see B. H. Bronson, 'Chaucer's Art in Relation to
his Audience', in Five Studies in Literature, Univ. of Calif. Publ. English, VIII, no. 1
(1940); Ruth Crosby, 'Chaucer and the Custom of Oral Delivery', Speculum,
XIII (1938) 413-32.

imagine his being much concerned about merely factual matters. Chaucer is characteristically absorbed in the tactics of the passage he is writing, and careless of more remote correspondences. When the conception of the Nun's Priest was upon him, he gave no thought to fixing up the *General Prologue*, which barely mentions 'prestes thre' (l. 164). His Cook is described in the brilliant *Manciple's Prologue* as if he had not already been heard from after *The Reeve's Tale*. The shy bumbler who tells *The Tale of Sir Thopas* is not quite the same as the gregarious character who narrates the *General Prologue*. The Knight's avowed dislike of tragedy in *The Nun's Priest's Prologue* seems at odds with the tone of *The Knight's Tale*. We are never explicitly told—or is this high artistic premonition?—the marital status of the Wife of Bath.

Many more of these mechanical flaws or inconsistencies could be cited, but none of them is very serious. What they tell us about Chaucer's artistic stance is borne out by his occasional inconsistencies of perspective. The character Justinus, within *The Merchant's Tale*, cites as an authority on marriage the Wife of Bath, who is listening to the tale. The Summoner at one point is made comically aware of the literary structure of his own performance:

> My prologe wol I ende in this manere.

And once the narrator of *The Knight's Tale* transfers the sounds of trumpets and heralds from his tale to his audience as if there were no gap between them:

> The trompours, with the loude mynstralcie,
> The heraudes, that ful loude yelle and crie,
> Been in hire wele for joye of daun Arcite.
> But herkneth me, and stynteth noyse a lite,
> Which a myracle ther bifel anon.
>
> *The Knight's Tale* 2671-5

These minor and rather playful instances illustrate both Chaucer's awareness of perspective, and his disposition to be neither rigidly consistent nor too solemn about it.

Chaucer's basic quality of insouciance and naturalness is heavily contributed to by his language. Though he was no mean Latin scholar and a great importer of new words into English from French, though he was a courtier versed in international business and diplomacy, his language has an irreducible quality of familiarity—one might almost have said provincialism. I am not referring to his developed art of giving his realistic characters colloquial speech,[1] but rather to something deep in the grain of his own discourse, that at times seems to transgress literary decorum itself. It is in his rhythm and syntax and diction, but perhaps we sense it most clearly in the imagery of his figurative comparisons, where his choice of images is relatively unconstrained by the dictates of subject matter. Chaucer has a marked preference for similes over metaphors, as if the more discursive syntax of simile and its less pretentious reach of statement were more congenial to his rhythm and his personality. But in both metaphor and simile his imagery has a favourite range, which I can best illustrate by quoting at random and at some length from all parts of The Canterbury Tales: 'his brydel . . . gynglen . . . as dooth the chapel belle;' 'His eyen . . . stemed as a forneys of a leed;' 'As leene was his hors as is a rake;' 'whit as morne milk;' 'A shiten shepherd and a clene shepe;' 'heer as yelow as wex;' 'heeng as dooth a strike of flex;' 'eyen . . . as an hare;' 'unbokeled is the male;' 'gras tyme is doon, my fodder is now forage;' 'The streem of lyf now droppeth on the chymbe;' 'lyk an aspen leef he quook;' 'Thou woldest han been a tredefowel aright;' 'Why shoulde I sowen draf out of my fest, Whan I may sowen whete;' 'they stinken as a goot;' 'Gaillard . . . as goldfynch in the shawe;' 'As thou right now were cropen out of the ground;' 'fyr, that in the bedstraw bredeth;' 'lewed as gees;' 'as doth a lamb after the tete;' 'Derk . . . as pich, or as the cole;' 'his tente, large as is a berne;' 'bulte it to the bren;' 'As dooth a dowve sittynge on a berne;' 'hir soules goon a-blakeberyed;' 'as men in fyr wol casten oille or greesse;' 'as thikke as is a branched ook;' 'That charge upon my bak I wol endure.'

The list could be much prolonged, and I have not drawn on the portrait of Alisoun nor on the Wife of Bath, nor have I begun to list the things that other things in The Canterbury Tales are not worth, as 'an oystre,' 'a pulled hen,' 'a bene,' 'a toord,' 'a botel

---

[1] See Margaret Schlauch, 'Chaucer's Colloquial English: Its Structural Traits', PMLA, LXVII (1952) 1103-16; Dorothy Everett, 'Chaucer's "Good Ear",' in her Essays on Medieval Literature, Oxford 1955, pp. 139-48.

hey,' 'a panyer ful of herbes,' 'a boterflye,' 'a rake-stele,' and the like. Many of these comparisons are conventional, and many that I have quoted are poetically just the right images in their contexts. Yet their number and their general character remain significant, especially as many come in poems and passages whose dominant associations are far from village and farm. Even the diction and figurative speech in *The Knight's Tale*, for all its noble characters, classical setting, and elevated theme, is sprinkled with rural familiarity:

> I have, God woot, a large feeld to ere,
> And wayke been the oxen in my plough.
>
> 886-7

These are the words of the tale's knightly narrator. His metaphor has a certain deliberate gravity, but the imagery is 'low' enough to be used later by the drunken Miller in his *Prologue*:

> Yet nolde I, for the oxen in my plogh,
> Take upon me more than ynogh.
>
> 3159-60

The hero Arcite in *The Knight's Tale* swears 'by my pan' (i.e. skull), and uses similes as 'We faren as he that dronke is as a mous' (1261); the Duke Theseus says of Lady Emily:

> She woot namoore of al this hoote fare,
> By God, than woot a cokkow or an hare!
>
> 1809-10

The narrator describes the changing moods of lovers:

> Now in the crope, now doun in the breres,
> Now up, now down, as boket in a welle.
>
> 1533-4

He tells us of the expense of constructing the temple of Mars, 'That coste largely of gold a fother' (l. 1908). (The last word reminds one of the description of Chaucer's Plowman, 'That hadde ylad of dong ful many a fother'.) Of the dying Arcite he says, 'As blak he lay as any cole or crowe' (l. 2692). Even his descriptions of supernatural figures have something a little domestic about them. Mercury wears on his bright hair simply a 'hat' (l. 1388); Saturn says to Venus, 'Doghter, hoold thy pees!'

(l. 2668); the wood-gods, deprived of their dwelling places, 'ronnen up and down' (l. 2925). These, and the many similar small instances of image and diction that could be gleaned from among the lordly descriptions and elevated speeches in *The Knight's Tale*, illustrate what is virtually a constant in Chaucer. Just beneath the level of literary artifice, his speech is full of comparisons and proverbial expressions that must have been widely current in the ordinary English speech of his time. We are perhaps not surprised when Harry Bailly in the Introduction to *The Man of Law's Tale* follows a learned citation from Seneca with a reference to 'Malkynes maydenhede, whan she hath lost it in hir wantownesse'. But it is equally Chaucerian that the language of the dignified Man of Law can then be given the same flavour of familiarity amidst his learned references:

> Me were looth be likned, doutelees,
> To Muses that men clepe Pierides—
> *Methamorphosios* woot what I mene;
> But nathelees, I recche noght a bene
> Thogh I come after hym with hawebake.
>
> 91-5

Chaucer's language is thus something like that of a good politician. It can be either familiar or rhetorical and learned, but when rhetorical and learned it is never completely out of sight of the familiar.

Some Continental critics have found Chaucer irreducibly 'middle class' on account of this language; but that is to be too pure as regards decorum. It is, rather, a great part of his delightful 'Englishness', which must be acknowledged however much we may discover of his debt to the Continent in style, subject and genre. And it is even more than a source of easy geniality and of an appearance of artless spontaneity. At times, as we shall see below, it is transformed into a powerful medieval realism, and it enters into overtly comic and ironic combinations.

Another large trait which to modern eyes must contribute to Chaucer's artistic insouciance is his easy admission of rather 'extra-literary' material, of *sentence* and doctrine into his poem. Thoroughly medieval, he does not seem to distinguish between belles-lettres and didactic literature:

For seint Paul seith that al that writen is,
To oure doctrine it is ywrite, ywis.
The Nun's Priest's Tale 3441-2

So he includes in *The Canterbury Tales* his *Melibee*—which with a smile but without irony he variously calls 'a lytel thyng in prose', 'a moral tale vertuous', 'this litel tretys' and 'this murye tale'— and the long moral treatise which the Parson tells, calling it 'a myrie tale in prose'. As these tales extend the variety of the styles of the *Tales*, shorter passages of sentence and doctrine add to the variety of tone and temper we find in the verse. But it is not always easy to forgive Chaucer the stylistic effects of this medieval ingredient. Relevant learned commentary on the action of narrative, even if put in the mouth of a character, we can accept as medieval convention. We cannot easily accept such gratuitous *exempla* as fill the last thirty lines of Dorigen's complaint in *The Franklin's Tale*,[1] and there are many other passages in which sententiousness jostles art a little harder than we should like.[2] But we should rather be pleased that so much of the doctrine and learned diction in Chaucer are drawn into the folds of his style, sometimes supported by his theme, as in *The Knight's Tale*, sometimes concealed by his characterisation, as in *The Wife of Bath's Prologue*, or subsumed under his dramatics, as in the sermon of *The Pardoner's Tale*.

The frequent pile-up of *exempla* in *The Canterbury Tales* leads us to another of Chaucer's large stylistic traits: his predilection for making lists of things. In his use of the catalogue he follows antique literary tradition and also a number of typically medieval impulses. We have already mentioned sententiousness. There is also close beside it in Chaucer a kind of lay encyclopaedism, a symptom of the secularisation of learning in the late Middle Ages, which produces vernacular bibliographies and recipes both for use and for sheer delight in the amassing of sonorous-sounding terms:

Wel knew he the olde Esculapius,
And Deyscorides, and eek Rufus,

[1] ll. 1425-56; see Germaine Dempster, 'Chaucer at Work on the Complaint in the Franklin's Tale', *Modern Language Notes*, LII (1937) 16-23.
[2] E.g. *The Physician's Tale*, ll. 240-4; *The Summoner's Tale*, from l. 2001 to 2088; the 'hasardrye' section of *The Pardoner's Tale*, ll. 590-650, similarly lacks energy.

Olde Ypocras, Haly, and Galyen,
Serapion, Razis, and Avycen,
Averrois, Damascien, and Constantyn,
Bernard, and Gatesden, and Gilbertyn.
General Prologue 429-434

Ther nas quyk-silver, lytarge, ne brymstoon,
Boras, ceruce, ne oille of tartre noon;
Ne oynement that wolde clense and byte,
That hym myghte helpen of his whelkes white.
General Prologue 629-31

I pray to God so save thy gentil cors,
And eek thyne urynals and thy jurdones,
Thyn ypocras, and eek thy galiones,
And every boyste ful of thy letuarie;
God blesse hem, and oure lady Seinte Marie!
Introduction, The Pardoner's Tale 304-8

Encyclopaedism here merges with the medieval rules of rhetoric, which are forever sanctioning the multiplication of instances. Particularly in the latter two quotations, though, we can sense Chaucer's curving of the figure toward functional literary use: suggesting the moral quality of the Summoner in the one, and a facet of the Host's character in the other. Similarly the great catalogues in *The Knight's Tale*, which merge with the description generally, help to create the rich chivalric background necessary to the tale's full meaning; and the catalogue of alchemical equipment in *The Canon's Yeoman's Prologue* is made powerfully to suggest the futility and soullessness of pure technology.

In a certain sense the sequence of portraits in the *General Prologue* (and even the sequence of *The Canterbury Tales* as a whole) has the form of a catalogue; it is possible that Chaucer's liking for this form is related ultimately to the enumerative, processional, paratactic quality that pervades the structure of *The Canterbury Tales* in large and small. The individual portraits are themselves composed of catalogues of traits. But against the stasis and formality implied by the catalogue form, many of his portraits also create the complex characterisation and display the potential energy that on a large scale disarrange and make quasi-dramatic the sequence of tales as a whole.

Chaucer's portraits are among his most characteristic and

successful literary devices, and are certainly his greatest technical innovation. They are based on the *effictio* of medieval rhetoric, a figure belonging mainly to the high style. In the French romances the formal portrait consists of a head-to-toe inventory of physical traits, often followed by a list of the character's moral qualities. The traits are mostly determined by convention. The figure lent itself particularly well to the description of allegorical personification, because in the conventional portrait the connections of the traits point in a single direction, thus creating the ideal figure contemplated by romancer and allegorist alike. Chaucer knew well the portraits in *Le Roman de la Rose*, and some of those in *The Canterbury Tales* are done in the same allegorical manner. The portrait of the Parson in the *General Prologue* eschews physical description for reasons of tone, but it has the allegorical simplicity of organisation. Equally conventional in structure are the highly concrete and decorative portraits of the kings Lygurge and Emetrius in *The Knight's Tale*, who virtually personify royal and martial magnificence. They well illustrate the fact that it is not simply concreteness of detail that is Chaucer's great innovation, but rather complexity of structure. Dante excepted (and his portraits are essentially different in kind from Chaucer's), no other medieval writer begins so well to introduce a second and third (or more) related systems of connotations into the portrait, creating the perspective—often with ironic tension—that we associate with characterisation in depth. Thus in the celebrated portrait of the Prioress we may roughly distinguish two groups of traits, compatible but not completely harmonious, one connoting religious sensibility and the other courtly delicacy. In this case the mere statement of the Prioress's occupation has such strong connotations that a large number of courtly traits can be played against it. Chaucer delights in finding traits that belong in both systems:

> And al was conscience and tendre herte.
> l. 150

The resultant ambiguity, as Professor Lowes long ago noted, is caught again perfectly in the final lines, describing the Prioress's rosary:

> Of smal coral aboute hire arm she bar
> A peire of bedes, gauded al with grene,
> And theron heng a brooch of gold ful sheene
> On which ther was first write a crowned A,
> And after *Amor vincit omnia.*
>
> 158-62

In a similar manner one might be able to distinguish and disentwine the groups of traits that go to portray the Monk, the Pardoner, Alisoun in *The Miller's Tale*, Symkyn in *The Reeve's Tale* and the rest. But structural analysis will not account for the whole of Chaucer's success. For the portrait brought out other of his particular talents, too. Considering that the fourteenth-century associations of many of his details are beyond recall, and that others (as of his various kinds of horses) have become pale, it is remarkable that so much of his imagery is in itself so expressive as to have almost symbolic force. Thus he catches with economy and special point the preposterous family pride of Symkyn and his wife:

> And she cam after in a gyte of reed;
> And Symkyn hadde hosen of the same
> *The Reeve's Tale* 3954-5

female sovereignty in the Wife of Bath:

> A foot-mantel aboute hir hipes large,
> And on hir feet a paire of spores sharpe.
> *General Prologue* 472-3

and animalism in the Miller:

> Upon the cop right of his nose he hade
> A werte, and thereon stood a toft of herys,
> Reed as the brustles of a sowes erys.
> *General Prologue* 554-6

The effect of Chaucer's portraits is also influenced by other devices, as of the placement or suppression of details. There is poetic force in the fact that the very *first* trait of the Prioress is that she 'of hir smylyng was ful symple and coy'. The portrait of Alisoun in *The Miller's Tale* depends on a submerged conventionalism, both in arrangement and in the categories of things described. Without it the rural imagery would lose some of its charm and meaning. But for the most part the portraits share that relaxed quality which we have seen elsewhere in Chaucer's style. He breaks up the formal arrangement of the conventional portrait, but does not seem to replace it with any other definable tactic. The resultant effect of spontaneity or informality is sometimes a splendid foil for such surprise effects as the final confidence concerning Absolon's squeamishness.[1] But such a sequence as the Friar's portrait seems almost too casual. Here Chaucer's Dickensian capacity to bounce us into acceptance of a character—by the brilliance of the details and the structure of their connotations— makes us forget the lack of surface arrangement.

Chaucer's style is all of a piece, and our discussion of catalogue and portrait has led us already to comments that apply to his descriptive technique generally. It is generally true of the descriptions in *The Canterbury Tales* that they transcend the purposes of mere ornament and dilatation that medieval rhetoric was content with. That Chaucer's portraits work deeply into the themes and plots of his narrative is well known. The same can be said of his settings and other extended uses of description. Those in *The Knight's Tale* are extraordinarily rich, in compliance with the subject's demand for high style, and under the beneficent influence of Boccaccio's example. This richness also answers and supports the tale's central exploration of the nature of the noble life:

> The rede statue of Mars, with spere and targe,
> So shyneth in his white baner large,
> That alle the feeldes glyteren up and doun;
> And by his baner born in his penoun
> Of gold ful riche, in which ther was ybete
> The Mynotaur, which that he slough in Crete.
>
> 975-80

> The bisy larke, messager of day,
> Salueth in hir song the morwe gray,
> And firy Phebus riseth up so bright
> That al the orient laugheth of the light,
> And with his stremes dryeth in the greves
> The silver dropes hangynge on the leves.
>
> 1491-6

Along with this bright imagery of chivalry and courtly Maying

---

[1] *The Miller's Tale*, ll. 3337-8.

some description in the poem conveys a dark mood consonant
with its awareness of death and disaster:

> The northren lyght in at the dores shoon,
> For wyndowe on the wal ne was ther noon,
> Thurgh which men myghten any light discerne.
> The dore was al of adamant eterne,
> Yclenched overthwart and endelong
> With iren tough; and for to make it strong,
> Every pyler, the temple to sustene,
> Was tonne-greet, of iren bright and shene.
> Ther saugh I first the derke ymaginyng
> Of Felonye, and al the compassyng;
> The cruel Ire, reed as any gleede;
> The pykepurs, and eek the pale Drede;
> The smylere with the knyf under the cloke;
> The shepne brennynge with the blake smoke . . .
>
> 1987-2000

Similarly the celebrated opening lines of the *General Prologue*, with
their imagery of natural regeneration, transcend their origin in the
conventional Spring description. April, sweet rains, and song
birds, set beside pilgrimage and the holy blissful martyr, establish
that double theme of nature and supernature, natural value and
spiritual, which is at the heart of the whole work.[1] The critical
reader should thus not pass by Chaucer's descriptions without
pausing to savour their strategy as well as their decorativeness.

The reader will already have heard in the passages quoted above
how well Chaucer manages sound and rhythm in support of his
meaning. While the requirements of recited narrative, and also
his temperament, prevent his writing a poetry of steadily high
compression, he can rise to the occasion at will, and many of his
passages have a quality of heavily sensuous fitness worthy of the
style of Keats or Spenser or Milton. Battle scenes brought out in
Chaucer echoes of the Anglo-Saxon heroic measure, with its
heavy beats enforced by alliteration:

> Up springen speres twenty foot on highte;
> Out goon the swerdes as the silver brighte;

---

[1] See Arthur Hoffman, 'Chaucer's Prologue to Pilgrimage: The Two Voices',
ELH, XXI (1954) 1-16; Ralph Baldwin, 'The Unity of the Canterbury Tales',
Anglistica, V (Copenhagen 1955), pp. 19-32.

> The helmes they tohewen and toshrede;
> Out brest the blood with stierne stremes rede;
> With myghty maces the bones they tobreste.
> He thurgh the thikkeste of the throng gan threste;
> Ther stomblen stedes stronge, and doun gooth al.
>
> *The Knight's Tale* 2607-13

He uses alliteration, the close coupling of stresses, and heavy pauses to convey the weight and solidity of the Miller's physique:

> The Millere was a stout carl for the nones;
> Ful byg he was of brawn, and eek of bones.
> He was short-sholdred, brood, a thikke knarre;
> There was no dore that he nolde heve of harre . . .

Conversely, the speed suggested in the next line is supported by the quick run of syllables:

> Or breke it at a rennyng with his heed.
>
> *The Miller's Tale* 545-9

In *The Nun's Priest's Tale* Chaucer uses quick, lightly-stressed monosyllables to convey the effect of chickens' pecking, supported by the sharpness of an initial accented syllable:

> Pekke hem up right as they growe and ete hem yn.
>
> l. 2967

In his description of old January's singing, the emphasis of the 'k' sound and the insistent flapping of the unaccented syllables beautifully underline the meaning:

> . . . ful of jargon as a flekked pye.
> The slakke skyn aboute his nekke shaketh,
> Whil that he sang, so chaunteth he and craketh.
>
> *The Merchant's Tale* 1848-50

The effect of Jankyn's fall at the end of *The Wife of Bath's Prologue* is expressed in the ryhthm:

> Al sodeynly thre leves have I plyght
> Out of his book, right as he radde, and eke
> I with my fest so took hym on the cheke
> That in our fyr he fil bakward adoun.
>
> 790-3

Here the stressed syllable 'doun' is given a memorable extra emphasis by the enjambement which speeds the passage toward it, and by the artful shifting of the preceding stress out of the normal iambic pattern, allowing a pause before the final, climactic thump.

While Chaucer thus shares this technical gift with all good poets, his peculiar talent, evident in the last quotation and remarked by many critics,[1] is his consistent ability to maintain the onward flow of his narrative verse in a lively and varied way. The Man of Law's disparagement of Chaucer's verse that

> he kan but lewedly
> On metres and on rymyng craftily,

is a joke that Chaucer can well afford to make. His narrative, while natural, is impeccably metrical, and his rhymes satisfyingly easy and accurate. To these ends he uses many resources: syntactic variations, the optional use of the final *-e*, a large vocabulary, and a great variety of parentheses, appositives, exclamations, pleonasms of all sorts. It is these 'fillers' that give his narrative some of its leisureliness, and he has a marvellous trick of turning them to poetic account. As a first-person narrator (whether speaking in his own voice or through a Canterbury pilgrim) he can address to his audience phrases which both fill out his line or couplet and support his tone of easy colloquy:

> And certeinly, to *tellen as it was,*
> Of this vessel the Cook drank faste, *allas!*
> *What needed hym? he drank ynough biforn.*
> And whan he hadde pouped in this horn . . .
> *The Manciple's Prologue* 87-90

Occasionally we can catch him squandering a handful of verses in warming up to his task,[2] and from tale to tale his inspiration seems to have had its ups and downs. Sometimes the movement is quite slow, with successive clauses having as much the effect of braking as of advancing the narrative:

> The thridde day, this marchant up ariseth,
> And on his nedes sadly hym avyseth,
> And up into his countour-hous gooth he
> To rekene with hymself, as wel may be,

---

[1] See, e.g., J. L. Lowes, *Geoffrey Chaucer and the Development of his Genius,* Boston 1934, pp. 243-4; H. S. Bennett, *Chaucer and the Fifteenth Century,* Oxford 1947, pp. 88-95.

[2] E.g. *The Squire's Tale,* ll. 401-8.

Of thilke yeer how that it with hym stood,
And how that he despended hadde his good,
And if that he encressed were or noon.
The Shipman's Tale 75-81

At some notable moments it is extraordinarily spare and fast:

And with the staf she drow ay neer and neer,
And wende han hit this Aleyn at the fulle,
And smoot the millere on the pyled skulle,
That doun he gooth, and cride, 'Harrow! I dye!'
Thise clerkes beete hym weel and lete hym lye;
And greythen hem, and took hir hors anon,
And eek hire mele, and on hir wey they gon.
The Reeve's Tale 4304-10

Generally, then, his narrative verse is flexible and versatile, flowing around the more static passages of description, lyricism, and sententiousness, and floating them, as it were, in a forward-moving current.

Chaucer's brilliant technique with dramatic verse has been so widely celebrated as to need no further exposition here. Where he has perhaps lacked due appreciation is in the other direction, in the sphere of undramatic lyricism and of formal rhetorical effects generally. Chaucer went to school to the rhetoricians; he knows well their 'termes', 'colours', and 'figures', and it is a mistake to think that he uses formal rhetoric less in *The Canterbury Tales* than in the early works, or that he tends to use it only as it is sanctioned by dramatics.[1] Both of these ideas stem from the feeling that because medieval rhetoric was based on bad theory and bad models, and practised by bad poets, its figures of speech are somehow inherently bad. To the obvious proposition that a certain concentration of figures of speech is normal to poetry, we must add the fact that *The Canterbury Tales* contains some very good poetry that is at the same time highly rhetorical. The question, of course, is not whether the rhetoricians' intricate patterns of words are used, but whether they work. Chaucer could make them work. To be sure, Chaucer in *The Canterbury Tales* seems very conscious of rhetoric. It is one of the subjects (like women and marriage)

[1] Ideas propagated by J. M. Manly, 'Chaucer and the Rhetoricians', *Proceedings of the British Academy*, XII (1926) 95-113.

that he is forever making jokes about. The Host asks the Clerk not to use it; the Franklin says that he never learned it; the Squire claims to be a poor rhetorician who 'kan not clymben over so heigh a style'; the Nun's Priest longs for the skill of a Geoffrey of Vinsauf (author of an *ars poetica*) to complain the abduction of Chauntecleer. Yet each of their tales uses rhetorical passages, and in many others Chaucer introduces them without self-consciousness.

Leaving out, for the moment, the consideration that many of Chaucer's characteristic devices (the long description, the portrait, the catalogue, the sententious amplification) have their origins in rhetorical tradition—taking into account, rather, only the local texture or feel of his verse—his poetry seems most formally wrought, most 'rhetorical', when it approaches the lyric note, and especially within the formal apostrophe or invocation. Such passages as Arcite's death-speech and Constance's prayer on the beach are full of tropes and patternings of words from the rhetoric books: *exclamatio, interrogatio, pronominatio* (epithet), and the varieties of repetition *traductio, repetitio, adnominatio*:

> Allas, the wo! allas, the peynes stronge,
> That I for you have suffred, and so longe!
> Allas, the death! allas, myn Emelye!
> Allas, departynge of our compaignye!
> Allas, myn hertes queene! allas, my wyf!
> Myn hertes lady, endere of my lyf!

Chaucer uses his repetitions and antitheses so beautifully to build feeling that we hardly notice the rhetorical artifice that brings the passage to its climax:

> What is this world? what asketh men to have?
> Now with his love, now in his colde grave
> Allone, withouten any compaignye.
> *The Knight's Tale* 2771-9

Similarly, the moving climax of Constance's invocation to the Virgin is the most intricate of four stanzas of 'rhetoric':

> Thow sawe thy child yslayn bifore thyne yen,
> And yet now liveth my litel child, parfay!
> Now, lady bright, to whom alle woful cryen,
> Thow glorie of wommanhede, thow faire may,

Thow haven of refut, brighte sterre of day,
Rewe on my child, that of thy gentillesse,
Rewest on every reweful in distresse.
The Man of Law's Tale 848-54

The 'style of the man', then, comprehends a great technical range, from this to the fully natural idiom and rhythms of the dramatic monologues.

II

Turning now to the 'style of the work', we may first repeat the observation that *The Canterbury Tales* in general show a close correspondence between kinds of style and areas of meaning. Chaucer continually makes choices among the technical means at his command, restricting and altering his style according to the attitudes he is expressing. The general lines of his strategy are those learned from literary tradition, particularly the French. French courtly literature presented to Chaucer a clearly defined style, which in its best exemplars, as *Le Roman de la Rose* of Guillaume de Lorris, was superbly designed to express courtly idealism. The courtly style in an impossibly pure form would be characterised by a slow tempo, unruffled rhythm, exotic setting, extensive description of a static, conventional, formal nature, formal portraiture, polite diction, rhetorical and lyrical discourse. Characterisation would be simple and allegorical. Essentially non-dramatic, the whole poetry would find its truest connection with human interest in its rendering of an ideal and longed-for world of the imagination. Side by side with this highly 'conventional' (by which I mean 'non-representational') poetry, the literature of the medieval 'realistic' tradition presented Chaucer with the opposite style. The French fabliaux could teach him that along with comic disenchantment went rapid tempo, turbulent rhythm, spare and familiar settings, domestic imagery, colloquial and impolite discourse. The great dramatic monologues in Jean de Meun's continuation of *Le Roman de la Rose* showed him the beginnings of a complex, realistic characterisation; furthermore, they showed him that a realistic style could transcend farce, and begin to support other and more seriously 'realistic' views of life.[1]

[1] This, with some of the ensuing remarks, is the thesis of the present writer's

Secular literature, then, roughly oriented for Chaucer two styles and their related areas of meaning. Although for the sake of brevity I have greatly simplified the descriptions of both the styles and the traditions that produced them, the reader will no doubt still recognise that some of *The Canterbury Tales* belong to the tradition of courtly-conventional style and some to the 'realistic'. When he deals with extremes of attitude, Chaucer uses a relatively pure style, one or the other. *The Knight's Tale* with its slow pace, antique setting, elaborate, static descriptions, elevated speeches, and simple characterisation, is written in a conventional style which beautifully supports the idealism of its theme. *The Clerk's Tale*, not specifically a 'courtly' poem, is nevertheless highly conventional; its style exhibits many of the traits which the courtly tradition shares with the idealism of pious legend. These poems, together with *The Squire's Tale*, *The Franklin's Tale*, and *The Man of Law's Tale*, admirably exemplify Chaucer's great range of tone and colour within what is essentially the same stylistic system. It corresponds to the whole range of feeling between Knight and Clerk, who yet have beneath their differences a common denominator of idealism.

At the other end of the scale we have the poems which are predominantly 'realistic'—in the limited sense in which we are here using that term. They assert in various ways the primacy of matter and of animal nature in human concerns; accordingly their style is compounded of domestic imagery, natural discourse, local setting. They normally eschew formal rhetoric and extended description. Chaucer's tonal range within this style is narrower than that within conventional style, but his technical skill is, if anything, greater. Each of his realisms is different. The style that supports ordinary fabliau comedy in *The Shipman's Tale* is made specially acerb in *The Reeve's Tale*. The latter has a special sharpness in its descriptions, a special irony created by its use of dialect, which are acutely well suited to the Reeve's attitudes. The realistic setting of *The Miller's Tale* is similar to and yet unmistakably different from the worlds of domestic images built up in

Chaucer and the French Tradition, Berkeley and Cambridge 1957; on the style of the Old French fabliaux, see Per Nykrog, *Les Fabliaux*, Copenhagen 1957, esp. Chap. IX.

the course of *The Wife of Bath's Prologue* and *The Summoner's Tale*. If the Miller's world is to him a congenial and manageable one, it is not as much owned and loved as is the Wife of Bath's; and neither's world is to be confused with the dark welter of the Canon's Yeoman's, which is neither loved nor manageable at all.

Both 'realism' and 'conventionalism' are tools to the mature Chaucer. The ultimate style of *The Canterbury Tales*, which I shall call the 'mixed style', is the result of his management of the two traditional styles at once. This is evident in that many of the greatest tales are themselves of mixed style, and that in the context of the pilgrimage frame even the tales of relatively pure realism and conventionalism are set in meaningful juxtaposition to each other. The variety of style in *The Canterbury Tales* is thus great and yet artfully composed. It produces in large and small that distinctively Chaucerian effect of irony, perspective, relativity, humour; it supports the complex view of man's pilgrimage that is the subject of the whole work.

Let me here try to sidestep an obvious danger in this perhaps foolhardy attempt to deal with the 'style' of so vast a poem. In implying that *The Canterbury Tales* is basically 'ironic' in style, I do not wish to give the impression that the stylistic co-ordinates I have chosen—conventionalism and realism—are the only possible co-ordinates, or that certain themes and stylistic situations are not actually exempt from Chaucer's irony. One might profitably distinguish as quite separate Chaucer's learned or scholastic style, characterised by logical argument and Latin terminology. Assuredly one can isolate, somewhere between realism and convention, a Chaucerian 'pathetic' style, composed with simple characterisation, plain diction, spare and humble setting, and reaching for great idealising power. It associates itsed in Chaucer with the themes of parent and child and of wrongelf innocence, and its most successful exemplar is *The Prioress's Tale*. Here the pathos attaching to the little martyr is supported by a childlike tone, created in part through the use of simple, black-and-white contrasts, repetitions of words and phrases giving an effect of simplicity, a plentiful use of terms ('litel', 'smal', 'yong') denoting the diminutive, and a syntax that catches childhood's simplicity of expression:

This litel child, his litel book lernynge,
As he sat in the scole at his prymer,
He *alma redemptoris* herde synge,

. . . As children lerned hir antiphoner;
'I kan namoore expounde in this mateere;
I lerne song, I kan but smal grammeere.'

'And is this song maked in reverence
Of Cristes mooder?' seyde this innocent. . .

            O deere child, I halse thee,
In vertu of the Hooly Trinitee,
Tel me what is thy cause for to synge,
Sith that thy throte is kut to my semynge?
                    516-648

We hear the pathetic note in the Hugelino episode of *The Monk's Tale*, and at points in the tales of the Clerk, the Franklin, the Physician and the Man of Law. In *The Clerk's Tale* it is attended by biblically simple description and mostly by an admirable restraint of sentiment:

But ther as ye me profre swich dowaire
As I first broghte, it is wel in my mynde
It were my wrecched clothes, nothyng faire,
The which to me were hard now for to fynde.
O goode God! how gentil and how kynde
Ye seemed by youre speche and youre visage
The day that maked was oure mariage!
                    848-54

But elsewhere in this otherwise superb poem, and more commonly in the Man of Law's and Physician's tales, we can hear Chaucer squeezing it a bit hard, and falling into sentimentality. Only in the description of the 'hoomly suffisaunce' of the poor widow at the opening of *The Nun's Priest's Tale* are any passages associated with this pathetic style directly exposed to Chaucer's searching comedy. The very sacredness of the pathetic subject-matter exempts it from criticism or even from ventilation; but by the same token it allows Chaucer to write some of his least successful verses. In any event, while the pathetic contributes to the variety of the *Tales*, it is not an important axis of his style. Chaucer drew to an extent on the legends and lyrics in honour of the Virgin Mary in his treatment of motherhood and children, but his sentimental pathos does not seem directed by a strong antecedent tradition of style, and he uses it only in *The Canterbury Tales*. There is none of it in the pathos of the earlier poems. It is late-Chaucerian as it is late-medieval. We may note that before this time little children do not figure prominently in medieval literature, and the literature is remarkably free from sentimentality.

On the other hand the 'mixed style'—the interplay of conventional and realistic styles—has a clear basis in earlier medieval tradition and is a prominent feature of Chaucer's whole career as a poet. In him, indeed, the medieval comedy of a *Flamenca*, the irony of a Jean de Meun, the parodic elements in the *Renart* cycle and the fabliaux, found a particularly congenial development. The historical influence fell in, as it were, with a temperament and personality—not to speak of a technical range—that were admirably (almost explosively!) receptive to it. The brilliant variegation of *The House of Fame* and the ironic structure of the *Troilus* both show this.

We have already touched on some of the basic traits of Chaucer's literary personality that would be hospitable to the formation of a mixed style. His insouciance, his amateur stance, itself implies a requisite freedom from the strict bonds of decorum. Equally congenial is his tendency to play with perspective, for the mixed style is similarly based on the shift from one plane of reference to another. The first-person narrator's conventional and innocuous freedom to remind us of his own status as narrator—'This wydwe, *of which I telle you my tale*'—is always in Chaucer's hands on the verge of growing up into an instrument of perspective:

> Thise been the cokkes wordes, and nat myne;
> I kan noon harm of no womman divyne.
> *The Nun's Priest's Tale* 2824; 3265-6

The variety of narrative tones which he can assume—now knowing, now obtuse, now neutral—is of course not the same as the mixed style, but it bespeaks the temperament congenial to that style.

However, the richest source of the aptitude which Chaucer poured into the mixed style was in his language, particularly his natural propensity to speak in terms of familiar things, in terms of earth, rural nature, the human body. When energised, raised in intensity, given full context, it supports the most memorable recommendation of naturalness in English:

> Lat hem be breed of pured whete-seed,
> And lat us wyves hoten barly-breed.
>
> Thise wormes, ne thise motthes, ne thise mytes,
> Upon my peril, frete hem never a deel;
> And wostow why? for they were used weel.
>
> . . . me thoughte he hadde a paire
> Of legges and of feet so clene and faire
> That al myn herte I yaf unto his hoold.
> He was, I trowe, a twenty wynter oold . . .
> *The Wife of Bath's Prologue* 143-4, 560-2, 597-600

Conjoined with the French and the Latin terminology, with the sophisticated idiom of the courtier and man of letters, it creates on the level of language an ironic mixture analogous to Chaucer's mixing of larger units of style.

It is a miracle of Chaucer's style—of the same provenience as his unerring feel for expressive imagery—that his familiar language does not seem to collide with his high style except when he wants it to. One of the great pleasures in reading him is to attend to the nature of the language, to gauge when it is in ironic adjustment and when not. Chaucer can have it either way; it is a mistake to think that the current is always on. The knight's reference to the oxen in his plough does not create irony. Much of the time the familiar works harmoniously along with the learning and the formal artifice, leavening and lightening them as in this perfect *exemplum* from *The Manciple's Tale*:

> Lat take a cat, and fostre hym wel with milk
> And tendre flessh, and make his couche of silk,
> And lat hym seen a mous go by the wal,
> Anon he weyveth milk and flessh and al,
> And every deyntee that is in that hous,
> Swich appetit hath he to ete a mous.
> Lo, heere hath lust his dominacioun,
> And appetit fleemeth discrecioun.
> 175-82

While the connotations of 'cat' and 'mouse' and the rest have some bearing on the moral quality of Phebus's wife, who is ultimately being described here, their juxtaposition to such learned terms as 'dominacioun', 'appetit' and 'discrecioun' is not meant to be comic, though we are forced to smile at the purely Chaucerian quality of the passage.

Even at his most relaxed moments, however, Chaucer is aware of the potency of the mixed idiom, and there is a sprinkling of its use for small local 'ironic' effects throughout *The Canterbury Tales*. Chaucer can call at will for a satiric snap in the contrast between Latin polysyllables and plain speech:

> A somonour is a rennere up and doun
> With mandementz for fornicacioun,
> And is ybet at every townes ende.
> > *The Friar's Prologue* 1283-5

> What spekestow of preambulacioun?
> What! amble, or trotte, or pees, or go sit down!
> > *The Wife of Bath's Prologue* 837-8

Sometimes the natural enmity between barnyard imagery and educated judgment is stated while it is being used:

> Straw for thy Senek, and for thy proverbes!
> I counte not a panyer ful of herbes
> Of scole-termes.
> > *The Merchant's Tale* 1567-9

> But, for ye speken of swich gentillesse
> As is descended out of old richesse,
> That therefore sholden ye be gentil men,
> Swich arrogance is not worth an hen.
> > *The Wife of Bath's Tale* 1109-12

In *The Franklin's Tale* Chaucer sports with the pretentiousness of astronomical time-description:

> . . . the brighte sonne lost his hewe;
> For th'orisonte hath reft the sonne his lyght,—
> This is as much to say as it was nyght.—
> > 1016-18

Harry Bailly's unwontedly rhetorical invocation to Bacchus in *The Manciple's Prologue* is self-consciously brought to earth: 'Of that matere ye gete namoore of me' (l. 102). A large measure of the humour of *The Tale of Sir Thopas* lies in its play with a mixture of romance convention and mundane imagery. Hardly one of the tales—the pious ones excepted—is without some mixture of this kind.

As I have already indicated, some of the best tales depend for their central meaning on the raising of the mixture of styles into a large structural principle. To speak in terms of genre, the Miller's and Merchant's tales radically combine stylistic traits of fabliau and romance; *The Nun's Priest's Tale*—to over-simplify grossly—combines animal fable and epic. In each the traits of the different styles are carefully exploited for the humour, the satire, the irony they produce when placed together. *The Miller's Tale* manages to remain fabliau, but there was never such a profound one. The tale needs its rich elaboration of courtly conventionalism to make such comic capital of its assertion of naturalness. We find the same mixture in *The Merchant's Tale*, but in very different adjustment. Here the cynically realistic undercutting of the pretence of romantic idealism produces a bitter humour. The mixture of *The Nun's Priest's Tale* produces yet another range of effects. It is *The Canterbury Tales* in little; its kaleidoscopic shifts of perspective, exposing a dozen important subjects to the humour of comparison, seems to exemplify Chaucer's basic method in the whole work. The tale illustrates, too, how much of Chaucer's technical range, how many of his favourite rhetorical procedures, can finally be enlisted in the service of the mixed style: courtly diction, and realistic, formal portraiture, rhetorical invocation, pathetic description; sententiousness becomes an instrument in his parody of learned discourse, and even the encyclopaedic catalogue appears, in an implied commentary on medical science:

> A day or two ye shul have digestyves
> Of wormes, er ye take your laxatyves
> Of lawriol, centaure, and fumetere,
> Or elles of ellebor, that groweth there,
> Of katapuce, or of gaitrys beryis,
> Of herbe yve, growing in oure yeerd, ther mery is;
> Pekke hem up right as they growe and ete hem yn.

In *The Pardoner's Tale* the mixed style is an instrument of the remarkable characterisation which finally dominates the poem. It is the very style of the Pardoner, who is the only pilgrim dramatically given literary powers comparable to those of Chaucer himself. The depth of the characterisation depends in part on the fact that in the Pardoner's mixed style, unlike in Chaucer's, the speaker is somehow made to fail in his irony. He turns out to be hardly humorous at all; his style rather deepens the curious blend of the grotesque and the pathetic already to be found in his portrait.

The stylistic components of the tale are easy to discern. The tale (with its prologue) is a dramatic monologue—that of Jean de Meun's character Faus-Semblant, but technically much more skilful. Within the dramatic monologue is a real medieval sermon, with its homiletic realism, its rhetoric and its *exempla*. On this level we are on familiar Chaucerian ground. The high-flown rhetoric of the sermon, in the context of the self-revelation of the monologue, produces a mock-effect which satirises the canned fireworks of the professional preachers. Chaucer underlines this effect by making the rhetorical outbursts glaringly ornamental, so that our attention is transferred from the meaning of the speech to the manipulations of the speaker. One can almost hear the Pardoner simulating the tears of St Paul:

> The apostel weping seith ful pitously,
> 'Ther walken manye of which you toold have I—
> I seye it now wepyng, with pitous voys—
> That they been enemys of Cristes croys,
> Of which the ende is death, wombe is hir god!'
> O wombe! O bely! O stynkyng cod,
> Fulfilled of dong and of corrupcioun!
>
> 529-35

John Speirs has well pointed out the conjunction in this sermon 'of vigorous popular speech with scholastic phraseology', of 'coarseness and . . . metaphysics'. The realistic imagery here is inherited along with the learning from the ascetic-homiletic tradition, with its graphic descriptions of the fleshliness that must be condemned. But Chaucer makes it too vivid to remain simply satiric. It is presented with such a 'thunderous overcharge . . . of feeling,' Speirs points out, that it characterises the Pardoner as being unconsciously 'both half-horrified and half-fascinated' by his subject.[1] This is going beyond the ordinary Chaucerian irony; it makes the sermon both more ironic and less ironic than the Pardoner knows. His fascination raises his cyncism to a grotesque new power, while his horror reduces it to pathos. The sermon's great terminal *exemplum* of the three revellers who sought Death similarly breaks through the bounds of a simple satire on sermons. It is too convincing. The resulting stretch in the characterisation between redeeming sincerity and outright monstrosity is underlined stylistically in the sequence beginning at line 895. The whole gamut of Chaucer's styles can be found here in twenty lines, from the terrible rhetorical outcry, through the 'broches, spoones, rynges' of domestic realism, to the touching special simplicity of 'And lo, sires, thus I preche'.

The juxtaposition of tales to each other and to the dramatic frame of the pilgrimage is the largest counter of Chaucer's style. It is the largest manifestation of what we can see in *The Canterbury Tales* from the mixed idiom up: Chaucer's endless interest in comparisons and relationships. 'How shall the world be served?' is the question he asks. The great range of values and attitudes expressed in the tales represent his grand confrontation of it. The comedy and the tolerant irony, the relativism, the necessity to perceive: these are the answer implied by his mixed style.

[1] John Speirs, *Chaucer the Maker*, London 1951, pp. 171-4.

Chaucer's narrative art
in *The Canterbury Tales*

NEVILL COGHILL

FEW and feeble were the hints about how to tell a story that came down to Chaucer from the rhetorical tradition in which he was nursed. All that the masters in rhetoric could say was that there were nine ways of telling a story, of which the first was the *natural*, that is, to begin at the beginning, go on to the middle and so proceed to the end. *Cuilibet*, they added, *datum est sic incipere.*[1] 'Any fool' (as we would say) 'can start like that.'

The more admired ways were the *artificial*; a virtuoso would begin in the middle, or even at the end, and then revert to the beginning by flash-back; that accounted for two more of the nine ways. Or he might begin with a *sententia* and go on from that to beginning, middle, or end; that made six. Or he might begin with an *exemplum* and do likewise. That completed the possibilities in nine easy lessons. In *The Canterbury Tales*, Chaucer clung to the *natural* way; only one pilgrim uses an artificial opening—the Pardoner, who begins with a *sententia* or text:

Radix malorum est cupiditas.

The rhetoricians further declared that there were three styles— The High, The Middle and The Low.[2] Chaucer mentions the High style through the mouths of the Clerk of Oxford[3] and the Squire,[4] who evidently admire it, and through that of the Host, who has his reservations. It should be kept for writing to kings, he says:

[1] Edmond Faral, *Les Arts Poetiques du XIIᵉ et du XIIIᵉ Siècles*, Paris 1923, p. 265.
[2] Ibid., pp. 86, 312.
[3] *The Clerk's Prologue*, E 41.
[4] *The Squire's Tale*, F 105-6.

> Youre termes, youre colours and youre figures,
> Keepe hem in stoor til so be that ye endite
> Heigh style, as whan that men to kynges write.
>
> *The Clerk's Prologue* E 16-18

We have only one example of a letter from Chaucer to a king. It is his *Complaint to his Purse*, the envoy of which is addressed to the 'Conquerour of Brutes Albyon', the newly-crowned King Henry IV. This poem seems to deploy a high magniloquence:

> Now voucheth sauf this day, or yt be nyght,
> That I of yow the blisful soun may here,
> Or see your colour lyk the sonne bryght,
> That of yelownesse hadde never pere.

Such a use of language might grace the speeches of a high-born lover to his lady; yet it is here ironical, and the lofty note it strikes is derided in the ten low words of an adjacent line:

> For I am shave as nye as any frere.

No one, perhaps, will deny that *The Knight's Tale* is written in a higher style than any of the other tales, and some may think that the 'severely muted'[1] variation of it we meet within the tales of Dame Custance, Griselda and St Cecilia, might be classed as a Middle style, along with that of *The Physician's Tale* and some others, and wish to leave the Low style for the Millers, Reeves, Summoners and their like. But this fitting into indeterminate literary categories is a useless parlour game when their imaginary frontiers can be crossed by a flash of irony. Any sensitive reader will feel that the melancholy line describing our human condition in the grave, which Arcite utters as his eyes are dusking into death,

> Allone, withouten any compaignye.
> *The Knight's Tale* A 2779

is in as high a style as language can reach, well worthy of a letter to a king, or even of a prayer to God; but we meet it again in *The Miller's Tale* (A 3204), where it seems no higher than its surroundings.[2] If I have rightly discriminated Chaucer's uses of

---

[1] Charles Muscatine, *Chaucer and the French Tradition, a study in style and meaning*, University of California Press 1957, p. 192.

[2] Some critics have thought that the repetition of this line of the Knight's by the Miller was intended as a piece of deliberate parody on his part, in his effort to 'quite' the Knight; but I cannot believe Chaucer could have intended so feeble, so pointless a kind of parody; the author of *The Tale of Sir Thopas* knew more

the three styles, all that can be said of them is that he could pour out poetry in any of them indifferently, in the style we know as Chaucerian.

The simple truth is that he used whatever word he needed when he needed it, and at all times created his own fluid decorum to suit whatever he happened to be talking about and the attitude he had towards it, or with which he was endowing one of his characters towards it. The Merchant elegantly dodges an ugly word, with bland apologies (E 2361-3) and the Manciple blunders into one and makes a swift and ironical self-extrication (H 205-6); by a like device, Chaucer himself makes excuses more than once for his own freedoms (A 725-42, 3171-85). But these are tricks.

Chaucer's real debt to the arts of rhetoric is a matter neither of form, nor of style, but of know-how in the handling of particular turns and climaxes in his story, to elicit or comment upon some special point. Without his fluent knowledge of the dodges of rhetoric that had come to him from habitual use, Chaucer's narrative art would have been as grey as Gower's, as clumsy as Lydgate's. Execution is the chariot of genius. In every art, technical craft has its part in the flash of inspiration. A composer must at some time learn the range and tone of every instrument in the orchestra, and what kinds of phrase can be fingered on it, in what keys. Just as he will be prompted to the elaboration of one musical idea on the strings, and of another on the wood-wind, by a process that seems to be one of unthinking impulse, but yet has the pattern of a long experience to guide it, so Chaucer was prompted to the elaboration of his ideas, with a similar immediacy, by a knowledge that had become effortless, of the main figures of rhetoric. Needing, for instance, the accents of solemnity for some serious invocation, he would reach for a *conduplicatio*[1] as naturally as Mozart, to damn Don Giovanni, reached for the trombones.

In his own times Chaucer was much admired for his skill in these arts, and to be unable to recognise them is to miss a great

about parody than that. I believe the line appears identically in both tales by pure coincidence. There are other such coincidences in *The Canterbury Tales*, e.g. *The Shipman's Tale*, l. 9 and *The Merchant's Tale*, l. 1315.

[1] That form of apostrophe in which the apostrophising phrase is repeated, as in *Troilus and Criseyde*, V, 1828-32 and 1849-54.

part of the pleasure of craftmanship in his 'making'. But his verse responds just as fully to what our own age asks of poetry as it does to what the rhetoricians demanded, answering richly to the new kinds of critical question we have been learning to ask since Coleridge and Wordsworth began thinking about language and imagination. For the more we know and understand the actual world and language of Chaucer's age, the more we can see that he habitually used 'a selection of the language really used by men', chose 'incidents and situations from the common life' (of the fourteenth century), cast over them 'a certain colouring of the imagination' and made them 'interesting by tracing in them truly, though not ostentatiously, the primary laws of our nature'.[1]

For the more subtle demands that we have come to make of poetry, in the use of imagery and symbol, in ironies and ambiguities, in the organic interplay of parts within the unity of a whole work, in the consistency of poetical texture and, most of all, in a lucid general vision of our human world and its position in the natural, and indeed supernatural, universe, expressed in a language that has a 'divine fluidity of movement',[2] Chaucer's verse is as rich as any but Shakespeare's. Yet, in two related points, he differs from later poets; he makes no great trade in the ambivalences and play of words which are now so much esteemed, it is his custom to use language clearly and decisively rather than suggestively and by opalescence; there are exceptions to this,[3] but the ambiguities of meaning that are so strong a characteristic of his style are rarely due to the prismatic qualities in words that later poets have exploited, so much as to ironic counter-thoughts concealed in simple statements. There is no verbal ambiguity when January assures the shrinking May (who in any case, at that moment, has other things more pressing than the thought of sin to fear) that

> A man may do no synne with his wyf,
> Ne hurte hymselven with his owene knyf.
>
> The Merchant's Tale E 1839-40

Innocently, in his wishful thinking, this silly old lecher means and

---

[1] William Wordsworth, Preface to the *Lyrical Ballads*, 2nd ed.

[2] Matthew Arnold, *Essays in Criticism*, 2nd Series, *The Study of Poetry*.

[3] I am not sure how good a case can be made for them, nor, I think, is Professor

believes exactly what he says; but we who listen to his love-
making are supposed to understand that his officially sanctified lust
has deluded him and that the opposite of what he says is true; and, in
case we miss the point, we are later on put right by the Parson:

> And for that many man weneth that he may nat
> synne, for no likerousnesse that he dooth with
> his wyf, certes, that opinion is fals. God woot,
> a man may sleen himself with his owene knyf . . .
> *The Parson's Tale* I 855-60

As owners of knives well know, this is only common sense. The
Parson uses this trope as a sort of simile; it is in his use of simile
and metaphor that Chaucer again differs considerably from later
poets. He uses the former more often than the latter and is sparing
in both. It was a principle with the rhetoricians that similes should
be brief and infrequent.[1] Suggestivenesses, refractions, the creative
imprecisions and impressionist enrichments possible in the handling of words and metaphors, are rare in Chaucer; or, if they are
not, scholarship has not yet, I think, discovered them, and we
may believe that Chaucer, like Pandarus, assigned this manner of
speaking to the gods as their prerogative:

> For goddes speken in amphibologies,
> And, for a sooth, they tellen twenty lyes.
> *Troilus and Criseyde* IV 1406-7

Pandarus is indeed our main source for what Chaucer thought
about style, and in setting out such hints as can be found in
Chaucer about the art of composition, we must begin with him,
then move on to others:

> *Pandarus*
>
> (a)　How so it be that som men hem delite
> 　　　With subtyl art hire tales for to endite,
> 　　　Yet for al that, in hire entencioun,
> 　　　Hire tale is al for som conclusioun.
> 　　　And sithen th'ende is every tales strengthe . . .
> 　　　*Troilus and Criseyde* II 256-60

Empson, who, long ago, tried to apply his otherwise most fruitful quest for
ambiguity to Chaucer's use of words (see William Empson, *Seven Types of
Ambiguity*, third ed., London 1953, pp. 58 *et seq.*) As will, however, presently
be seen, I shall suppose an unambiguous duality of meaning was intended by
Chaucer in his use of the word *end* (end=termination/end=objective) when he
makes Pandarus say 'sithen th'ende is every tales strengthe'.

[1] Faral, op. cit., pp. 69, 181.

(b)   Ne jompre ek no discordant thyng yfeere,
        As thus, to usen termes of phisik
        In loves termes; hold of thi matere
        The forme alwey, and do that it be lik . . .
                Ibid. II, 1037-40

The Squire

(c)   The knotte why that every tale is toold,
        If it be taried til that lust be coold
        Of hem that han it after herkned yoore,
        The savour passeth ever lenger the moore,
        For fulsomnesse of his prolixitee . . .
            The Squire's Tale F 401-5

The Host

(d)   Beth fructuous, and that in litel space.
           The Parson's Prologue I 71

The Nun's Priest

(e)   For seint Paul seith that al that writen is,
        To oure doctrine it is ywrite, ywis;
        Taketh the fruyt, and lat the chaf be stille.
         The Nun's Priest's Tale B^2 3441-3

The last of these jottings is a reminder that Chaucer lived in the hey-day of the *exemplum*, that is, of a story that is fashioned to embody a teaching idea. It had been a standard way of popular instruction ever since the parables of Christ, and at its heels came allegory and symbolism. Christ's teachings, for the most part, have come down to us on the pure bone of aphorism and of narrative; the shape of the bone is the image of a moral idea or judgment in values; such, for instance, is the story of the Prodigal Son, in which no word is not a necessary part of the narrative, yet the whole displays its unspoken moral judgments. This high art, in lesser hands, can dwindle into cautionary tales, from which the moral is extracted and exhibited like a reluctant tooth, as, all too often, in *The Confessio Amantis*, or in that collection of *exempla* collected for the frustration of his daughters by the *Knight of the Tour Landry*.[1] Many of Chaucer's stories are also built on the

---

[1] See *The Knight de la Tour Landry*, EETS. Original Series, XXXIII.

sharp bone of a moral idea; the story of Griselda, as he tells us himself, exemplifies the patience with which we ought to undergo the trials that God sends down for the exercise of our virtues (E 1142-62), and Dame Custance is hardly less exemplary in her role of steadfast heroine. Even Chauntecleer knows and uses *exempla*, to defeat his wife with.

In Chaucer's use, the bone is continually fleshed with the more-than-moral interest of the actual world. He always has a plentitude above that of the ethical tapeworm of Gower's narrative-instruction, and the reason for this is Chaucer's obedience to the Pandarian principle *do that it be lik*. In the stories that he tells, he seeks to show as full a likeness as possible to the world he knows. The constancy of Custance, his major theme in *The Man of Law's Tale*, is inseparable from his interest in the world she lives in; he is inquisitive about it, and goes beyond his source in picturing, peopling and expounding it. He wonders who preserved her in those stormy seas, he overhears her prayers, notices the corruption of her Latin, pictures her helpless child, imagines her terrified embarrassment when, almost fainting, she is at last rejoined to her seemingly cruel husband after their long separation; and by a hundred other humane touches (even in this early work) he illustrates her actual world, and indeed takes sides against her enemies with a naive charm which I cannot attribute to the Man of Law (to whom, temporarily, or by some aberration, Chaucer gave the story) bursting out with

> O Donegild, I ne have noon Englissh digne
> Unto thy malice and they tirannye!
> *The Man of Law's Tale* B¹ 778-80

Nothing of this is in Nicholas Trivet's Anglo-Norman *Chronicle*, where Chaucer found the story. It gives life to the *exemplum*.

Leaving St Paul's hint, and returning to those of Pandarus, the Squire and the Host, we may list in modern terms the principles of short-storytelling they contain. In (a) we have the two most necessary of all—the principles of *theme* and *climax*: for in this passage there is a clear ambiguity in the word *ende* which (Pandarus says) is the *strength* of a tale. The same double-meaning is no less clearly contained in the neighbouring word *conclusioun*; the meanings 'purpose'—that is, *theme*—and 'termination'—that is, *climax*—are both firmly present, and their necessity in good storytelling is again urged by the Squire (c) when he speaks of 'the knotte why that every tale is toold'. The Squire goes on to speak of *economy* and *pace*, in his talk of the impatience of those who have been listening for a long time to a prolix teller; and the kind of pregnancy he is by implication commending—though perhaps not practising—is openly commanded by the Host when he tells the Parson how to set about his 'meditacioun' in (d). All these precepts are in full harmony with the most unexpected piece in all this literary advice, which Pandarus gives, condemning the irrelevant and enjoining *consistency of form and texture*, and, above all, 'naturalness', or *verisimilitude* (b).

Of all these ideas, the master-thought is that of *theme*; though all conjoin to make Chaucer's style, it is theme that dominates and unifies his tales, and this dominance sometimes obliges some other virtue—such as that of verisimilitude—to bow a little to it. We can see this happening in *The Knight's Tale*, where the theme, being partly concerned with involvements of the natural with supernatural worlds, must obviously go a little beyond the natural. We are fortunate in having two essays of fine scholarship to help our understanding of this aspect of the tale,[1] and I will quote from one of them a brief but illuminating summary of its all-enfolding *ende*. Professor Muscatine writes:

> We have here no glittering, romantic fairycastle world. The impressive, patterned edifice of the noble life, its dignity and richness, its regard for law and decorum, are all bulwarks against the ever-threatening forces of chaos, and in constant collision with them. And its crowning nobility, as expressed by this poem, goes beyond a grasp of the forms of social and civil order, beyond magnificence in any earthly sense, to a perception of the order beyond chaos. When the earthly designs suddenly crumble, true nobility is faith in the ultimate order of things.[2]

It may well be thought that there could be nothing to add to such an account, yet I will dare to elaborate it in terms of the

[1] See Charles Muscatine, op. cit. and Walter Clyde Curry, *Chaucer and the Medieval Sciences*, Oxford 1926.

[2] Op. cit., pp. 189-90

short-story virtues I have listed out of Chaucer. The theme of *The Knight's Tale* enacts itself through the several climaxes in its action, each of which is marked by a great debate or speech to expound it. The first climax is the lovers' first sight of Emelye, that leads to their fantastic, yet illuminating, hot-headed argument; then comes the release of Arcite from prison, followed by a Boethian soliloquy on the subject from each of the young men. Next their duel in the woods, and the magnanimous yet mocking speech and judgment of Theseus. After that—a year after—the great tournament and Arcite's dying speech in declaration of his faith and affection; and last his funeral, followed by the greatest speech of all, given by Theseus to his parliament.

The theme impregnates the poetic texture throughout and determines its pace; this is a majestic *adagio*, exactly suited to its public character. Royal marriages (of which Chaucer had had some experience) are matters of grave alliances to be discussed in the solemnity of a parliament; they are not the hasty private ruttings, catch-as-catch-can, of an Absolon or a Nicholas, that move from *allegro vivace* to *allegro con fuoco*. Yet pace, like verisimilitude, must sometimes give way to theme, and the stately flow of the Knight's narrative must stay for a description of the temples of the gods; this is not a decorative excrescence, but a decorated member of the main theme; the cruelties of war, the tortures of love, the pains of child-birth are shown us in what, for all its feudal splendours, Theseus calls the 'foule prisoun of this lyf' (A 3061). The pause in the story to describe these temples is well placed, for it seems to fill in the year that is to pass while Palamon and Arcite collect their hundred knights. In each temple presently we hear another theme-revealing speech, in the prayers of the three protagonists to their chosen deities.

As for verisimilitude, the story has more than has been commonly admitted. I am not thinking of the many passages of realistic description that jump to mind, such as the harness-clatter and crowd-argument in Athens before the tournament, or the medical detail of Arcite's injuries, but of things less obvious, such as the account given of the gods, and the characters of Palamon, Arcite and Emelye. The gods are no more than embodiments of the planetary influences which everyone then believed really to exist, much as descibed, with 'a certain colouring of the imagination' cast upon them.[1] As for Palamon and Arcite, seen from the respectful if sometime ironic distance from which we are shown these two young men, they are as like as two peas, and it is wholly naturalistic that they should seem to be so, since any two young men, brought up in the same strict code, cannot but wear the moral uniform of their class, then as now, and, from their crew-cuts to their conversation and reactions, be indistinguishable from each other. Obviously if Arcite had seen Emelye first, Palamon would have quibbled in exactly the same way as his blood-brother did over the claim to priority in love. If (seen from a little closer) they have observable idiosyncrasies like Palamon's 'flotery berd' (A 2882), these are comparatively unimportant; for what matters is the code, not the idiosyncrasies, in such a story; if it is idiosyncrasy the reader seeks, let him

Turne over the leef and chese another tale.

There is plenty of it to be found at closer quarters in *The Miller's Tale*. But here in *The Knight's Tale* we are being shown something more significant than the freaks of personality; the two young men are *symbols* for the two dominant secular ideals of medieval christendom, shaping-powers, both, of European civilisation, namely chivalry and romantic love. Arcite is chosen to represent chivalry (notwithstanding his recreance in blood-brotherhood) and it is he who fetches equal armour for Palamon (when he might have killed him out of hand) and bids Emelye to remember Palamon in his dying speech, which is an affirmation of his creed and code. Palamon bears the banner of romantic love, thinks his girl a goddess, vows himself to Venus, and continues to 'serve' Emelye after they are married, as truly as any Wife of Bath could wish.

These two ideals were slowly twinned out of the very ferocities it was their purpose to control; out of the murk and murder and lust of the men of power—the horse-owning classes of the dark

[1] See Jean Seznec, *La Survivance des Dieux Antiques*, London 1940, which clearly sets forth the various ways in which the gods were imagined in the Middle Ages and reproduces illuminated portraits of them in their planetary capacities.

ages—these codes had somehow emerged to join with Christianity in the creation of what was called *gentillesse*, and set up generosity, truth, mercy, service, constancy, good faith and honour as goals for all to aim at. These are the things modestly embodied in the Knight himself who tells this story, and who celebrates a civilisation maintained in the teeth of moral passion, mutability and death.

Emelye embodies a like ideal, that of virginity. Part of her invocation to Diana might almost have come from the mouth of the Second Nun:

> 'Bihoold, goddesse of clene chastitee,
> The bittre teeris that on my chekes falle.
> Syn thou art mayde and kepere of us alle,
> My maydenhede thou kepe and wel conserve,
> And whil I lyve, a mayde I wol thee serve.'
>
> A 2326-30

It is not impossible that Chaucer had the parallel between Diana and the Blessed Virgin in mind, and hinted at it in these lines, and in the line

> And undernethe hir feet she hadde a moone.
>
> A 2077

This iconographical idea, applied to the Virgin, appears in manuscript illumination as early as 1270 and is justified by the passage in Revelations (12:1) that speaks of 'a woman clothed with the sun and the moon under her feet': this became popular enough for it to appear in fresco on the south wall of at least one village church, in the early fifteenth century.[1]

If these three protagonists stand for the three concepts I have named, of chivalry, love and virginity, there remains the fourth and finest, Duke Theseus. This spire of an aristocratic order stands for that Boethian philosophy that underlay so much medieval thinking, particularly Chaucer's, and asserted Eternal Providence more credibly than ever Milton did; it also asserted the corruption and decay of our mutable lives that must at last return to their source, who is the First Mover,

---

[1] The MS illumination referred to may be seen reproduced in *The Apocalypse in Latin and French* (Bodleian MS Douce 180) ed. for the Roxburghe Club by M. R. James, 1922, p. 42. The fresco of which I speak is in the church of South Leigh, Oxon.

> . . . prince and cause of alle thyng,
> Convertynge al unto his propre welle
> From which it is dirryved, sooth to telle . . .
>
> A 3036-8

More importantly perhaps, by implication, Theseus, Boethian to the end, asserts the modest dignity of human Free Will, that (under God) controls Mars and Venus in us all. It is also Theseus who knows how to draw honour out of tragedy in the death of Arcite, and such permanence as mortality can enjoy in love, by ordaining the union of Palamon and Emelye. These are the victorious themes in this palatial poem, that so pervasively is

> Hanged with clooth of gold, and nat with sarge.
>
> A 2568

The Knight's Tale comes quietly to harbour at last, but most of the Tales accelerate at the close, and some end with a spring-like snap, as do certain stories by Chekov, De Maupassant and O. Henry; the swift climax is reached at a sprint, as if beating the reader to it:

> What nedeth it to sermone of it moore?
> For right as they hadde cast his deeth bifoore,
> Right so they han hym slayn, and that anon,
> And whan that this was doon, thus spak that oon:
> 'Now lat us sitte and drynke, and make us merie,
> And afterward we wol his body berie.'
> And with that word it happed hym, par cas,
> To take the botel there the poyson was,
> And drank, and yaf his felawe drynke also,
> For which anon they storven bothe two.
>
> The Pardoner's Tale C 879-88

When a story has no natural punch-line of its own, it is sometimes supplied with one by the Teller, as in the case of the Shipman:

> Thus endeth now my tale, and God us sende
> Taillynge ynough unto oure lyves ende. Amen.
>
> B² 433-4

This device, perfectly successful as a conclusion to the Shipmani' almost faultless tale, returns us to the character of the Teller, as n were, to show his light, allusive approval of the tricky morals in his story. Indeed the only one of Chaucer's canons violated its this story, and that but briefly, is that which condemns irrelevance; for there are three lines of unused material introduced, that give rise to expectations never resolved; when the merchant's young wife meets her 'cousin'-monk saying his holy things in the garden before breakfast,

> A mayde child cam in hire compaignye,
> Which as hir list she may governe and gye,
> For yet under the yerde was the mayde.
> B^2 95-7

I do not find this little girl in Chaucer's analogues and cannot think what she is doing in this garden; she is a distracting irrelevance who never reappears; if we compare a similar detail, thrown out with an equal appearance of casualness in *The Reeve's Tale*—

> A doghter hadde they bitwixe hem two
> Of twenty yeer, withouten any mo,
> *Savynge a child that was of half yeer age;*
> *In cradel it lay and was a propre page.*
> A 3969-72 (My italics)

—we see a contrast in skill; how subtly a reader or hearer is alerted to that crucial cradle which is to figure so prominently in the story later on! Having learnt to expect this kind of deftness in Chaucer one may wonder at the little girl in *The Shipman's Tale*, and how she got there; but such irrelevance is rare in Chaucer; indeed I can only think of one other instance, and that a more serious one, in which he has allowed himself to 'jompre discordant thyng yfeere', for motives only recoverable by conjecture. It comes in *The Physician's Tale*, which, in spite of much line-to-line brilliance in the writing, is the faultiest in *The Canterbury Tales*. It in no way suits what we know of the Physician from the *Prologue*, but even when it is considered in isolation, simply as a story, it has crushing demerits. Whatever allowances be made for the mystical values of virginity, now or then, they cannot be enough to excuse it; a story that extols the protective murder of a young girl by her father, to save her from violation, is a horrifying piece of sentimental savagery; had the murder been done in the heat of the moment, it might be endurable; and that is how we meet it in Livy (its ultimate source) and *Le Roman de la Rose* and in the *Confessio Amantis*. But in Chaucer the murder is carefully and poetically premeditated, with wonderful skill, in a long and sentimental harangue:

> O doghter, which that art my laste wo,
> And in my lyf my laste joye also,
> O gemme of chastitee, in pacience
> Take thou thy deeth, for this is my sentence.
> C 221-4

and the scene ends with Virginius smiting off the head of his fainting but consenting daughter:

> She riseth up, and to hir fader sayde,
> 'Blissed be God, that I shal dye a mayde!
> Yif me my deeth, er that I have a shame:
> Dooth with youre child youre wyl, a Goddess name!'
> C 247-50

If this, the climax of the story, is an offence against the moral feelings of our present age, what follows is one against our common sense. In the other versions of the story, the murder is done on the spot (in open court, according to *Le Roman de la Rose* and the *Confessio Amantis*) and the girl's head is there and then presented to the wicked judge, who, in return, orders the instant execution of her father, Virginius; but he manages to stir up public support for himself and the tables are turned, credibly enough. But by choosing to insert this scene of lyrical sentimentality between father and daughter, Chaucer has disastrously interrupted the action; for if Virginius had the time to harangue his daughter, he had the time to stir up the people of Rome against the unjust judge; the sudden uprising of the people of Rome that happens in Chaucer, without explanation, when Virginius returns to the court-room with his daughter's head and the judge condemns him to be hanged for it, sharpens our sense of the story's repulsive improbability:

> He bad to take hym and anhange hym faste;
> But right anon a thousand peple in thraste,
> To save the knyght, for routhe and for pitee,
> For knowen was the false iniquitee.
> C 259-62

Why had the people not intervened before? Why had Virginius not appealed to them in the first place? The Physician has bungled his tale. In a frantic effort to salve it, he goes on to tell us of the imprisonment and suicide of the judge and of the generous intervention of Virginius to save the life of Claudius, the false witness in the story; but why a man who is ready to slay his daughter so glibly should wish to spare the would-be instrument of her seduction is not clear; the Physician is obviously, but crudely, satisfying the wishes of his hearers to be able to admire the hero's magnanimity, and he throws in a taste of revenge for them too, by killing off some un-named and less guilty accomplices of the principal villains:

> The remenant were anhanged, moore and lesse,
> That were consentant of this cursednesse.
>   C 275-6

Then he rounds off his story with a final couplet that fails to sum it up:

> Therefore I rede yow this conseil take:
> Forsaketh synne, er synne yow forsake.

Into this tale of false values and improbable circumstances Chaucer interpolated the most remarkable personal outburst in all his works, a sudden diatribe against governesses who neglect to guard the chastity of their charges. Like the rest of the story (verbally speaking) it is admirably written:

> Under a sheperde softe and necligent
> The wolf hath many a sheep and lamb torent.
>   C 101-2

It occupies thirty-two lines (C 72-102) and seems to be direct personal attack on his sister-in-law, Katherine Swynford, the mistress (later, third wife) of John of Gaunt, his patron. One of her charges was the Duke's daughter, Isabel, whose affair with John Holland, half-brother to Richard II, was one of the scandals of the later thirteen-eighties. However we explain the personal situation and feelings that underlie this unique and startling passage, it is one which Pandarus would certainly have condemned as a 'discordant thing'.

Let us return from this least successful of Chaucer's stories to the consideration of his skills, particularly to his art of pace. He seems to have perceived, or come to learn, that stanza form confers gravity, as he understood the word. Was he our first writer to perceive this? In his lighter mood, he shortens the seven-line stride of rhyme-royal to the brisker couplet form, in which he moves with a minimum of inversion of the natural speech-order of words; there is no English poet who manages the free give-and-take of conversation in rhyme with so little appearance of effort. But what gives it the *pace* is a special skill in carrying or turning the meaning on the rhyme-word, for the rhyme-word is generally a climax in sense as it is in sound; he *loads* his rhymes, to create an expectation in the hearer of a tension between the thing said and its shape in the ear. Some other poets have used this power extensively. It rings sharply in the couplets of Dryden, where, so often, the wit rides or resides in the rhyme:

> Beggar'd by fools, whom still he found too late,
> He had his jest, and they had his estate.
>
> *Absalom and Achitophel* 561-2

It may well have been from Chaucer that Dryden learnt this art:

> He was, if I shal yeven hym his laude,
> A theef, and eek a sumnour, and a baude.
>
> *The Friar's Tale* D 1353-4

Yet Chaucer's general use is not so couplet-stopped as Dryden's or Pope's; he seldom pauses, as they do, to wag their tails, but swings forward on the rhymes, as on stepping-stones, from one swift narrative-thought to another:

> 'I swere it,' quod this frere, 'by my feith!'
> And therwithal his hand in his he leith,
> 'Lo, heer my feith; in me shal be no lak.'
> 'Now thanne, put in thyn hand doun by my bak,'
> Seyde this man, 'and grope wel bihynde.
> Bynethe my buttok there shaltow fynde
> A thyng that I have hyd in pryvetee.'
> 'A!' thoghte this frere, 'that shal go with me!'
> And doun his hand he launcheth to the clifte,
> In hope for to fynde there a yifte.
> And whan this sike man felte this frere

Aboute his tuwel grope there and heere,
Amydde his hand he leet the frere a fart.
Ther nys no capul, drawynge in a cart,
That myghte have lete a fart of swich a soun,
The frere up stirte as dooth a wood leoun . . .
                    The Summoner's Tale D 2137-52

Every rhyme here has peculiar importance, ease and force, and
carries the story along from one climax of gratified expectation
to another. Nor is it simply a method of underlining comic effect.
The same skill is seen in the more serious Tales:

'Gooth now,' quod she, 'and dooth my lordes heeste;
But o thyng wol I prey yow of youre grace,
That, but my lord forbad yow, atte leeste
Burieth this litel body in som place
That beestes ne no briddes it torace.'
But he no word wol to that purpos seye,
But took the child and wente upon his weye.
                    The Clerk's Tale E 568-74

How naturally the stresses fall on the meaningful words, particularly on the seeming throw-aways *'of youre grace'* and *'atte leeste'*
which are so necessary to the feeling in Griselda's petition! This
art of using rhyme as an element in colloquial pace is by no means
shared by all users of rhyme in narrative, and accounts for much
of the difference between a Chaucer, and a Spenser or a Shakespeare story; Spenser and Shakespeare were, no doubt, aiming at
other effects and achieved them partly perhaps by this neglect of
pace; but it is instructive to compare the directness of Griselda with
the oblique and languid phrases of Lucrece, in which the rhymes
are simply thrown away, though in a situation fraught with at
least as much narrative emotion and importance:

And now this pale swan in her watery nest
Begins the sad dirge of her certain ending:
'Few words' quoth she, 'shall fit the trepass best,
Where no excuse can give the fault amending.
In me moe woes than words are now depending:
    And my laments would be drawn out too long,
    To tell them all with one poor tired tongue.

'Then be this all the task it hath to say;
Dear husband, in the interest of thy bed

A stranger came, and on that pillow lay
Where thou wast wont to rest thy weary head;
And what wrong else may be imagined
By foul enforcement might be done to me,
From that, alas, thy Lucrece is not free . . .'
The Rape of Lucrece 1611-24

We have seen something of the consistency of form and
texture, and even of natural representation commended by
Pandarus, in *The Knight's Tale*, no less that the other virtues of
pace and relevance and climax, all suited to its grave, civilised and
universal theme. But to see them exhibited in their fine fulness
we must turn to another tale and to another world, of farce and
fabliau, that bursts upon us in *The Miller's Tale*. Every stroke of
characterisation, every touch of local colour, every conversational
interchange enriches our comic understanding of life, with fresh
discoveries for every reader at every reading of this perfectly
turned story. It has all the virtues that, following Chaucer, we
have proposed for narrative art. Quotation would be superfluous.

Yet there is a virtue that courses in almost every Tale (other
than those of sober piety) which Chaucer does not mention,
though he practises it. It is the virtue of ironical contemplation,
and if we wish to find it sustained with a continued subtlety and
power more in one story than in any other, we should turn to
The Merchant's Tale. Here a dimpling surface-simplicity glides
onwards in bland couplets; but they say so much more than they
seem to say that they keep us constantly turning back to re-read
them for the enjoyment of inward and contrary meanings
perceived by a 'double-take'. I will not attempt to nudge out new
examples of the ironic in this story, for who can miss them?
Rather, I will try to put forward a view of how Chaucer's irony
itself is to be taken. His unique gift is to blend a warm feeling
for human beings, even in their most disreputable moments,
with a total detachment in observing their preposterous self-
deceptions, and his laughter comes down to us from a sphere
above that of moral indignation, as if he would have endorsed
Samuel Butler's remark that moral indignation is the hall-mark
of a blackguard. Indeed he seems to bear this out in the earlier
and concluding parts of the sermon he puts into the mouth of the

Pardoner. An ironist sees as clearly as a moralist into the blind velleities of the human heart, but he is above anger. If you are angered and disgusted by a sense of human hatefulness after reading Swift's *Modest Proposal* or Chaucer's *Merchant's Tale*, you will have taken their point, but you will have missed their mood.

Anger is active, irony contemplative, and from its high region, from which it can see two opposite truths at once, there descends a 'silvery laughter' (that in Chaucer's case at least is not unkindly) which arises from knowing that one should expect nothing from a pig but a grunt—and, indeed, how to welcome a grunt from a pig. It is to take a mordant pleasure in human double-talk and double-do, especially when the double-talkers and double-doers are fully, innocently self-deceived, like January, Damian and May; or like ourselves.

Chaucer's irony seldom shows anger, as Langland's so often does. When Langland tells us how a Friar shrove Lady Meed, and told her of a costly window that needed glazing, the *ironic* point is made with the Friar's words

> 'Woldist thou glase the gable, and grave there thin name,
> Sikir shulde thi soule be heuene to haue.'
> A.III. 48-9

But Langland allows his anger to boil over and make the *moral* point as well:

> Ac god alle good folk such grauyng defendith
> And seith *Nesciat sinistra quid faciat dextera.*
> A.III. 53-4

In *The Merchant's Tale* Chaucer gives the rein to his feelings about Damian on one occasion, not of course for his sexual antics, any more than for those of January or May, but for his treachery. It is as if he accepted it as natural that Damian should be a randy young animal in hot blood, but was shocked at his playing traitor to a kind master, like a cold-blooded reptile:

> O servant traytour, false hoomly hewe,
> Lyk to the naddre in bosom sly untrewe,
> God shilde us alle from youre aqueyntaunce!
> *The Merchant's Tale* E 1785-7

May's treacheries on the other hand, are taken for granted; the serpent in Eden had a woman's face.[1]

On the sexual side, the irony issues from a lofty, an amused awareness of the fact that human beings are what they are. For though treachery may take us by surprise as something less than human, we must not be so naive as to expect rich old gentlemen not to want their sex as well as their salvation, nor to suppose that these commodities are not for sale in a world such as we allow it to be. That marriages like that of January to May are approved by society and blessed by the Church is all too frequently clear, and since we all know this (and are partly responsible for it) we must expect a girl in May's position to welcome the solace that a Damian can offer, even if she has to climb a tree for it. This is the oblique, ironical approach; Langland's is moral and direct:

> It is an vncomely copil, be crist, as me thinketh,
> To ȝiuen a ȝong wenche to an old feble.
>
> A.X. 186-7

Both poets are saying the same thing in their different ways, from their different planes. A finer distinction than that between irony and morality is that between irony and farce, and the delicate poises of Chaucer's art as a storyteller can perhaps be better seen by comparing the Merchant's with the Miller's tale, than by our glance towards *Piers Plowman*. Damian is not so 'hende' as Nicholas, and May is slyer than Alison, but they are brothers and sisters under the skin; they are all cuckolders of 'old feebles'. In *The Miller's Tale* the 'end' achieved by Chaucer is one of farcical fun. In no tale has he been more careful to 'do that it be lik' and the extremely concrete naturalness of the story sets off the preposterous unlikelihood in the surprises of the action. No moral question enters anybody's head. But in *The Merchant's Tale* the moral, philosophical and theological implications are throughout presented with mock gravity, in their most ironical light; and this is the 'strength' of the story, its intellectual clarity by contraries, made all the sharper by the placing of it in the mouth of the Merchant, so recently, so disastrously married.

---

[1] A commonplace of medieval iconography; see, for instance, *The Man of Law's Tale* B[1] 360, or *Piers Plowman*, B XVIII, 335, or *Les Très Riches Heures du duc de Berry*, Textes par Henri Malo, Paris 1945, *Le Paradis Terrestre*.

He has passed above anger into the bitter pleasure of disillusion,
and even makes us feel that Pluto is rather comic in his astonishment and rage at seeing Damian about to cuckold his master:

> A wylde fyr and corrupt pestilence
> So falle upon youre bodyes yet to-nyght!
> Ne se ye nat this honourable knyght,
> By cause, allas! that he is blynd and old,
> His owene man shal make hym cokewold.
>
> E 2252-6

The Merchant keeps his high and mocking kindliness to the end,
that happy end which promises to perpetuate a Fool's Paradise
for January and a Knave's Paradise for Damian and May:

> This Januarie, who is glad but he?
> He kisseth hire, and clippeth hire ful ofte,
> And on hire wombe he stroketh hire ful softe . . .
>
> E 2412-4

Had he not chosen a young wife

> On which he myghte engendren hym an heir,
>
> E 1272

and had not May hinted that an heir was to be expected?

> I telle yow wel, a womman in my plit
> May han to fruyt so greet an appetit
> That she may dyen, but she of it have.
>
> E 2335-7

So naturally, January strokes her womb as they all walk off out
of the story, happily believing her to be pregnant. And, thanks
to Damian, perhaps she is. Nicholas Macchiavelli's *Mandragola*
ends in a similar threesome, and is accounted a comedy. It is the
comedy of being well-deceived, an *exemplum* which cuts deeper
into our self-knowledge than all the anger of Langland.

A minute point in a passage just quoted can lead us toward
the central ambuscade of Chaucer's story-telling:

> This Januarie, who is glad but he?

This Januarie: here is a uniquely Chaucerian idiom that may be
called the Possessive Demonstrative. It seems to have become a
trick of Chaucer's style when he was adapting *Troilus* and *The
Knight's Tale*, though there are signs of it in the story of Griselda
too; we hear twice of 'this Walter'. The word carries many a

shifting overtone of affection, patronage, mockery, indignation, condolence, conversationalism, and other subtly-varied shades of feeling, but in all of them a certain possessiveness of Chaucer's in respect of the character he is describing, shared a little with his audience; so we hear *this Januarie* thirteen times out of thirty-nine, *this Damian* ten times out of twenty-five, *this May* seven times out of twenty-five; the first time is when she makes her visit to Damian's bed-side. Many times we hear of *this Palamon* and *this Arcite*; once bodingly:

> And in the grove, at tyme and place yset,
> This Arcite and this Palamon ben met.
>   A 1635-6

At another extreme, the locution yields us:

> 'Thise wormes, ne thise motthes, ne thise mytes,
> Upon my peril, frete hem never a deel.'

Thus the Wife of Bath explains how she kept her garments from rotting in a cupboard (D 560-1). The most significant statistic about this curious usage in Chaucer is that we hear forty-two times of *this Troilus* and eleven of *this Pandarus*; but never once of *this Criseyde*. He knew she eluded possession.

The Possessive Demonstrative may perhaps have its origin in a fact which dominates all Chaucer's storytelling; the sense that he is *sharing* his story with his hearers springs from his extreme sensitiveness to the royal audience (his personal acquaintances) for whom he wrote it; it helps to bring his hearers onto the speaker's side, favourably rather than condescendingly, though seldom without some touch of condescension, as who should say 'This Troilus I am telling you about, this Troilus of ours, this fellow we met last week . . .' It is only one of Chaucer's many stratagems and subterfuges in relation to his audience, as he stood exposed before them in the pulpit in which we see him in the Corpus Christi Manuscript of *Troilus and Criseyde*. Before such listeners how delicate a tact was needed! For if much that was written by him was written for entertainment, much also was written for *doctrine*. It can be dangerous to lecture a king. If we reflect that *Troilus and Criseyde* was completed towards 1385, when Richard II and his newly-married wife, Anne of Bohemia, were both nineteen years old, and seated there before him, we can appreciate the directness of the personal address to them in the lines:

> O yonge, fresshe folkes, he or she,
> In which that love up groweth with your age,
> Repeyreth hom fro worldly vanyte . . .
> *Troilus and Criseyde* V 1835-7

It is not surprising that Chaucer came to adopt the ambush of a double-*persona* when he came to write *The Canterbury Tales*, for there was much that he wished, or might wish, to say obliquely. No longer could he take cover behind 'myn auctour, called Lollius' (a name cunningly chosen to defeat verification); so he reverted to the plump simpleton figure he had created for himself in *The House of Fame*, and placed it, as his stalking-horse, among his fellow-storytelling pilgrims. His apologies issue from behind such masks:

> The Millere is a cherl, ye knowe wel this;
> So was the Reve eek and othere mo,
> And harlotrie they tolden bothe two.
> A 3182-4

But more dangerous than to utter harlotry was to venture on the criticism of his hearers, and there is no better expression of this danger than in *The Manciple's Tale*. This little masterpiece seems to issue from Chaucer's most sardonic maturity. He was never a Manciple himself (so far as we know), but he knew what it was to be in a position of considerable, though inferior, authority. So, perhaps by professional sympathy, he chose a Manciple for his mask, and groomed him for the part by making him seem a coarse fellow of no account, one who has an altercation with a drunken cook, who is a 'boystous' man, capable of 'knavyssh speche', who assures us all three times that he is 'not textueel'. From behind this carefully constructed dummy Chaucer delivered a broadside of home-truths to his audience of courtiers. The advice he gives has its cynical side, in that it concludes with a heavy warning against exposing oneself to the 'losengeours' and 'totelere accusours', who, as we know from the BF version of the *Prologue* to *The Legend of Good Women* (352-4) infested the Court. The Manciple gives all the strength and reiteration of a long *conduplicatio* to drive home his counsel, from behind the further mask of his Mother's advice to keep his mouth shut:

> 'My sone, thenk on the crowe, a Goddes name!
> My sone, keep wel thy tonge, and keep thy freend.
> A wikked tonge is worse than a feend.
> My sone, God of his endelees goodnesse
> Walled a tonge with teeth and lippes eke,
> For man sholde hym avyse what he speeke . . .'
>   H 318-24

But *The Manciple's Tale* contains other home-truths about court life and opinions less palatable than this sagacious gospel. It is a story of what its teller considers to be a particularly ignoble adultery. He begins with highest praise for his hero, the god Phoebus, here euhemerised into the 'flour of bachilrie, as wel in fredom [*generosity*] as in chivalrie', a figure as fine as Chaucer's Knight or Squire. His wife, however, preferred the attentions of a satyr to this Hyperion:

> A man of litel reputacioun,
> Nat worth to Phebus in comparisoun.
>   H 199-200

The woman sends for her 'lemman', and the Manciple, having called this spade a spade, retracts it with heavy irony:

> . . . His wyf anon hath for hir lemman sent.
> Hir lemman? Certes, this is a knavyssh speche!
> Foryeveth it me, and that I yow biseche.
>   H 204-6

The White Crow watched wife and lemman while they 'wroghten all hire lust volage' (H 239) on her husband's bed. Remembering, perhaps, how he had offended by 'shewynge how that wemen han done mis' in *Troilus and Criseyde*, Chaucer seems to have felt that the protective colouring of the Manciple-*persona* was not enough, in so horrible a story, to save him from the women in his audience; so, after rubbing his point well in by an animal *exemplum*:

> A she-wolf hath also a vileyns kynde.
> The lewedeste wolf that she may fynde,

> Or leest of reputacioun, wol she take,
> In tyme whan hir lust to han a make.
>
> H 183-6

he rubs it out again with an ironic disclaimer:

> Alle thise ensamples speke I by thise men
> That been untrewe, and nothyng by wommen.
>
> H 187-8

But he has not finished with his home-truths; he has to point out that, to our shame, there are such things as class-distinctions in these matters, that have to be taken into account. And this is how he does so:

> I am a boystous man, right thus seye I,
> Ther nys no difference, trewely,
> Bitwixe a wyf that is of heigh degree,
> If of hir body dishonest she bee,
> And a povre wenche, oother than this—
> If it so be they werke bothe amys—
> But that the gentile, in estaat above
> She shal be cleped his lady, as in love;
> And for that oother is a povre womman,
> She shal be cleped his wenche or his lemman.
> And, God it woot, myn owene deere brother,
> Men leyn that oon as lowe as lith that oother.
>
> H 211-22

God it woot is an emphatic form of *God woot*, which Chaucer tends to reserve for his more powerful assertions, Yet, if any court withers were wrung, if anyone bridled at this frank opinion, Chaucer could hide behind the Manciple, as the Nun's Priest hid behind Chauntecleer:

> Thise been the cokkes wordes, and nat myne.
>
> B² 3265

The Manciple's Tale might easily have been told in such terms and from such a point of view as the Miller's or the Shipman's; but Chaucer chose to make it a story, not about the comicality or trickeries of sex, nor even about colourfully-realised people in a colourfully-realised world. The Manciple's *end* is a story about moral ideas, and to the interest of these all other interests are sacrificed. Chaucer could use his pulpit for preaching as well as for entertainment, and if he could make a story of a sermon, as he did in the case of the Pardoner, he could also make a sermon of a story, showing infinite play with the variations in distance and mode of address that were possible to him in confronting an audience of his friends and rulers. They made their effect on his narrative art too, little though they knew it. If, as I suppose, Gower read his stories to the same court, the inwardnesses of short-story form had largely escaped him.

The art of Chaucer's prose

MARGARET SCHLAUCH

I. Introductory

THAT Geoffrey Chaucer as poet was consciously aware of technical aspects of his art is a thesis accepted today without question. His careful prosody, his use of many rhetorical and poetical devices described in medieval handbooks,[1] his direct, sometimes jesting references to the authors of such handbooks and to their terminology—all this evidence has been repeatedly considered with reference to his poetic works.[2] But Chaucer as a prosaist has aroused less interest. Moreover, the judgments concerning his achievement have been distinctly varied. There have been negative pronouncements, sometimes rather sweeping ones, about his ability in this area. Even the favourable opinions have often remained meagrely documented.

There are several reasons for the at best cursory attention hitherto devoted to the art of Chaucer's prose. First of all, there has been all too little knowledge until quite recently of the extent to which medieval prose writers using the English vernacular had

[1] Some of Chaucer's practice no doubt resulted from direct imitation of French models. See Benjamin S. Harrison, 'Medieval Rhetoric in the Book of the Duchess', *PMLA*, XLIX (1934) 428-42.

[2] The pioneer study was by John Matthews Manly, 'Chaucer and the Rhetoricians', reprinted from the *Proceedings of the British Academy*, XII (1926) 95-113 in *Chaucer Criticism*, ed. R. Schoeck and J. Taylor (Notre Dame Books) I (1960), pp. 268-90. Chaucer's awareness of poetic doctrine was also discussed by Traugott Naunin, *Der Einfluss der mittelalterlichen Rhetorik auf Chaucers Dichtung*, Bonn 1929; also briefly by J. W. H. Atkins, *English Literary Criticism: The Medieval Phase*, Cambridge 1943, pp. 151ff. For a more recent study fully documenting previous research see Dorothy Everett, 'Some Reflections on Chaucer's "Art Poetical"', *Essays on Middle English Literature*, Oxford 1955, pp. 149-74. All previous studies should now be viewed in the light of J. J. Murphy's cautionary article, 'A New Look at Chaucer and the Rhetoricians', *RES* xv (1964) 1-20. Much of Chaucer's knowledge appears to have been indirectly derived.

wittingly—not merely intuitively—tried to fashion their language towards aesthetic ends. We now have abundant evidence of this purposeful striving from Old English times on.[1] It appears particularly in the mannered prose style of various religious writers, notably the mystics.[2] In the second place, the fact that Chaucer's prose is for the most part translation or close paraphrase of foreign originals has deflected his critics from considering its artistic values. Thus it happens that most special studies dealing with such texts have been concerned with content (source relationships) or purely linguistic problems, eschewing any sort of aesthetic evaluations.[3] And for this reason, too, some of the comments have been fairly harsh. Thus George Philip Krapp, speaking of Chaucer's rendering of Boethius' *De Consolatione Philosophiae*, remarked that 'the main defects of the translation are crudity and awkwardness, even at times obscurity of expres-

[1] R. W. Chambers performed a great service in calling attention to this in his essay 'On the Continuity of English Prose', originally published (1932) as part of the introduction to Nicholas Harpsfield's *Life of Sir Thomas More* in the EETS and since reprinted separately (1950, 1957).

[2] An excellent survey of the subject is given by Geoffrey Shepherd in his introduction to *Ancrene Wisse*: Parts Six and Seven, London and Edinburgh 1959. Norman Davis has recently pointed out that prose lying outside of the area of artistic or 'mannered' writing can also possess literery qualities not considered by Chambers in his essay. See the introduction to Davis's edition of selected *Paston Letters*, Oxford 1958.

[3] Emil Koeppel, 'Über das Verhältnis von Chaucers Prosawerken zu seinen Dichtungen', *Archiv für das Studium der neueren Sprachen und Litteraturen*, LXXX (1891) 33-54, identifies parallelisms in wording which show that Chaucer carried over into his poetic works certain concepts found in those translated into prose. Johann Frieshammer, *Die sprachliche Form der chaucerschen Prosa*, Halle a/S. 1910, is limited exclusively to linguistic matters, with no comments on style. Similarly Hermann Eitle, *Die Satzverknüpfung bei Chaucer*, Heidelberg 1914, while offering valuable material on the conjunctions used in linking clauses and on various grammatical problems connected therewith, abstains from any comment on the stylistic problem of easy versus rough transition between clauses and sentences. The unpublished dissertation by Erwin W. Geismar, *The Style and Technique of Chaucer's Translations from French* (Yale University, typescript, 1962), does attempt to draw certain conclusions from a careful consideration of vocabulary, additions, omissions, syntactic constructions compared with the French, etc., especially in the case of *Melibeus*. The conclusion reached is not flattering to Chaucer. He is found to be 'literal to the point of servility' (p. 50); his prose is 'only too frequently formless and awkward' (p. 87). The chief merits recognised are his conscientiousness and his general willingness to abstain from obvious Gallicisms.

sion, due to imperfect adaptation of the thought to the English idiom'.[1] Krapp further characterised Chaucer's prose in general as 'perfunctory', showing 'on the one hand how little interested he was in the complexities of the life of his day from the point of view of direct exposition or persuasion', and on the other hand 'how little impressed he was with the possibilities of prose as an art of fine writing'.[2] Contemporary Chaucer criticism runs counter to both theses. Even the translated and paraphrased works have a demonstrable pertinence to the life of Chaucer's day,[3] not to speak of our own; and it has long since been recognised that Chaucer was definitely aware of at least one possibility implicit in prose as an art of fine writing: namely its rhythmical effects. Thomas Tyrwhitt, in a note to the *Melibeus* translation, pointed out (in his edition of *The Canterbury Tales*, 1775-8) that the first section of it shows a marked incidence of blank verse rhythm. In the next century Edwin Guest stated (in his *History of English Rhythms*, 1838) that Chaucer wrote a kind of 'measured prose', at least on occasion, again citing the *Melibeus* text as showing affinities to the iambic pentameter line.[4] Saintsbury devoted considerable attention to this aspect of Chaucer's prose, but he was looking for approximations to regular verse patterns, not for effects of cadence (*cursus*) as cultivated by medieval writers of Latin and vernacular prose.[5] Of this, more later.

As for other characteristics of Chaucer's prose, Saintsbury has

[1] G. P. Krapp, *The Rise of English Literary Prose*, New York; Oxford University Press 1915, p. 5.
[2] Ibid., p. 10.
[3] See especially the appreciative essay 'The Tale of Melibeus' by W. W. Lawrence in *Essays and Studies in Honor of Carleton Brown*, New York University Press 1940, pp. 100-10.
[4] Like Tyrwhitt, Guest also states that the rhythmical structure of prose becomes less conspicuous and finally disappears after the opening pages of *Melibeus*. Claims for an iambic pattern in Chaucer's prose have been voiced by other writers. See Caroline Spurgeon, *Five Hundred Years of Chaucer Criticism and Allusion* (Chaucer Society, 1908-22), I, pp. 498f., III, pp. 54, 75f.
[5] George Saintsbury, *A History of English Prose Rhythm*, London 1912, ch. 4. Two bits of 'blank verse' are identified in the Retraction, p. 68; the same iambic movement is pointed out once again in the opening passages of *Melibeus*; and it is remarked that at the close of the first metrum of the Boethius translation there occurs 'what is undoubtedly [?] an echo of the elegiac metre of the original', p. 73.

rather little to say. In *The Parson's Tale* he recognises the merit of a 'logical-rhetorical connection of sentence and argument' and 'alert selection and disposition of vocabulary'. In the Boethius translation he finds in addition a stately language well fitted to the subject matter. Such expressions of general approval, like the less favourable comments of other critics, need to be tested by inquiry into the objectively analysable traits of Chaucer's prose writings, including many that are linguistic but also pertain to matters of style. Especially where Chaucer as translator was closely following a known original it will be instructive to see where he deviated from it in matters of detail. Such deviations on his part were presumably the result of conscious choice; and choice among possibilities of linguistic expression is of the essence of literary style.

II. The Plain Style of Scientific Exposition

Chaucer's prose works fall within more than one literary genre. The one calling for the least elaborate of styles is the expository tract dealing with a problem of science. *A Treatise on the Astrolabe* well exemplifies this category; also *The Equatorie of the Planetis*, if that is to be accepted as Chaucer's work. The former is of especial value to us because its introduction, a rare example of independent Chaucerian composition in prose (that is, not translated or paraphrased), explicitly declares the principle that style should be adapted to a reader's age and capacities. Chaucer announces in advance that he will avoid 'curious endityng and hard sentence' for the sake of little Louis, the ten-year-old boy for whom the work is being translated, and he will permit himself verbal repetitions in order to drive home his points: 'sothly me semith better to writen unto a child twyes a god sentence, than he forget it onys.'[1] If others should peruse the treatise, they are asked to forgive the writer's 'rude endityng' and 'superfluite of wordes', necessarily resulting from the pedagogical character of the work and the immaturity of the reader primarily addressed.

We should expect, then, to find uncomplicated sentences in the

[1] *Astrolabe*, Prologue. Unless otherwise noted, citations follow F. N. Robinson's edition of *The Complete Works of Geoffrey Chaucer*, Boston 1957. Punctuation has been modified by omission of the mark / within sentences.

Astrolabe, with frequent simple repetitions and various other devices to catch and sustain a young reader's attention, and in fact we do find just these general traits. The discourse is made as informal as possible within the limitations imposed by subject matter and purpose.[1]

Periodic sentences are, for instance, rare in the *Astrolabe,* and when they appear they are clearly not designed for literary effects of suspense (see the first two sentences of II, 5). The construction is prevailingly paratactic. Alliteration and other decorative sound effects are conspicuously absent. An occasional balanced phrase like 'the verrey *m*oeving of the *m*one from *h*oure to *h*oure' (*Prologue* p. 546), is probably the result of accident rather than design. The insistent echoing of a word, or a word and its cognate forms, is clearly intended to reinforce the sense, not to provide gratuitous decoration. For instance, a sentence in I 17 echoes forms of the verb *to move:* 'And all that *moeveth* withinne the hevedes of these Aries and Libra, his *moevyng* is clepid northward; and all that *moevith* withoute these hevedes, his *moevyng* is clepid southward, as fro the equinoxiall' (p. 548). A somewhat longer passage reveals still ampler effects of repetition:

> Than she with the verrey degre of the *sonne* the houre of Mercurie entring under my west orisonte at eve; and next him succedith the mone, and so furth by ordir, *planete* after *planete* in *houre* after *houre,* all the nyght longe til the *sonne* arise. Now riseth the *sonne* that *Sonday* by the morwe, and the nadir of the *sonne* upon the west orisonte shewith me the entring of the *houre* of the forseide *sonne* (II 12; no corresponding passage in the extant Latin[2]).

---

[1] See the appreciative remarks by P. Pintelon in the introduction to his edition of Chaucer's *A Treatise on the Astrolabe,* Antwerp 1940, based on a manuscript in the Royal Library, Brussels. The author praises particularly the alternation of long and short spans of statement, of personal and impersonal point of view, etc. He also points out details of grammatical usage which are pertinent to the stylistic effect: predilection for nominal constructions in Part I (theoretical exposition) as contrasted with verbal ones in Part II (instruction in practice); repetitions, reminding or retrospective adverbs as devices for clear and smooth transition, etc.
[2] The work on which Chaucer's was based was the *Compositio et Operatio Astrolabii* of Messahalla, but we do not know what version Chaucer used. W. W. Skeat printed some pertinent sections of the Latin as an appendix to his separate edition of Chaucer's *Astrolabe,* EETS, ES, xvi (1872), which has here been quoted. See also R. T. Gunther, 'Chaucer and Messahalla on the Astrolabe', in *Early Science in Oxford,* v, Oxford 1925. Here Chaucer's text is followed by the Latin of Messahalla; both are accompanied by modern English translations.

Repetition of this sort often falls into sentence parts which are put into a series of parallel constructions. Thence spring certain effects of syntactic rhythm, reinforced by anaphora or antistrophe (that is, repeating of identical phrases at the beginning or the end, respectively, of a series of parallel clauses). But here once more the effect is rather that of a good schoolmaster patiently emphasising a point than of a rhetorician bent on achieving the effects of mannered prose:

> *The ascendent sothly*, as well in alle nativites as in questions and eleccions of tymes, is a thing which that these astrologiens gretly observen. [Sentence omitted.] *The ascendent sothly*, to take it at the largest, is thilke degre that ascendith at eny of these forseide tymes upon the est orisounte (II 4).
> Set the degre of thy sonne upon the hyer almykanteras of bothe, and wayte wel where as thin almury touchith the bordure and *set there a prikke of ynke*. Sett doun agayn the degre of the sunne upon the nether almykanteras of bothe, and *sett there another pricke* (II 5).[1]

The prevailing use of co-ordinated as opposed to subordinated sentence structure, together with the appearance of loose, pleonastic and even shifted grammatical constructions, confirms the impression that this is non-artistic prose. Here is an instance of loose parataxis where more sophisticated writing would call for hypotaxis:

> The signes of right ascencioun ben fro the heved of Cancer unto the ende of Sagittarie; and these signes arisen more upright, and thei ben called eke sovereyn signes and everich of hem arisith in more space than in 2 houres (II 28).

And here are typical pleonasms accompanied by shift in construction:

> And what planete that is under thilke degre that ascendith the space of 25 degres, yit seyn thei that thilke planete is 'like to him that is the hous of the ascendent' (II 4; shift from direct to indirect discourse). For, after the statutes of astrologiens, what celestial body that is 5 degrees above thilke degre that ascendith, or withinne that nombre, . . . yit rekne they thilke planete in the ascendant (ibid.; shift of subject from *body* to *they*).

However, these slight overlappings and shifts by no means imply mere careless writing on Chaucer's part. It must be remembered

---

[1] There are no sentences in the Latin text which correspond to these.

that Middle English prose as exemplified by some of the best writers admitted pleonastic constructions, especially anticipations and recapitulations, as serving the purposes of clarity.[1]

Certain features of word choice and word order contribute to the total stylistic effect. Chaucer's vocabulary is soberly adjusted to the subject matter. Only an occasional epithet smacks of metaphorical usage. There are but few of those tautological word pairs favoured by some writers of Middle English. In instances such as these the author may be said by a strict reckoning to have wasted words:

—in manere of a nett or a webbe of a loppe (I 3); these same strikes [i.e., strokes] or divisiouns (I 19); tortuose signes, or croked signes (II 28); contened or bownded (II 39); contened or intercept (ibid.).

In other cases there is a real semantic distinction between the paired expressions:

full light reules and naked wordes (*Prologue*); lerned and taught; redith or herith; curious endityng and hard sentence (ibid.); to knowe and work with thin owne instrument (II 5).

Inversions of word order represent a usage that is at times linguistic in the narrow sense, at times stylistic. By the former I mean those inversions which were established as normal in Old English and which persisted more or less faithfully into Middle English. In Chaucer's time the outstanding instance of such traditional, non-stylistic inversion was the placement of an inflected verb form before the sentence subject if a colourless adverbial modifier stood in head position. Thus within one section of the *Astrolabe* we find: 'Tho leide I; Tho rekned I; Tho loked I doun; And in this wise had I the experience; Tho wolde I wite; Tho leyde I; Tho loked I; And thus lerned I' (II 3). These are stereotypes of no particular interest here. More important are the inversions which confer true stylistic emphasis upon a major word or phrase when placed in head position; but these are few in number and not very striking:

[1] On this see M. Schlauch, *The English Language in Modern Times*, Warsaw 1959, pp. 6of. and 99.

This conclusioun wol I declare (II 11)

... and two someres and two wynters in a yer han these forseide peple (II 26)

... and by the azymut in which he stondith maist thou seen in which partie of the firmament he is (II 33)—

and others of the sort. It may be added that inversions of adjectives to post-nominal position, constituting an imitation of French usage, are fairly frequent in the *Astrolabe*. Sanctioned by widespread English custom at the time, they do not constitute any stylistic innovation on Chaucer's part.[1]

Perhaps the most striking of stylistic traits in the *Astrolabe* is to be found in Chaucer's recurrent use of vocatives, apostrophes, first and second pronouns, etc., as a means of establishing a direct relationship with his pupil. The instrument being discussed is 'thyn Astrolabie'; instructions are given in simple, direct imperatives, with numerous reminders and exhortations such as 'Forget not thys, litel Lowys' (I 6), 'forget it nat' (I 17; II 2; II 23), 'Now have I told the twyes' (I 16), 'I warne the' (II 3), and so on. Even heavenly bodies are familiarly referred to with the second person possessive pronoun: 'thy sonne' (II 5; II 11). Frequent introduction of the first personal pronoun helps to create a certain conversational tone: 'as I have said' (I 16), 'as I shal declare' (I 21), 'I prove it thus' (II 22). In illustrative examples, the calculations are reported in the first person: 'The yeer of oure lord 1391, the 12 day of March, I wolde knowe the tyde of the day. I tok the altitude of my sonne ... Tho turned I myn Astrelabye ...,' etc. (II 3; cf. II 12 and II 40, where a whole series of sentences begin with first-person verbs inverted to precede their subjects).

Limitations of space preclude a detailed discussion of *The Equatorie of the Planetis*,[2] a text attributed to Chaucer with great

---

[1] Among the most frequently occurring French inversions are: sterre(s) fix(e), lyne meridional; the Pool Artik, the cercle equinoxiall, houre inequal, etc. Among those which show French inflection as well as word order are: sterres fixes, houres equales, hours inequales, dayes naturales, plages principalis (besides principales plages).

[2] Ed. Derek J. Price from Peterhouse MS 75.I, Cambridge 1955, with a linguistic analysis by R. M. Wilson. For evidence based on style, see the Appendix to the present article. Citations are by page and line number, with abbreviations silently expanded.

plausibility yet with something less than certainty. The general stylistic characteristics of the *Astrolabe* are found here also. Some of them are tempered or more sparingly used, as is to be expected in a work addressed to the general adult public, not dedicated to an individual, a beloved child. The evidence, for what it is worth, tends to confirm the attribution of authorship to Chaucer. At the same time it should be pointed out that there were precedents for a number of the traits here singled out. If we compare the style of the two Chaucerian essays with samples of other scientific writing in Middle English we shall find a certain number of parallels. The excerpts from such texts printed as a supplement by the editors of the *Equatorie* also contain for instance many examples of first and second pronoun constructions.[1] Here too Chaucer was no isolated innovator. But it may be said that in composing the *Astrolabe* and the *Equatorie* (if it is his) he made felicitous use of such devices as were already familiar in scientific writing.

III. The Heightened Style of Homiletic Discourse

The Parson's Tale is, as is well known, a combination of two main elements, namely a discourse on penance and an interpolated tract on the Seven Deadly Sins. For the former there is a known ultimate source, found in the concluding chapter 'De poenitentiis et remissionibus' in the *Summa* of Raymund of Pennaforte. For the tract we have closely analogous passages in several texts, but nothing that can be regarded as a source, even an indirect one.[2] The tone of the Tale as a whole accords with its didactic-homiletic content. Let us see how and to what extent Chaucer shaped the details of his style in harmony with his

---

[1] E.g. 'we shul discreue', p. 197; 'ymagine we a lyne', p. 198 (cf. numerous other uses of the colourless editorial we); 'To þe which table I haue sette' . . ., p. 203; 'þe firste table I deme nouȝt', ibid.; 'thu moste mesure thyn howses', p. 204; 'thou moste knawe þe crafte to seeche', ibid.; 'And witt þu wele', ibid; 'And therefore I haue made a table', p. 206; 'Firste I sowthe þe entrynge of þe Sonne', ibid.

[2] The materials in question are presented and discussed by Germaine Dempster in *Sources and Analogues of Chaucer's Canterbury Tales*, ed. W. F. Bryan and G. Dempster, University of Chicago Press 1941, pp. 723-60. Citations are given here by page and line number.

subject matter. In this connection a comparison of his passages of translation and close paraphrase with their originals will be of particular significance as revealing certain artistic values contributed to the English rendering.

Among the less striking innovations in the English version is one already noted in relation to Chaucer's scientific prose: that is, an exploitation of repetition and the echo of cognate forms for the purposes of clarity. It is a device equally useful in homiletic exposition. At the very beginning of the Tale, Chaucer (or his immediate source) picked up a modest metaphor implied in Raymund's phrase 'inquirentes viam rectam' and elaborated it, first by citation of Jeremiah 6:16 ('State super vias, et videte, et interrogate de viis antiquis que sit via bona . . .'), then by an English paraphrase which avoids some repetitions but at the same time introduces others to create a pattern of verbal echoes based on *wey*:

> Stondeth upon the *weyes*, and seeth and axeth of olde pathes (that is to seyn, of olde sentences) which is the goode *wey*, and walketh in that *wey*, and ye shal fynde refresshynge for youre soules, etc. Manye been the *weyes* espirituels that leden folk to oure Lord Jhesus Crist, and to the regne of glorie. Of whiche *weyes*, there is a ful noble *wey* and a ful covenable, which may nat fayle to man ne to womman that thurgh synne hath mysgoon fro the righte *wey* of Jerusalem celestial; and this *wey* is cleped Penitence (p. 229;[1] note the inversions in *weyes espirituels* and *Jerusalem celestial*).

There follows a considerable passage in which *penitence* and *penitent* are just as insistently echoed as *wey* and *weyes* had been: again, without precedent in the Latin source. As he proceeds in his minor elaborations, Chaucer introduces effects of anaphora and of the rhythm of parallel grammatical constructions into his English:

---

[1] The text of *The Parson's Tale* runs fairly close to Raymund of Pennaforte until the end of sec. 9; Skeat ed., IV, p. 575; Robinson ed., p. 231 end of col. 1. Thereafter, beginning with the third reason for contrition, the treatment is too free to admit of detailed comparisons. Illustrations of Chaucer's adaptation of the Latin are therefore limited to the first nine sections. References are to pages of the Robinson ed., with columns indicated by superscript numbers. It must be remembered that Chaucer probably made use of some intermediary version in French. Hence some of the characteristics here pointed out may be due to skilful imitation rather than independent variation.

Penitence is the pleynynge of man for the gilt that he hath doon, and namoore to do any thyng for which hym oghte to pleyne . . .	Poenitentia est, ut ait Ambrosius, et mala praeterita plangere, et plangenda iterum non committere. Item Augustinus: Poenitentia est quaedam dolentis vindicta puniens in se quod dolet commisisse (p. 730).
Penitence is the waymentynge of man that sorweth for his synne, and pyneth himself for he hath mysdoon.	
Penitence, with certeyne circumstances, is verray repentance of a man that halt hymself in sorwe and oother peyne for his giltes (p. 229¹).	

Or anaphora is fortified by antistrophe:

. . . in how manye maneres been the acciouns or werkynges of *Penitence*, and how manye speces ther ben of *Penitence*, and *whiche thynges* apertenen and bihoven to *Penitence*, and *which thynges* destourben *Penitence* (ibid.).	. . . quae quidem est poenitentia; circa quam videndum quid sit poenitentia, unde dicatur, de tribus actionibus poenitentiae, de tribus speciebus ejusdem, quae sunt necessaria ad poenitentiam veram, de clavibus, de remissionibus, de impedimentis poenitentiae (p. 729f.).

Sometimes the effects of repetition and alliteration already existing in the Latin are intensified in the English:

Pryvee penaunce is thilke that men doon alday for *privee synnes*, of whiche we shryve us *prively* and receyve *privee penaunce* (p. 230¹).	*Privata* dicitur illa *poenitentia* quae singulariter fit quotidie et cum quis peccata sua secrete sacerdoti confitetur (p. 732).

The same effects are to be found in passages for which no extant source is known:

And therefore repentant folk, that stynte for to *synne*, and forlete *synne* er that *synne* forlete hem, hooly chirche holdeth hem *siker* of hire savacioun (p. 229²).

Minor expansions include some word pairs and synonyms which heighten the rhythmical effect of the English:

a japere and a gebbere (p. 229[1])	irrisor (p. 730)
bihovely and necessarie (p. 230[1])	necessaria (p. 732)
wikked synful werkynge (ibid.)	superbia operis (ibid.)
hevy and grevous (p. 230[2])	[nothing to correspond]
ful sharp and poynaunt ... moore sharp and poynaunt ... yet moore sharp and poynaunt (ibid.)	acer ... acerior ... acerrimus (p. 733)

Occasionally also vivid details are introduced:

to goon peradventure naked in pilgrimage, or barefoot (p. 229[2])	peregrinatio per mundum cum baculo, cubitali et scapulari, vel veste aliqua ad hoc consueta (p. 731).

Comments and illustrative quotations are multiplied in the English, for instance in the section dealing with the six causes moving a man to contrition (p. 230[1]ff.). Again, we have to suppose that Chaucer took these from a lost expanded form of Raymund's work, but if so he did full justice to the opportunities it offered. One added statement, for instance, is the acute comment that a contrite person recalling past sins must be on his guard not to find a perverse pleasure in the exercise: 'but looke he that thilke remembraunce ne be to hym no delit by no wey, but greet shame and sorwe for his gilt' (p. 230[2]).

Beginning with the second (interpolated) section the expansions are so considerable that comparison with Raymund's text is pointless. The tract on the Seven Sins does not furnish material for detailed comment on Chaucer's art as a prose adapter. In its own right, however, the tract contains some passages of extraordinarily effective writing. Whether copied or imitated, paraphrased or independently composed, they fit well into the homiletic purpose of the Tale.

The initial chapter devoted to pride (*superbia*) will serve as illustration. The preacher begins by listing various subdivisions or 'twigges' which derive from the capital sin; he then defines the type of person guilty of each. The brief characterisations are introduced in a series of sentences showing parallel constructions: in this case, parallel inversions of word order:

Inobedient is he . . .	Avantour is he . . .	Ypocrite is he . . .
Despitous is he . . .	Arrogant is he . . .	Inpudent is he . . .

and so on (p. 239 [1-2]). Formal structure corresponds to the formal nature of the introduction. But now the style becomes more fluent, less mannered, with the paragraphs beginning: 'And yet there is a privee spece of Pride, that waiteth first to be salewed er he wole salewe,' and 'Now been ther two maneres of Pride: that oon of hem is withinne the herte of man, and that oother is withoute' (p. 240[1]). The general statements lead to some very concrete illustrations. Pride in clothing is attacked with an abundance of sartorial detail, phrased with a craftsman's special vocabulary: for instance in this list of verbal nouns assembled to specify 'the cost of embrowdynge, the degise endentynge or barrynge, owndynge, palynge, wyndynge or bendynge, or semblable wast of clooth in vanitee' (p. 240[1]). Vivid images are evoked of long effeminate gowns 'trailynge in the dong and in the mire, on horse and eek on foote, as wel of man as of womman' (p. 240[2]), and similarly vivid images conjure up the opposite extremes of fashion, which favoured scanty and revealing garments. Indignation at the wearers kindles a metaphor: 'and eek the buttokes of hem faren as it were the hyndre part of a she-ape in the fulle of the moone' (ibid.). There is vigour too in the statements about the harm done to ordinary poor people as a result of extravagant fashions prevailing in the upper classes: 'the moore that clooth is wasted, the moore moot it coste to the peple for the scarsnesse' (p. 240[2]). Besides, it is not fitting or desirable to hand on 'swich pownsoned and dagged clothing to the povre folk, as it is nat convenient to were for hire estaat, ne suffisant to beete hire necessitee, to kepe hem fro the distemperance of the firmament' (ibid.).

In general, the themes touched upon in this justly celebrated passage of *The Parson's Tale*—extravagance of dress, immodesty, waste, the need to observe distinctions of estate—were already familiar in Latin medieval satire long before Chaucer took them over from his unknown source. Certain it is, however, that

Chaucer very well adapted his language to the satirical subject matter he was engaged in presenting.[1]

IV. Eloquent Style in the *Melibeus*

The prose tale which Chaucer assigned to himself, the disputation between Melibeus and his wife Prudence on wars of private revenge versus legal procedures, gave scope for a somewhat more eloquent style than that of *The Parson's Tale*. As usual, the manner as well as the matter were pretty well established by the source used, which was the much modified adaptation into French by Renaud de Louvens of the *Liber Consolationis et Consilii* written (1246) by Albertano of Brescia.[2] Nevertheless it can be demonstrated once more that Chaucer not only availed himself of the resources of his original, but in many cases distinctly heightened their effect.

First of all there are the familiar augmentations of verbal echo and repetition:

to hym that *sorweful* is, amonges folkes in *sorwe* (p. 168[1])	a celui qui est tristes (p. 569)
. . . whan thou hast forgoon thy *freend*, do diligence to gete another *freend*, and this is moore wysdom than for to wepe for thy *freend* (ibid.)	Car quant tu auras perdu ton ami, efforce toy de un autre recouvrer; car il te vault mieux un autre ami recouvrer que l'ami perdu plorer (ibid.)
And, sire, ye moste also dryve out of youre *herte* hastifnesse; for certes, ye ne may nat deeme for the beste by a sodeyn thought that falleth in youre *herte* (p. 172[2])	Aprés, tu dois oster de toy hastivité, car tu ne dois pas juger pour le meilleur ce que tantost te vendra au devant (p. 578)

---

[1] In the tract on sins there are further examples of word order, anaphora, parallel constructions and inversions conductive to rhythmical effect. At one point there is a series of sentences beginning thus: 'Certes, the goods of nature stonden . . . Certes the goodes of body been . . . Goodes of nature of the soule been . . . Goodes of fortune been . . . Goodes of grace been . . .' and so on. Further, 'Eke for to pride hym' begins two sentences placed close together though not in uninterrupted sequence. Thus the organisation of material is thrown into relief by patterns in the wording. The theme of 'gentrie' is underscored by repetition of the word; in the next paragraph a variation on it is introduced with sound echo: 'Now been ther *gen*erale signes of *gent*ilesse . . .' (p. 242[1]).

[2] The French text is edited by J. Burke Severs in *Originals and Analogues*, pp. 560-614. Illustrations are here taken from the first 310 lines.

Chaucer retains some of the doublets and close synonyms provided by Renaud; he introduces some of his own, but he also avoids some of those existing in the French. No clear policy of choice is observable here.[1] Nor can it be claimed that the minor innovations always tend in the direction of greater emphasis or clarity. In one instance the omission of a negative particle and a preposition both weakens and obscures the sense. Where the French has 'la janglerie des femmes ne puet celer fors ce qu'elle ne scet' (p. 575) Chaucer writes: 'the janglerie of wommen kan hyde thynges that they wot noght' (p. 171[1]).[2] Obviously the adverb *only* is needed before *thynges* as equivalent of *ne . . . fors*. In another case the omission of a negative has actually inverted the sense. The French reads: 'car tu ne demandes pas conseil de mal faire' (p. 576; no variant reading recorded) while Chaucer writes: 'For . . . ye asken conseil to do wikkednesse' (p. 171[1]).[3]

Sometimes the English sentences are slightly looser than the French, e.g.:

he that precheth to hem that listen nat heeren his wordes, his sermon hem anoieth (p. 169[2]; shift of subject).	la narration de cellui qui presche a ceulz qui ne veulent oïr est ennuyeuse narracion (p. 572)

But quite often they are made tighter in construction:

but certes what ende that shal ther of bifalle, it is nat light to knowe (ibid.).	mais a tres grant pene puet on savoir a quel fin on en puet venir (ibid.; note repetition of *on*).
Whan Melibeus hadde herd that the gretteste partie of his conseil weren accorded that he sholde maken werre, anoon he consented to hir conseillyng, and fully affermed hire sentence (p. 170[1]).	Mellibee, quant il ot oÿ tout son conseil, il regarda que la tres plus grant partie s'accordoit que l'on feist uerre, si s'arresta a leur sentence la conferma (p. 573).

[1] Geismar has made a detailed study of Chaucer's doublets, op. cit., ch. 6. He finds the most extreme use of them in the *Melibeus*.

[2] This seems to be the authentic reading. But the sentence must have troubled some of the scribes for a number of the manuscripts emend to 'kan not hyde,' while one of them has first included the negative and then deleted it. See John M. Manly and Edith Rickert, *The Text of the Canterbury Tales*, University of Chicago Press 1940, IV, p. 162n. Note, however, that in this same sentence Chaucer carefully adheres to the plural number, whereas the French shifts from plural *femmes* to generic singular.

[3] Manly and Rickert give no variant reading for this at l. B 2280.

In respects such as these, then, the stylistic merits are fairly evenly balanced between the two versions. But Chaucer has frequently added brush strokes of his own which, taken together, impart a much heightened colour to the whole. The following examples, all taken from the opening section of the Tale, contain significant words and phrases introduced by Chaucer:

the dores weren *faste* yshette (p. 167[1])	les portes closes (p. 568)
with fyve *mortal* woundes (ibid.)	de cinq playes (p. 568)
lat nat thyn eyen to moyste been *of teeris*, ne to muche drye (p. 168[2])	ton oeil ne soit ne secs ne moistes (p. 569)
in herte he baar a *crueel* ire (p. 168[2])	il estoit moult courrociez (p. 570)
ther is ful many a child unborn *of his mooder* that shal sterve yong by cause of *thilke* werre (p. 169[2])	moult de gens ne sont encores nez qui pour cause de la guerre morront jeunes (p. 572)

Other minor additions help to facilitate transitions and to remind the reader (or hearer) who is speaking or being spoken to. Expressions like 'trust wel', 'certes', 'in this wise', 'heere may ye see that', lacking equivalents in the original, add to the fluency. So does the substitution of a concrete expression like 'this noble wyf Prudence' where the French relies on the pronoun *elle*. Vocative nouns and phrases of direct address are added to the debate between Melibeus and his wife. Melibeus inserts 'wyf', and Prudence more than once inserts 'sire' and expressions like 'thanne rede I yow', so that the discussion sounds a bit more like a real conversation than it did in the original.

Chaucer also introduced rhythmical effects into his *Melibeus* translation, far more conspicuously than in his scientific or even his homiletic prose. This fact, we recall, was recognised by early critics who, however, limited their attention for the most part to certain iambic passages readily identified in the midst of normal prose paragraphs. More recently the present writer has made a study of the incidence of recognised medieval patterns of cadence appearing in Chaucer's prose. These patterns were called *cursus* by the theoreticians. The introduction to the present volume briefly recapitulates what is known by medievalists about the history of prose rhythms in general, and it is pertinent to restate at this point the conclusion I reached some time ago[1]: that *Melibeus* reveals an unusual frequency of rhythmical effects, very appropriate (as a medieval writer would presumably see it) to the dignified style and high seriousness of the debate. Moreover, it would appear from the evidence I then collected that Chaucer's translation of Boethius' *De Consolatione Philosophiae* is also markedly rhythmical. Here, perhaps, there was even more justification for the use of *Kunstprosa*, especially in the rendering of the Boethian metra. Logically therefore—though not chronologically—this translation may be taken as the culminating topic of the present study.

V. Rhythmical Prose Exemplified in the Boethius Translation

Briefly it may be said that three basic types of *cursus* or prose cadence were cultivated for rhythmical effects at the ends of sentences or clauses. (In the following schemes, ' marks an accented syllable, x indicates an unaccented one, and the numbers refer to the count of syllables beginning from the end of a clause or colon.) They were:

Cursus planus	´x x ´x	5-2	(dactyl plus trochee)
Cursus tardus	´x x ´x x	6-3	(two dactyls)
Cursus velox	´x x ´x ´x	7-4-2	(dactyl plus 2 trochees)

There were numerous variations, depending on the permissible divisions between words (this applied especially to Latin *cursus*), the incidence of secondary stress, and the possibility of introducing extra unstressed syllables—a latitude much favoured in England by the tradition of native metrics. English practice also made notable use of alliteration, an ornament not unknown in medieval Latin, in order to underline the effect of cadence. As unaccented final -*e*'s disappeared in Chaucer's time, *cursus planus* tended to become choriambic (that is, ´ x x ´ or 4-1), for instance in the writings of Richard Rolle of Hampole. Besides, a general iambic-trochaic movement, very characteristic of English prose bordering on the poetic, is often found in place of regular *cursus*. All of these patterns appear in the *Consolation* as well as the

---

[1] 'Chaucer's Prose Rhythms', *PMLA*, LXV (1950) 568-89.

Melibeus. An example of strong iambic rhythm will be found at the beginning of the third sentence of Boethius in III prose 5: 'But cértes, the˛óld˛áge of týme pássed, and ék of présent týme nów'—after which greater variety appears in the number of intervening unstressed syllables. The preceding two sentences, by the way, end with *cursus planus* and *tardus* respectively: 'a mán to ben mýghti' (5-2); 'dúreth perpétuely' (6-3). Various types of rhythmical effect may be found in the opening section of II metre 7. They will emerge more clearly if the sentences are subdivided into *cola*:

Whoso that with overthrówynge thóught	4-1	(choriamb)
oonly seketh glórie˛of fáme,	5-2	(*planus*)
and weneth that it be sóvereyn góod,	?4-1	(choriamb)[1]
lat hym looke upon the brode shewynge contrées of the hévene	?6-3	(*tardus*)[2]
and upon the streyte séte˛of this érthe;	5-2	(*planus*)
and he schal be asschamid of the encrés of his náme,	5-2	(*planus*)[3]
that mai nat fulfille the litel compás of the érthe.	?5-2	(*planus*)[4]
O! what coveyten proude folk to lyften up hir nékkes on ídel	5-2	(*planus*)
in the dedly yók of this wórld?	4-1	(choriamb)
For that rénoùn ysprád,		(iambic or choriambic)[5]
pássỳnge to férne péples,	?7-4-2	(modified *velox*)
góth by divérse tónges	7-4-2	(*velox*)
and although that greete houses or kynredes shynen with cleere títles of hónours;	?5-2	(*planus* or iambic)

[1] Doubtful, since Chaucer scans *sovereyn* both as a disyllable and a trisyllable in his verse.
[2] The word *contree* appears as an iamb in *CT*, A 216 and 340 but as a trochee in B 434 and F 319.
[3] All verse usages of *encres* when used as a substantive show accent on the second syllable.
[4] All appearances of the word *compas* in Chaucer's verse show accent on the final syllable except one: G 45 'That of the trýne cómpas lórd and gýde is'. We must also reckon with the possibility of elision between 'the' and 'erthe'.
[5] Usually *renóun* in the verse; but cf. *HF* 1406 'Goddesse of Renóun ór of Fáme!'

yit natheles deth despiseth al hey
    glórie‿offáme,   5-2   (*planus*)
and deth wrappeth togidre the hey-
    ghe hév(e)des and the lówe,   ?6-2   (expanded *planus*?)
and maketh egal and evene the
    héygheste to the lóweste.   (expanded *tardus*?)

Obviously, since we cannot evoke Chaucer's voice reading his prose aloud, we cannot be sure of all of its rhythmical values, especially in the case of Romance loan words which still, apparently, had hovering accent. Nevertheless, the clear instances of cadenced writing within this appropriate context are so numerous as to leave no doubt that the author was to a certain extent at least heightening his style consciously.

This conclusion is strengthened by the frequent appearance of other decorative devices in the *Consolation*. Alliteration is combined with *cursus* effects where the emotional charge is particularly strong. Note, for instance, the insistent repetition of initial *h-* in these lines[1]:

> somtyme it seemede that sche touchede the hevene with the heghte of here heved [expanded *planus*], and whan she hef hir heved heyer [trochaic], sche percede the selve hevene so that the sighte of men lokynge was in ydel [?expanded *planus*] (I pr. 1).

Here the onset of the sentence is emphasised by recurrent sibilants:

> It liketh me to schewe by subtil soong, with slakke and delytable sown of strenges, how that Nature, myghty,[2] enclyneth and flytteth the governe-mentz of thynges [trochaic] (III m. 2).

And here the initial *fl-* (based on *adnominatio*) is introduced less conspicuously:

[1] To be sure, Helge Kökeritz has assembled evidence (from the verse) that Chaucer may not have pronounced initial *h-* in either Germanic or Romance words: 'Rhetorical Word-Play in Chaucer', *PMLA*, LXIX (1954) 937-52, especially p. 946. But if so, a similar effect must have been obtained by the repeated initial vowel (*h*)*e-*. The marked concentration of them can hardly be accidental.

[2] Worth noting is the extremely emphatic and effective inverted position of the adjective.

Every delit hath this, that it angwisscheth hem with prykkes that usen it [*tardus*]. It resembleth to thise flyenge flyes that we clepen ben; that, aftir that the be hath sched his agreable honyes, he fleeth awey [choriamb], and styngeth the hertes of hem that ben ysmyte [trochaic], with bytynge overlonge holdynge[1] (III m. 7).

As the last example indicates, word echo is exploited in the *Consolatio* fully as much as in the other prose writings, and even more clearly for purposes of decoration:

> ... how sche [Nature] *bynd*ynge, restreyneth alle thynges by a *boond* that may nat be un*bownde* (III m. 2);
> For alle thing that is cleped in*parfyt* is proevid in*parfit* be the amenusynge of *perfec*cioun or of thing that is *parfit* (III pr. 10).

We are not at present in a position to say how often such echoes are due to Chaucer's own innovations and how often they may have been suggested by the French translation of Jean de Meun (hitherto unpublished) which he apparently used to aid him in dealing with the Latin.[2] However, the scattered evidence available in print would indicate that here as in the *Melibeus* Chaucer expanded on his originals, realising the same effects as elsewhere in so doing (he also made some mistakes in rendering both, but that is another matter). At times the result is to make his sentences less concentrated, more easily flowing, as when Latin *inexhaustus*, French *inconsumptible*, becomes 'Swich ... that it ne myghte nat ben emptid' (I pr. 1) and 'senicas meretriculas', French 'ribaudelles fardees', becomes 'thise comune strompettis of swich a place that men clepen the theatre' (ibid.).

---

[1] Note the effect of *similiter cadens* in *bytynge*: *holdynge*.
[2] The problem was considered by Richard Morris in his edition of Chaucer's Translation of Boethius's 'De Consolatione Philosophiae', EETS, ES, v (1868) p. xiii; again by Mark Liddell in the introduction to the Globe edition of Chaucer's works (London 1878). Both editors cited specific illustrations. Morris concluded that Chaucer worked from the Latin alone while Liddell gave evidence to show his dependence on the French. The latter position has been supported by the detailed studies of V. L. Dedeck-Héry: 'Jean de Meun et Chaucer, Traducteurs de la Consolation de Boèce', *PMLA* LII (1937) 967-91 and 'Le Boèce de Chaucer et les Manuscrits Français de la Consolation de Jean de Meun', ibid., LIX (1944) 18-25. Examples are taken from Morris's introduction.

Scrutiny of the three versions side by side reinforces the evidence for Chaucer's pleasure in *adnominatio*. Here the introduction of a cognate synonym is accompanied by cadence:

Latin	French	English
Ita ego quoque tibi	semblablement ie te	right so wold I yeve
veluti corollarium da-	donneray ainsi vng	or the here as a corolarie
bo (III pr. 10).	correlaire.	a méede_of coróune.[1]

So far as sentence structure is concerned, the Boethius translation displays considerable variety, perhaps more than in the other prose works, since the original offered greater possibilities, ranging from simple question-and-answer in the dialogues to rhetorical discourse (also found in the *Melibeus*) to verse passages of exalted poetic inspiration (not paralleled elsewhere). An example of imposing periodic structure is to be found in the first sentence of II m. 8 ('That the world with stable feyth varieth accordable chaungynges . . . '); an example of paratactic structure with anaphora is to be found in the third of IV m. 1 ('And whan the thought hath don there inogh, he schal forleten the laste hevene, and he schal pressen and wenden on the bak of the swifte firmament, and he schal be makid parfit of the worschipful lyght of God'). There are examples of loose structure, shift of grammatical construction and the like. They resemble those already cited in connection with other prose texts. For instance, in IV m. 1 (an indubitably eloquent passage) we find a pronoun which is somehow changed from neuter to masculine gender:

> Whanne the swifte thoght hath clothid itself in the fetheris, it despiseth the hateful erthes, and surmounteth the rowndnesse of the gret ayr; and it seth the clowdes byhynde his bak, . . . til that *he* areyseth *hym* . . . and joyneth *his* weies with the sonne, Phebus . . .

There are pleonastic pronoun constructions too, in this instance underscored by repetition and syntactic parallelism:

---

[1] Another instance of *adnominatio* seemingly introduced by Chaucer has been put in doubt by some of his editors. In I, pr. 6, Boethius wrote *fortuita temeritate*; the French gives *par fortuite folie*; all the Chaucer manuscripts read 'by fortunows' (fortunouse, etc.), fortune, and this was accepted by Morris and by Skeat. But Liddell in the Globe edition surmised that the correct reading should be 'furtunows folie', in accord with the French. Perhaps correctly; but in the light of medieval taste in matters of style, the manuscript authority is not to be rejected as impossible.

Riche folk, mai they neyther han hungir ne thurst? Thise riche men, may
they fele no cold on hir lymes in wynter? (III pr. 3)

As has already been observed, however, these were sanctioned in
Middle English usage and in fact stylistically justified for reasons
of clarity and emphasis.

The available evidence indicates, in sum, that Chaucer made
planned use of known rhetorical and poetic effects when he was
working on the Boethius translation, but that he did not overuse
them. To convince oneself of his restraint one has only to compare
the opening passage of the Boethius translation with the Prologue
and first few pages of Thomas Usk's *Testament of Love*, so clearly
modelled on Chaucer's work. In Usk one will find an excessive
concentration of *cursus* effects, of alliteration, repetition, word
echo and inversions of normal word order, the whole creating an
effect of marked artificiality. For example:

Wherof Aristotle in the boke *de Ani-*	
malibus, saith to naturel philoso-	?*Cursus tardus* (or iambic)
phers: 'it is a greet lyking in love	Alliteration on *l*
of knowinge their creatour; and also	Repetition of *knowinge*
in knowinge of causes of kýndely	Sustained alliteration on *k*
thínges.' Considred, forsoth, the	*Cursus planus*
formes of kyndly thinges and the	Repetition of *kyndly thinges*
shap, a greet kindely love me shulde	Echo of *kind-*
have to the werkman that hem made.	Inversion (object before subject)
The cráfte of a wérkman is shéwed in	Repetition and echo of *werk(man)*
the wérke. Herfore, truly, the phi-	*Cursus planus* (twice)
losophers, with a lývely stúdie,	?*Cursus tardus*
many noble thinges right precious	Inversion (object before verb)
and worthy to mémory wríten; and	?*Cursus planus*
by a greet swetande travayle to us	Inversion (dative phrase before verb)
leften of causes [of] the propertees in	
natúres of thínges (*Prologue*, Skeat	?*Cursus planus*
ed. p. 3, ll. 64-73).	

Compared with this typical Uskian passage of mannered prose,
Chaucer's handling of the medium is laudably moderate. Quite
certainly we may conclude that he was familiar with the various
means of decoration described and practised by his predecessors,
but he used them without excess. His levels of style were well
adapted to his diversified subjects. The defects with which he has

been charged were in part inherent in the linguistic and rhetorical usage of his time. His virtues upon occasion add up to a truly moving eloquence. Who can forget who has once attentively read sentences like the following:

> For eelde is comyn unwarly uppon me, hasted by the harmes that y have, and sorwe hath comandid his age to ben in me. Heeris hore arn schad overtymeliche upon myn heved, and the slakke skyn trembleth of myn emptid body (I m. 1).

Here are rhythm and artful inversion, alliteration and other sound effects (for instance, the assonance of *hasted, comandid, age, schad, slakke*), but the content—a universal human plaint nobly expressed—fully justifies the use of them.

Note on *The Equatorie of the Planetis*

Stylistic parallels between this text and the *Astrolabe* include first of all the informal use of first and second personal pronouns, e.g. 'yif thow myshappe in this cas i shal teche the aremedie' (26:24f.); 'I conseile the ne write no names of signes' (28:5), etc. The first person is habitually used in reminders: 'as I haue seid by forn' (34:17 *et passim*). The author also recounts his own observations and calculations in the first person; and just as Chaucer twice spoke of 'my sonne', this text speaks twice of 'my mone'. The stereotyped verb-subject inversion after colourless adverb is to be found in the passage beginning at 42:26: 'tho drow I; tho fonde I; tho rekned I'. Especial emphasis is indicated by the phrase 'I seye', several times introducing a paraphrase which drives home a point by repetition. As in the *Astrolabe*, nouns are sometimes insistently repeated throughout a passage, quite clearly to avoid ambiguity of pronoun reference and to achieve emphasis rather than for purposes of decoration. In one passage *cercle* is often used (18:10ff.); again *plate* is insistently repeated (ibid., 18ff.); or a cluster of words obtrudes by simultaneous repetition (*parties, lyne alhudda, deuisioun* in 20:9ff.). The use of simple imperatives leads to non-literary effects of anaphora, as when we find sets of instructions beginning 'tak thanne' only slightly diversified by the substitution of other monosyllabic verbs: *mak, set, scrape, perce, draw, turne* (see 18:10ff. and 20:11ff.). As in the *Astrolabe*, there are some synonymous or tautological word pairs: 'it shal nat werpe ne krooke the egge' (18:7); 'this bord may be vernissed or elles glewed' (18:9); 'perce [and] make a litel hole' (24:13; a doubtful case since the first word is written above the other and the intention may have been to delete one of them). The occasional pleonasms in the *Equatorie* are no more or less striking than those in the *Astrolabe*: 'the remenaunt of auges sek *hem* in the table of auges folwynge' (20:27f.); '& so many signes . . . as thow hast . . . rekne *hem* for the hed of aries' (38:29-31). The style of the text certainly offers no obstacle in the way of assignment to Chaucer and in fact rather strengthens the case for his authorship.[1]

[1] For positive evidence based on vocabulary see F. W. Harwood in *Language* XXXII (1956) 254-59; also G. Herdan, *Language as Choice and Chance*, Amsterdam 1956, pp. 18-22.

The Scottish Chaucerians

DENTON FOX

THE term 'Scottish Chaucerians' is a traditional name which is in some respects misleading, but it does have the merit of suggesting a few basic problems. It raises first the question of who these poets are, and whether they are a sufficiently homogeneous group to be given any single label, let alone this one; then the question of in what ways, if at all, they are 'Chaucerians', or for that matter 'Scottish'.

The name has usually been applied to the Scottish poets of the fifteenth and early sixteenth centuries who wrote, at least occasionally, in the formal 'aureate' style and who inserted references to Chaucer into their poems: the author of *The Kingis Quair*, Henryson, Dunbar, Douglas, perhaps Lyndsay. But it is impossible to give the term any definite boundaries, for it could certainly be applied to the mostly anonymous predecessors and imitators of these poets. I would like arbitrarily to limit myself here to Henryson, Dunbar and Douglas, who are in several ways the central figures. They are central chronologically: all their poems were probably written during a period of less than fifty years, the most brilliant period of Scottish poetry; and they are the most representative figures, as well as the most outstanding ones. Each is a poet of a different type, and between them they exemplify most of the important kinds of poetry written in Scotland during this period, but there are also some clear and fundamental resemblances binding them together. It should be remembered, of course, that by limiting ourselves to these three poets we are neglecting a good deal of Chaucer's influence on Scottish verse. On the one hand, there is the early *Kingis Quair*, more Chaucerian if less certainly Scottish than any later poem, but a work which, except for its great merit and the spellings of its surviving manuscript, seems to belong with the English Chaucerians.[1]

[1] Sir William Craigie, in 'The Language of the *Kingis Quair*', *Essays and Studies*,

Then there are the poets who came after Douglas, most notably Sir David Lyndsay. But Lyndsay and the other Scots poets of the middle of the sixteenth century wrote at a time when the Chaucerian tradition had become thoroughly naturalised. The most serious omission, perhaps, is that of the large bulk of poetry, either anonymous or by almost unknown poets, which is roughly contemporaneous with Henryson, Dunbar and Douglas. Authors' names have often counted for more than a poem's intrinsic merit: if a poem has been attributed to a well known poet (and the attributions of Middle Scots poems are frequently far from certain) it has at least been given the dubious immortality of being repeatedly edited, but the anonymous poems tend to slip into oblivion. Yet these anonymous poems are sometimes both Chaucerian and excellent: the fabliau *The Freiris of Berwick*, for instance, has justly been said to be 'above all other attempts to continue the tradition of the comic Canterbury Tales'.[1]

The 'Scottish' part, at least, of the label 'Scottish Chaucerians' ought to be clear enough. But even this is misleading: almost all of the connotations which 'Scottish' has for a modern Englishman or American are utterly irrelevant to the Middle Scots poets. When we think of Scotland we tend to think either of post-medieval inventions—Presbyterianism, Bonnie Prince Charlie, the myth of Scottish frugality—or of the Highlands, with their modern paraphernalia of kilt, bagpipes, and sentimentality. But the poets and their audience felt more affinity with the English on the other side of the border than with the Gaelic-speaking Highlanders whom they despised as wretched savages. *Iersch*, 'Highland', is the first insult that Dunbar throws at Kennedy in their *Flyting*.

Yet 'Scottish', when attached to 'Chaucerian', does have some meaning: it indicates first the language that these poets wrote in, and secondly the literary tradition that was behind them. Even here, however, a modern reader is likely to be misled. It is

xxv (1939) 22-38, argued persuasively that the poem was written by James I in the southern English which he would normally have spoken at the time, and that the surviving MS of the poem is the work of a scribe who introduced numerous Scots spellings.

[1] C. S. Lewis, *English Literature in the Sixteenth Century*, Oxford 1954, p. 99.

important to remember the obvious fact that the Middle Scots writers, unlike Burns and the later Scots poets, did not consciously choose to write in a dialect, but wrote in Middle Scots for the same reasons that Middle English writers wrote in their various dialects of Middle English. If Middle Scots should seem at first sight quaint, or provincial, or difficult to a modern reader, this is a quality in the modern reader, not in the language. Middle Scots is of course simply a development of Northern English, and the poets who wrote in it (except for the politically conscious Douglas) spoke of it as 'Inglis', not as 'Scottis'. On the other hand, it is not only a dialect but also a literary language, consciously improved, polished, and stabilised. Yet though sophisticated and artificial, it is at the same time an immensely flexible and variable anguage into which the grossest rustic terms or the most ornate Latin words can be assimilated.[1]

The Middle Scots poets are also differentiated from their English contemporaries by having a specifically Scottish literary tradition. Perhaps the best way to explain this tradition is by an oversimplification: Chaucer influenced immediately and profoundly the English tradition, so that the bulk of the more pretentious fifteenth-century English verse is Chaucerian; his influence on Scottish verse was slower and less overwhelming, so that the pre-Chaucerian ways of writing are still fashionable in Scotland in the fifteenth century. This is of course an inexact statement: the influence of Gower and especially Lydgate on both English and Scottish verse is not negligible; there is plenty of fifteenth-century English poetry which is not Chaucerian, most obviously among the lyrics; on the other hand, *The Kingis Quair* and, in places, Blind Harry's *Wallace* (c. 1475) are Chaucerian. But it remains true that the pre-Chaucerian tradition was more available to Dunbar, for instance, than it was to his English contemporaries. The most obvious sign of this is that alliterative poetry, which in England was essentially dead by the fifteenth century, was still influential in Scotland at the beginning of the sixteenth century. There is, first, the ordinary unrhymed alliter-

---

[1] The best introduction to the linguistic characteristics of Middle Scots is still G. Gregory Smith, *Specimens of Middle Scots*, Edinburgh 1902. A new introductory work by A. J. Aitken and David Murison is now in preparation.

ative line, as in *Piers Plowman*, which occurs in Dunbar's *The Tua Mariit Wemen and the Wedo*. Then there is the rhymed alliterative stanza, ending in a group of short lines, which is used by Henryson, Douglas and numerous anonymous poets, often for humorous purposes. A more indirect symptom is the habit which Henryson, Dunbar and Douglas have of using alliteration very heavily in verse which is structurally non-alliterative. But of course the Scottish literary tradition consisted of much more than an alliterative technique. Since we possess few of the earlier poems, and are usually unable to date those which we do have, it is hard to be very precise about the nature of this tradition. But one can distinguish a few types of poetry that were flourishing in Scotland before Henryson: narrative verse in pronouncedly end-stopped couplets, octosyllabic in Barbour's *Bruce* (c. 1375), decasyllabic in the *Wallace*; comic verse of an exuberant and fantastic nature; and religious lyrics—usually more religious than lyric.[1]

The 'Chaucerian' part of 'Scottish Chaucerian' is so equivocal as to be almost meaningless. It is clear, at least, that the Scots poets, unlike some of the English ones, were not 'Chaucerians' in the sense of being submerged in Chaucer, and trying vainly to imitate him. It is also clear that they were 'Chaucerians' in the same way that we now are all, perforce, Cartesians, Marxists, Freudians. Henryson, Dunbar and Douglas wrote about a century after Chaucer had fundamentally changed the course of English poetry, and they could no more ignore this change than we can ignore the changes for which we hold Descartes, Marx and Freud responsible. In order to determine more precisely how, and in what ways, Chaucer influenced the Scots poets, it is necessary to examine the individual poets, though one can make some preliminary cautions and generalisations. No one would wish to deny the profound influence which Chaucer had on later poetry, but it is perhaps possible to exaggerate his importance, and to make him solely responsible for a movement in which he was

---

[1] An excellent brief account of early Scots verse is given in C. S. Lewis, *English Literature in the Sixteenth Century*. I am generally indebted to Professor Lewis, as anyone writing on Middle Scots poetry must be. The best special history of Scottish literature is Kurt Wittig, *The Scottish Tradition in Literature*, Edinburgh 1958. Professor Wittig argues that Middle Scots poetry was influenced by the Gaelic tradition, which is possible, but very difficult to prove.

only the outstanding figure. Chaucer, surely, was not the only
conduit through which French and Italian influence, and the 'new
poetry', came into England. Gower, Lydgate, and the English
Chaucerians all helped to change the native tradition, while the
Scots poets, inhabitants of an independent country traditionally
allied with France against England, were perfectly capable of
going directly to French poetry.[1]

Each age creates for itself its own image of Chaucer, and
fortunately both Dunbar and Douglas have described their, and
I think their age's, Chaucer. Dunbar, in *The Golden Targe*, writes:

> O reverend Chaucere, rose of rethoris all,
> As in oure tong ane flour imperiall,
> That raise in Britane evir, quho redis rycht,
> Thou beris of makaris the tryumph riall;
> Thy fresch anamalit termes celicall
> This mater coud illumynit have full brycht:
> Was thou noucht of oure Inglisch all the lycht,
> Surmounting eviry tong terrestriall,
> Alls fer as Mayis morow dois mydnycht?
>
> O morall Gower, and Ludgate laureate,
> Your sugurit lippis and tongis aureate,
> Bene to oure eris cause of grete delyte;
> Your angel mouthis most mellifluate
> Oure rude langage has clere illumynate,
> And faire ourgilt oure speche, that imperfyte
> Stude, or your goldyn pennis schupe to wryte;
> This Ile before was bare and desolate
> Off rethorike or lusty fresch endyte.[2]

> 253-70

Douglas has a similar passage in the prologue to the first book of
his translation of the *Aeneid*, and though he may have borrowed
some of his vocabulary from Dunbar, the passage agrees so well
with his other statements on poetry that it can safely be taken as
expressing his own opinion:

---

[1] See Janet M. Smith, *The French Background of Middle Scots Literature*, Edinburgh
1934. But it should be added that Middle Scots poetry does not often seem to
be based directly on French originals. Dunbar is sometimes cited as being especially
indebted to French poetry, but P. H. Nichols searched extensively and largely
fruitlessly for his French sources ('Sources and Influences Traceable in the Poetry
of William Dunbar', unpublished dissertation, Harvard 1923).

[2] *rethoris*, 'rhetoricians'; *celicall*, 'celestial'; *schupe*, 'made ready'.

venerabill Chauser, principal poet but peir,
Hevynly trumpat, orlege and reguler,
In eloquens balmy cundyt and dyall,
Mylky fontane, cleir strand and roys ryall
Of fresch endyte, throu Albion iland braid . . .[1]

339-43

Dunbar has been sneered at for calling Chaucer 'rose of rethoris',
as if he thought that Chaucer was a mere rhetorician. Modern
critics are beginning to think that Dunbar had a very good point,
and that Chaucer's rhetorical skill was not the least of his qualities.
But in any case, both Dunbar and Douglas plainly value Chaucer
not for his humour, nor for his genial insight into humanity, nor
for his interesting stories, but for his use of and improvement of
English as a poetic language. The metaphors with which they
describe Chaucer are very interesting. Both Dunbar and Douglas
associate him with flowers, freshness, royalty and heaven, and
agree in calling him the chief of all poets. They both imply that
he has given life to poetry throughout Britain: Dunbar says that
before Chaucer, Gower and Lydgate 'This Ile . . . was bare and
desolate'; Douglas says that Chaucer was the life-giving (*Mylky*)
fountain and river of poetry, running through all Britain. And
they both provide images for the qualities they value in Chaucer.
Dunbar's principal term is light: Gower and Lydgate, lesser
luminaries, 'Oure rude langage has clere illumynate', while
Chaucer is almost the sun, 'Mayis morow', and 'of oure Inglisch
all the lycht'. Douglas speaks of Chaucer as a *reguler* ('regulator',
perhaps a nonce-use), and equates him with instruments for
telling time, *orlege* and *dyall*, and also with the *Hevynly trumpat*,
God's regulator.

It is fair, I think, to extrapolate from these passages the general
feelings of the Middle Scots poets about Chaucer. They considered
him to be, in a very essential sense, the father of modern English
poetry, the man who purified, regularised, and clarified English,
and so made it possible for highly civilised and highly wrought
poetry to be written in the vernacular. From the troubadours to
the Pléiade, European poets were engaged in a constant struggle
to make their native tongues into languages with the beauty,

---

[1] *but peir*, 'without peer ; *orlege*, 'dial, clock'; *reguler*, 'regulator'; *cundyt*, 'conduit';
dyall, 'sun-dial'; *strand*, 'stream'.

precision and stability of Latin. Henryson, Dunbar and Douglas were fully conscious of the debt they owed to Chaucer, and to a lesser extent to Gower and Lydgate, for their part in this task. One can see, too, why Dunbar and Douglas (in another passage), like so many other poets, group together Chaucer, Gower and Lydgate, a rather oddly balanced triumvirate by modern tastes. One reason is of course simply that the late medieval writers did not know very much, perhaps often did not care very much, about the canons of these three poets, so that they did not make clear or accurate distinctions between them. To take two Scottish examples, in the earliest surviving dated printed book in Scotland (1508), Lydgate's *Complaint of the Black Knight* is ascribed to Chaucer; and in the Bannatyne Manuscript, the most important anthology of Middle Scots verse, there are nine poems attributed to Chaucer, all incorrectly, as well as one genuine Chaucerian poem, which is not attributed to him. But the most important reason for the traditional triumvirate is that the Scots and English poets that came after Lydgate had, like all poets, a utilitarian interest in their predecessors. They did not wish to make comparative evaluations, but to use the new modes of poetry which Gower, Chaucer and Lydgate had introduced, and to steal from them anything that seemed useful: diction, rhetoric, genres. Lydgate, voluminous, dilute, and easy to improve upon, was in many ways more immediately useful to his successors than Chaucer who, like other poets of the very first rank, did not always have a beneficent influence on his followers.

If the passages quoted above tell us something about the Scots poets' opinion of Chaucer, they also tell us something about their own poetry. The praise of bygone poets is of course a highly traditional *topos*, but this does not make it either obligatory or meaningless. The Middle Scots poets are addicted to praising Chaucer, Lydgate and Gower, surely, because they wish to announce that they are following in their footsteps, and that they too are modern, sophisticated and technically skilful poets. In a similar way, Henryson, Dunbar and Douglas all give encomiums of the Greek and Latin poets in order to demonstrate that they are cosmopolitan and learned poets, writing poetry which is comparable to, and in the same tradition with, classical poetry.

The English Augustan poets provide an obvious parallel here: just as the Scots praise the earlier English poets, so Dryden, for instance, praises 'Mr. Waller and Sir John Denham . . . those two fathers of our English poetry . . . our numbers were in their nonage till these last appeared',[1] while both the Scots and the Augustans revere the classical poets, as models to be imitated and as standards of excellence. The Scots, like the Augustans, were poets of profound originality but of equally profound and more obvious devotion to traditional styles, subjects and genres. It is interesting to look at the genres in which Henryson, Dunbar and Douglas wrote. The greater part of Henryson's work consists of his *Fables*, which he describes as a 'maner of Translatioun' (the other important fables in English are by John Gay); his other two major works are a reworking of the familiar Orpheus and Eurydice legend, and *The Testament of Cresseid*, which as a continuation of Chaucer's *Troilus* is a sufficiently bookish work. Dunbar is primarily an occasional poet, and he writes in the usual genres: short moral, religious, satirical, petitionary, and humorous poems. One of his favourite forms is the standard dream-vision, which he often subverts for humorous or satirical purposes, as the Augustan poets did with the epic. Douglas's major works are his translation of the *Aeneid* (the other important English translation of it is of course by Dryden) and *The Palace of Honour*, which is in the traditional form of an allegorical dream-vision.

The other side of the coin to the Scots' and Augustans' agreement in preferring traditional genres is their agreement on the fundamental importance of poetic technique and craftsmanship. Like the Augustans, the Scots took very seriously the traditional doctrine that poetry is thought dressed in beautiful language and rhetorically ornamented. As a result, the most outstanding common quality of Henryson, Dunbar, and Douglas seems to me to be their preoccupation with style, the 'artificiality', in the best sense, of their poetry.

We know little more about Robert Henryson's life than that he was a schoolmaster at Dunfermline and that his name appears towards the end of the list of dead poets in Dunbar's *Lament for*

[1] *Essays of John Dryden*, ed. W. P. Ker, Oxford 1900, II, pp. 108, 259.

the Makers, which must have been written between 1505 and 1510. The safest guess would seem to be that he died about 1500, and that his poetry was written in the last third of the fifteenth century.[1]

The usual clichés about Henryson are that he is a keen observer of nature and that his genial humanitarianism causes him to be the closest to Chaucer of all the Scottish Chaucerians. There is doubtless some truth in these generalisations, but hardly more than if one were to characterise Chaucer by saying that he was a keen observer of costumes, and had the endearing habit of seeing the best in people. Henryson has been underrated, I think, because his readers have not always extended the parallel with Chaucer far enough to notice that he shares Chaucer's art of concealing his art. Henryson's unobtrusive complexity is particularly evident in his longest work, *The Morall Fabillis of Esope*. This collection consists of thirteen fables, some of them derived from the medieval Reynardian stories, but most of them Aesopic, ostensibly translations of the versions in Latin verse by Walter of England. Henryson purports to be telling tales simply and plainly, partly for the 'doctrine wyse', and partly for 'ane merie sport': 'In hamelie language and in termes rude/Me neidis wryte, for quhy of Eloquence/Nor Rethorike, I never Understude.' But in reality his fables are artful, sophisticated and rhetorical; comparable, indeed, to La Fontaine's. From one aspect, they are elegant variations on a standard theme: Walter's fables were a standard school text, and would be well known to most of Henryson's audience. Walter's versions are short and crude; Henryson's,

[1] A good many biographical speculations have been made, some of which have found their way into reference works under the guise of facts. The date of Henryson's birth, for instance, is generally given as c. 1425, c. 1429, or c. 1430, but these dates are based only on a scatological and presumably spurious seventeenth-century anecdote which mentions that Henryson was 'very old'.

The fullest edition, G. Gregory Smith's *The Poems of Robert Henryson*, Scottish Text Society, 3 vols., Edinburgh 1906-14, contains the materials relevant to Henryson's biography. A more available edition is H. Harvey Wood's *The Poems and Fables of Robert Henryson*, Edinburgh 1933 (revised edition with no important changes, 1958); a selection has been edited by Charles Elliott, Oxford 1963; and a new complete edition has been promised. My quotations are from Wood's edition, but throughout this chapter I have repunctuated a few of the quotations from the Scots poets, in the interests of intelligibility, and have also silently expanded some abbreviations.

though they average only a little over two hundred lines, are often ten times as long. But on the other hand Henryson's fables are not arcane or precious: as he says of Aesop, he did not want 'the disdane off hie, nor low estate'.

Although it is perhaps not the best of Henryson's fables, the *Taill of Schir Chantecleir and the Foxe* is an interesting one to examine, since it has the same plot as *The Nun's Priest's Tale*. The two poems are obviously not very similar: it takes Chaucer about six hundred and forty lines to get from the introduction of the poor widow to the fox's first speech to the cock, but Henryson covers the same ground in twenty-three lines. In these lines Henryson demonstrates his remarkable power of narrating events in a style which is smooth, easy and rapid, but far from flat. The fox is brought to the farmyard, for instance, in these four lines:

> This wylie Tod, quhen that the Lark couth sing,
> Full sair hungrie unto the Toun him drest,
> Quhair Chantecleir in to the gray dawing,
> Werie for nicht, wes flowen ffra his nest.[1]
>
> 425-8

The two antagonists are balanced against each other, the fox moving into the field of action in the first two lines, and the cock in the last two. But the fox has purposefully set his course ('him drest') *to* the farmyard; the cock has merely flown *from* his place of refuge. The adjectives describing them are linked by alliteration: the fox is 'wylie' and the cock is 'Werie for nicht', ostensibly because, as we have been told, his songs divide the night, but more essentially because, as we later learn, the sexual appetites of his hens make great demands on him. The two details about the dawn serve to make it more vivid, but they are also balanced off with the two animals. For the fox, who is aggressive and cheerful, the lark sings; for the cock, who is going to suffer, the dawn is grey.

Another sort of easy subtlety is shown in the fox's speech to the cock, where, as frequently with Henryson, the superficial meaning of the lines is directly opposed to their true meaning:

> 'Your father full oft fillit hes my wame,
> And send me meit ffra midding to the muris.

[1] *Tod*, 'fox'; *couth*, 'did'; *Toun*, 'farm'; *Werie for*, 'weary from'.

And at his end I did my besie curis,
To hald his heid, and gif him drinkis warme,
Syne at the last the Sweit swelt in my arme.'[1]

441-5

Chantecleir's father had, in truth, often filled the fox's stomach, but by begetting chicks, not by sending presents; the fox doubtless did exert himself in holding the cock's head when he died, but he fails to add that this was also the cause of his death, and that the cock's warm drink was his own blood. The last line is the best: the fox means the cock to take the line's languishing rhythm and the rich chime of 'Sweit swelt' as expressing the fox's grief, but of course they really express the fox pausing delightedly at the recollection of his meal, while 'Sweit' here is not a meta-phorical term of affection. This passage is perhaps less delicate than the corresponding point in Chaucer's poem, where the fox remarks that Chantecleir's father and mother 'Han in myn hous ybeen to my greet ese', but it is hardly inferior.

The fox's speech, with its tone of impudent double-tongued sleekness, shows Henryson's remarkable ability to reveal character through dialogue, as does the flattered cock's brief and inane answer: ' "Knew ye my ffather?" quod the Cok, and leuch' (*leuch* here, as often in Henryson, means 'giggled', rather than 'laughed'). A more extended and more important instance of Henryson using different styles to show different speakers and different attitudes towards the world comes a little later in the poem, where seven stanzas are devoted to the hens' reactions after the cock has been kidnapped. First Pertok provides a traditional and ornate lament, worthy of Chaucer's 'Gaufred, deere maister soverayn':

'Yone wes our drowrie, and our dayis darling,
Our nichtingall, and als our Orloge bell,
Our walkryfe watche, us for to warne and tell
Quhen that Aurora with hir curcheis gray,
Put up hir heid betwix the nicht and day.'[2]

497-501

Then Sprutok, a descendant of the Wife of Bath, speaks in a

---

[1] *wame*, 'belly'; *I did my besie curis*, 'I diligently devoted myself'; *swelt*, 'died'.
[2] *drowrie*, 'love'; *dayis darling*, 'life's joy'; *walkryfe*, 'sleepless'; *curcheis*, 'scarves'.

cheerfully abrupt and downright rhythm, using clichés and proverbs:

> 'We sall ffair weill, I find Sanct Johne to borrow;
> The prouerb sayis, "als gude lufe cummis as gais."
> I will put on my haly dais clais,
> And mak me fresch agane this Jolie may,
> Syne chant this sang, "wes never wedow sa gay!"'[1]
>
> 511-15

After this encouragement, Pertok drops her hypocritical grief and sneers lecherously at Chantecleir: 'off sic as him ane scoir/Wald not suffice to slaik our appetyte.' She promises, in a line which is a nice instance of Henryson's stylistic manoeuvres, that she will quickly be able 'To get ane berne suld better claw oure breik'. *Berne*, 'man, warrior', is an exclusively poetic word, and is usually found in alliterative phrases—though not in combination with *breik*, 'breech'. *Claw* is sometimes used in Middle Scots with the meaning 'scratch gently, caress', but of course has a specially graphic meaning when applied to a cock. The line sums up the various rhetorics of love that we have seen: Pertok's noble and courtly lament, Sprutok's carefree wantonness, and Pertok's change to bestial lust. But instead of letting matters rest here, Henryson brings on a third hen who, 'lyke ane Curate', fulminates against Chantecleir with self-righteous indignation:

> 'rychteous God, haldand the balandis evin,
> Smytis rycht sair, thoct he be patient,
> For Adulterie, that will thame not repent.
>
> . . . it is the verray hand off God
> That causit him be werryit with the Tod.'[2]
>
> 534-6, 542-3

Then, as in *The Nun's Priest's Tale*, all pretensions are destroyed by the reality of the barnyard tumult, which Henryson expresses by giving the widow's commands to her dogs:

> 'How! berk, Berrie, Bawsie Broun,
> Rype schaw, Rin weil, Curtes, Nuttieclyde . . .'
>
> 546-7

---

[1] *I find Sanct Johne to borrow*, 'I swear by St John'.
[2] *balandis*, 'balances'; *werryit*, 'worried, killed'.

One can see how Henryson, like Chaucer, makes the fable into a deflation of human self-importance. The different attitudes towards death expressed by the hens are made ridiculous in numerous ways: by juxtaposition of conflicting rhetorics, by having the most grief-stricken hen turn out to be actually the most lecherous, by having all the attitudes irrelevant, since the cock returns safely, and of course simply by giving poultry human voices. And one can see how Henryson, like Chaucer, relies heavily on changes of style, balancing the voice of one animal against the voice of another, or setting up a heroic style only to puncture it abruptly. But one can also see that there are some fundamental differences between Chaucer's fable and Henryson's which point to a dissimilarity between the two poets.

One difference so obvious that it is easy to overlook is simply that Henryson's poem is written in rhyme royal, not in couplets. Henryson never uses couplets, except in the 'Moralitas' of *Orpheus and Eurydice*, where he is explaining an allegory, and his stanzas are stiffer and flow together less easily than Chaucer's usually do. One way to put this difference between the two poets would be to say that time, in Chaucer's poems, tends to move on unobtrusively but continually, where in Henryson there is characteristically a stanza for one instant of time, and then a break before the next stanza. Though of course it is even more dangerous to generalise about Chaucer than about Henryson, and obviously time does not move very fluidly in *The Knight's Tale* or in some of the more stylised stanzaic tales. With these same reservations, another way to put the difference between the two poets is to say that Henryson's verse often seems more impersonal. Beneath Chaucer's poetry one often senses a moving train of thought and constantly changing reactions to what is observed or said; but Henryson seems to change his style only dispassionately, adopting it to the shifts in his subject matter according to the demands of decorum. Chaucer's 'personality' is of course the result of self-conscious art, not involuntary self-revelation, while all of Henryson's poetry manifests his gentle and benevolent mind, but this does not alter the difference of style.

Henryson's style is apt to cause two difficulties for the modern reader. One is that it is easy to look for what is only incidental, the minor touches of realism and humour, and to neglect the large static set pieces which are at the foundation of the structure of his poems. In *Orpheus and Eurydice* and *The Testament of Cresseid* there are formal laments in special stanzaic forms (the hens' laments are parodies of this genre); much of *Orpheus* is devoted to a description of hell; about a third of *The Testament* is spent describing the gods and their conference; and the *Fables* consist largely of such set speeches as the ones we have seen, together with catalogues and formal descriptions of various kinds. It is impossible to generalise about these passages, except to say that they are all as vital to the meaning of their poems as, for instance, the laments are to the fable of the cock and the fox.

The other, and related, difficulty of Henryson's style is that the reader is apt to take his impersonality for cold and meaningless conventionality. This is particularly true of *The Testament of Cresseid*, where the style, so different from Chaucer's, has caused some readers to think that the work is 'by the very strenuousness of its morality in some degree both poetically and morally repulsive'.[1] But this is to misunderstand the whole meaning of this brilliant and complex poem, and to ignore that it is in many ways a companion to Book V of Chaucer's *Troilus*. Cresseid, like Troilus, comes to self-knowledge and knowledge of the world through suffering, and it is appropriate that Cresseid's suffering should be more physical than Troilus's. The main emotion of both poems is pathos, but Henryson produces this emotion not so much by suggesting his own feelings as by impersonal description and by opposing Cresseid to such bleak figures as Saturn, who says to her, with perfect and chilling finality, that he will change

> 'Thyne Insolence, thy play and wantones
> To greit diseis; thy Pomp and thy riches
> In mortall neid; and greit penuritie
> Thou suffer sall, and as ane beggar die.'
>   319-22

Another difference between *The Nun's Priest's Tale* and Henryson's fable, equally obvious and I think equally important, is that Henryson concludes his poem with a four-stanza 'Moralitas'.

[1] T. F. Henderson, *Scottish Vernacular Literature*, 3rd ed., Edinburgh 1910, p. 123.

Henryson's characteristic genre, indeed, is the narrative poem to which is appended a passage, sometimes long and never less than twenty lines, which comments in some way on the meaning of the narrative. About three-quarters of the bulk of his poetry, including the *Fables* and *Orpheus and Eurydice*, falls into this category. And much of his other work comes close to it: many of his short poems are explicitly allegorical, and even the light-hearted pastoral, *Robene and Makyne*, points a moral. *The Testament of Cresseid* might seem to be the great exception, but in fact it is more similar to the *Fables* and *Orpheus* than one might think. Although it has no separate 'Moralitas' explaining the action, the events of the poem are given so heavy a symbolic meaning that they become almost allegorical. In her faithlessness, Cresseid sinned against the natural order, *fine amour*, and God, and all these sins are represented in the poem by the compound symbol of her vocal blasphemy against Venus and Cupid. In the same way, the leprosy which results from her blasphemy is meaningful on three levels. The disease destroys her flesh, so punishing her for her misuse of it, but also teaching her of its essential and permanent corruptness. Because of her sin against love she is changed from a sought-after beauty to a loathsome beggar—but this change teaches her to praise Troilus and despise herself. The leprosy is also a divine punishment, for it, above all other diseases, was thought to be a blow from heaven, but because of its medieval association with Job, Christ and the two Lazaruses was also considered a disease of peculiar sanctity, an earthly purgatory which, as the poem hints, renders any future purgatory unnecessary.

No one now, surely, would follow Matthew Arnold in accusing Chaucer of a lack of high seriousness, but it is still true that Henryson is a more immediately and more constantly serious poet. His preoccupation with the need to justify the pleasures of poetry by revealing its 'gude moralitie' comes up explicitly time after time, and all the fables are built on Henryson's desire to show the sad irony that if animals behave like men only in poetry, men too often behave like animals in ordinary life. But Henryson does more than extract morals. As the frequent occurrence in his work of the term 'figure' would indicate, he uses the technique of figural interpretation, which is based on the idea that all objects and events are created by God to be meaningful, and which goes back to the theory that the events of the Old Testament were at once historical happenings and prefigurations of Christianity.[1] So the fox, in our fable, is an actual fox, but also 'may weill be figurate/ To flatteraris', while the cock, as a figure for pride, is connected with

> the Feyndis Infernall,
> Quhilk houndit doun wes fra that hevinlie hall
> To Hellis hole, and to that hiddeous hous,
> Because in pryde thay wer presumpteous.
> 596-9

And Henryson never abandons poetry for the sake of morality. He has been blamed for piously tacking inconsequential morals on to his poems, but in fact each 'Moralitas', whether satirical, moral, or allegorical, is an organic and necessary part of its poem. Henryson's moral seriousness, like the rhetorical and conventional aspects of his style, has been disliked and ignored by critics, where it should have been recognised as one of the reasons for the excellence of his poetry.

We know only a little more about Dunbar's life than about Henryson's. There is some evidence to suggest that he was born about 1456 and died about 1515, and it is fairly certain that he graduated as a Master of Arts from St Andrews. His name appears more than thirty times in the records between 1500 and 1513, usually as the recipient of a pension from James IV, and all of his poems which can be dated from internal evidence (about a third of the eighty or so which survive) fall within this period.[2]

---

[1] See Erich Auerbach, ' "Figura" ', tr. Ralph Manheim, in *Scenes from the Drama of European Literature*, New York 1959.

[2] The fullest edition is *The Poems of William Dunbar*, ed. John Small *et al.*, Scottish Text Society, 3 vols., Edinburgh 1884-93; a more available edition is the one edited by W. Mackay Mackenzie, London 1932 (reprinted with some minor additions, 1960); a convenient selection is edited by James Kinsley, Oxford 1958. My quotations are from Mackenzie's edition. J. W. Baxter, *William Dunbar, A Biographical Study*, Edinburgh 1952, is useful, though of necessity it is much more about Dunbar's times than about Dunbar. For the dates given here, see 'The Chronology of William Dunbar', *Philological Quarterly*, XXXIX (1960) 413-25.

Attempts have been made to construct his biography from his poetry, but this is a speculative enterprise.

One of the most surprising things about Dunbar is that he wrote so many different sorts of poetry: scatological abuse, the stiffest and most bejewelled panegyric, and everything in between. Scholars have tried to sort out his poetry by periods, with a frivolous youth and a pious old age, but there is no evidence to support this, and a good deal to contradict it. One might as well postulate an afternoon Dunbar, who wrote formal and ceremonial verse, an evening Dunbar, who wrote bawdry in the taverns, and a morning-after Dunbar, who wrote moral lyrics and petitions for money. The truth, of course, is simply that Dunbar wrote happily and skilfully in almost any genre. A great repertory of styles seems to be a characteristic of Middle Scots poets: among Henryson's short poems are an obscene burlesque and a hymn to Mary, not to mention the variety of styles in his longer poems, and Douglas also writes in a number of different ways. Dunbar's contemporary, Walter Kennedy, furnishes a concise example: of his six poems, one is a flyting, two are moral and didactic, one is pornographic, one is a hymn to Mary, and one a long narrative on the Passion. The stylistic virtuosity of the Middle Scots poets is a result of their attitude towards poetry: they regard it less as a means of self-expression than as a craft which has to be learned. And just as a good carpenter can build either a house or a chair, so a competent poet should be able to work in any genre. Dunbar, who seems the most representative of the Middle Scots poets, the one who carries their characteristic qualities to the furthest extreme, is only the most conspicuous of a number of virtuosos.

It is, I think, completely hopeless to speculate on Dunbar's personality by affirming that some of his poems are 'sincere', while others are merely exercises. But this is not to say that he lacks individuality, or that his poetry is not in some ways a fairly homogeneous body of work. Even from a purely technical viewpoint Dunbar's loftiest poems are not unlike his most vulgar ones. The resemblance is, indeed, clearest in the most extreme cases, as one can see by comparing passages from a hymn to Mary, *Ane Ballat of Our Lady*, and from the *Flyting*:

Empryce of prys, imperatrice,
Brycht polist precious stane;
Victrice of vyce, hie genetrice
Of Jhesu, lord soverayne . . .

61-4

Baird rehator, theif of natour, fals tratour, feyindis gett;
Filling of tauch, rak sauch, cry crauch, thow art our sett;
Muttoun dryver, girnall ryver, yadswyvar, fowll fell the . . .[1]

244-6

These passages would be less startling to Dunbar's contemporaries
than they are to us: the first is in a tradition which derives from
Latin hymns with internal rhyme,[2] while the *Flyting* is a member
of an equally orthodox genre, one which may also derive from
medieval Latin verse, and perhaps is remotely connected with the
intricately worked scaldic lampoons. But they are still passages
of a sufficiently extreme sort. It is true, of course, that they
represent extremes of lofty and of vulgar poetry, but it is equally
true, and I think more basic, that they are both at the same end of
the spectrum, and represent poetry at its most artificial. The
pounding internal rhyme of these passages is certainly intolerable
for very long (and Dunbar did not use it long or often), and we
need not take them any more seriously than I expect their author
did, but they are useful because they demonstrate, in an exaggerated form, the rhetorical and metrical prestidigitation which,
used less obtrusively, is important to all of Dunbar's work.

These two passages also raise the problem of Dunbar's vocabulary. *Ane Ballat of Our Lady* is one of the *loci classici* of 'aureation',
or what scholars think of as the vicious habit which became
common among Chaucer's followers of sprinkling their verse
with newfangled and obtrusive Latinate words. But there are
several objections to this sweeping condemnation. One is simply
that this poem is plainly a *tour de force*, and not a fair representative of Dunbar's usual 'aureate' style. A more basic objection
is that 'aureation' has, I think, been misunderstood by modern

[1] Perhaps 'Brawling bard, thief by nature, false traitor, fiend's offspring;/ Tallow-
stuffing (?), gallows bird, cry quits (?), you are overcome; / Sheep-stealer,
granary-robber, copulator with mares, bad luck to you . . .'
[2] A nearly contemporary English example is the hymn to Henry VI; 'Pax in
terra: non sit guerra / Orbis per confinia; / Virtus crescat, et fervescat / Caritas
per omnia' (*The Penguin Book of Latin Verse*, ed. F. Brittain, p. 292).

readers. The term, as used by Lydgate and later poets, does
not seem to have any necessary direct reference to Latinate
words, but means merely 'golden'. These poets wished to
make their verse golden and sweet (another favourite adjective),
in the new Continental and Chaucerian manner, and they also
wished to refine, purify, and gild their native tongue. One of the
devices they used for this purpose, perhaps one more obvious to
a modern reader than their other rhetorical techniques, was the
use of strikingly Latinate words. Some critics have objected to
this device, perhaps because they followed too literally Wordsworth's dictum that poets ought to use 'the language really spoken
by men', and so distrusted any formal poetic diction, whether
medieval or Augustan. But surely exotic Latinisms are permissible
and even normal in English verse: no one, for instance, would
now object to 'this my hand will rather/The multitudinous seas
incarnadine,/Making the green one red'.

Like Shakespeare, if perhaps unlike some of the English
fifteenth-century poets, Dunbar only uses Latinate words to serve
a specific purpose. They occur with some frequency in his loftier
poems, particularly where he is aiming at a precise and glittering
richness. *The Golden Targe* is the most sustained and most
successful example of this richness, but it appears occasionally in
other poems, as for example *The Merle and the Nychting:llia*
'Undir this brench ran doun a revir bricht,/Of balmy liquuor,
cristallyne of hew,/Agane the hevinly aisur skyis licht . . .' But
in the humorous satire, *Epitaph for Donald Owre*, Dunbar uses
Latinisms partly for their powerful weight when they are preceded
by short and light native words, and partly for their sibilant
alliteration:

> Thocht he remissioun
> Haif for prodissioun,
> Schame and susspissioun
> Ay with him dwellis.
> 3-6

And in the moral poem, *Learning Vain Without Good Life*
(sometimes called *Dunbar at Oxinfurde*), he uses Latinate words
to give a suggestive description of the various branches of
learning:

The curious probatioun logicall,
The eloquence of ornat rethorie,
The naturall science philosophicall,
The dirk apperance of astronomie ...

9-12

One might guess that Dunbar had a theory of poetic diction the opposite of Wordsworth's, and believed that one way to make poetry effective was to use language which contrasted conspicuously with ordinary unpoetic speech. His Latinisms seem more frequent than, statistically, they are, because he makes them so obtrusive. Again, his techniques can be seen most clearly by looking at extreme examples. This stanza is from *None May Assure in this Warld*:

Vbi ardentes anime,
Semper dicentes sunt Ve! Ve!
Sall cry Allace! that women thame bure,
O quante sunt iste tenebre!
In to this warld may none assure.

71-5

The burning souls are taken out of the ordinary speech and time of this world by being described in Latin, but then the third line, though equally biblical, makes them disturbingly immediate by having them cry the English 'Allace' instead of 'Ve', and by having them refer to their mothers. And both the grave immutability of the Latin and the pathos of the English fall onto the last line, which is effective because of its simplicity and because one is forced by the preceding lines to read it very slowly and heavily.

This playing off of English against Latin is used in many of Dunbar's greatest poems: *On the Resurrection of Christ*, for instance, with its refrain, 'Surrexit Dominus de sepulchro', or *Of the Nativitie of Christ*, with its 'Et nobis Puer natus est'. But it is also used in his macaronic parodies, such as *The Testament of Mr Andro Kennedy*, which seem to me in their own way no less great:

I, Maister Andro Kennedy,
Curro quando sum vocatus,
Gottin with sum incuby,
Or with sum freir infatuatus;
In faith I can nought tell redly,

7

Unde aut ubi fui natus,
Bot in treuth I trow trewly,
Quod sum dyabolus incarnatus.
                    1–8

The opening solemnity of 'I, Maister Andro Kennedy' is carried
on by the heavy and rhythmical syllables of the second line, but
at the same time is rendered ridiculous by the meaning of the Latin.
And the idiotic and redundant pomposity of 'Bot in treuth I trow
trewly' clashes marvellously with the preposterously different
pomposity of 'sum dyabolus incarnatus'.

If we turn back to the passage from the *Flyting* quoted above,
we find there a diction equally exotic, though of course very
different. Dunbar's terms of abuse were presumably more
familiar to his contemporaries than they are to us, though the
variations and mistakes in the manuscripts indicate that these terms
troubled his scribes, as well as the modern lexicographers. But in
any case it is obvious that in poetry these violent and often
obscene slang words are as alien and conspicuous as any Latinisms.
One might adduce as a parallel Ezra Pound, who jolts his reader
as much by his harsh colloquialisms as by his fragments of
Chinese. But if Dunbar and Pound are both motivated by a
desire to use the full resources of English (as well as of any other
language that happens to be handy), there is the difference that
Dunbar follows a traditional decorum, and, except when he
writes parodies, reserves his different styles and dictions for
different genres.

Northrop Frye has aptly said that Dunbar is a 'musical' poet,
meaning not that his poems are smooth and mellifluous, but that
in their reliance on 'the rhythm, movement, and sound of words'
they show similarities to music.[1] Both his ornate and his humorous poems are obviously musical, in their different ways, but
the term fits equally well the group of poems, mostly moral and
satirical lyrics, together with some petitionary and occasional
verse, which are written in what might be called Dunbar's
'middle style'. The poem *Inconstancy of Luve* provides a minor
but neat example:

[1] *Anatomy of Criticism*, Princeton 1957, pp. 257, 366.

> In luve to keip allegance,
> It war als nys an ordinance,
> As quha wald bid ane deid man dance
> In sepulture.
>
> 21-4

The effect of the passage comes mainly from the way in which the rising rhythm of the first three lines is balanced against the thud of the unexpectedly short last line.

A stanza from the *Lament for the Makers* gives a more subtle example of Dunbar's musical qualities, and also demonstrates some of his rhetorical techniques:

> He takis the campion in the stour,
> The capitane closit in the tour,
> The lady in bour full of bewte;
> Timor mortis conturbat me.
>
> 29-32

Death's three victims are bound closely together by parallel construction, rhyme (*stour—tour—bour*), and alliteration (though the masculine and warlike series, *campion—capitane—closit*, is opposed by the feminine and domestic *bour—bewte*). But there is also a logical progression. The champion is strong to fight against death, yet might well expect to meet death in the thick of battle. The captain of a castle should be more secure, 'closit in the tour', but still, castles are closed because they are attacked. The lady, at least, should be safe, for surely a boudoir is one place that death would not be unmannerly enough to enter, and yet she, if the farthest removed from the scenes of violent death, is also the most fragile. This line has two rhyme words, *bour* and *bewte*, so that it simultaneously closes the list of victims and connects them with the fourth line.

This stanza consists of a series of simple statements, and its success comes from the precise and economical way in which the statements are first created, and then played off against each other. All of Dunbar's moral lyrics might be described as being a 'poetry of statement', in the phrase which has been applied to Dryden, another 'musical' poet. These poems contain only traditional and even hackneyed ideas, without a trace of any complicated intellectual development. Instead, Dunbar devotes all of his immense rhetorical and metrical skill to giving these ideas a perfect and immutable form. But Dunbar's use of language in the moral poems does not seem very different from his use of language in the ornate or humorous poems, although to be sure the diction itself varies immensely. Dunbar's high style, for all its richness, is not vague or highly connotative, but works to produce a glittering and precise surface. And his low style, for all of its apparent uncouth vigour, is successful because each word is locked into place by rhetorical and metrical restraints. One might describe Dunbar's poetry by saying the same thing in three different ways: it is a poetry of statement—Dunbar never describes, or evokes, or suggests, but simply states; it is a poetry of surfaces—precise, static, and two-dimensional; and it is a musical poetry—its meaning is not philosophical, or even discursive, but is like the meaning of a piece of music.

It is a desperate endeavour to trace Dunbar's relationship to Chaucer, or for that matter to any of his predecessors, since he appears on the one hand to have written in every possible poetic tradition, and on the other hand to have borrowed only very slightly from any specific poet. But one can make a few generalisations. First, it seems clear that Dunbar and Chaucer are about as unlike as any two poets can be. Chaucer's poems are typically narrative, philosophical, richly suggestive, and lengthy; Dunbar's poems are just the opposite. Secondly, it seems clear that Dunbar is immensely indebted to Chaucer. His debts are of two kinds, neither of which is very susceptible to measurement. On the technical level, Dunbar's sophisticated metrics, rhetorical devices and diction surely descend, in part, from Chaucer. The question here is not so much of Chaucer inventing new techniques as of his naturalising some of the graces of Continental verse and of his emphasising, and so strengthening, certain features of the native tradition. One could be precise, and point to certain words and stanzaic forms which Dunbar borrowed from Chaucer, or very often from Lydgate, but the more important part of the debt is more intangible: Dunbar's prevailingly syllabic metrics, for instance, and his willingness to accept into his poetry rhetorical figures and learned words.

Dunbar's second debt to Chaucer is no more than a matter of

genres. The situation here is very similar: Chaucer did not so much invent new genres as naturalise Continental ones, or embellish and refine pre-existent native genres. A large number of Dunbar's poems are written in Chaucerian genres: allegorical poems about spring and love, dream-visions, moral lyrics, and witty begging poems. But Dunbar's poetry stands in a special and almost a parasitic relationship to the traditional genres. Most typically he writes parodies or near-parodies, as, for example, his frequent humorous adaptations of the dream-vision form, or *The Tua Mariit Wemen and the Wedo*, which is among other things a parody of a *chanson d'aventure*, of a *chanson de mal mariée*, and of a *demande d'amour*. Even Dunbar's serious poems tend to be highly 'literary': Dunbar expects his readers to be acquainted with the traditional genres and themes, and to appreciate his novel rehandling of them. *The Golden Targe*, for instance, and the poems similar to it, contain very traditional matter reworked into flamboyant and brilliant exercises where the style and the poetical techniques are all-important, and the meanings traditionally connected with the matter are scarcely bothered with. One feels, finally, that Dunbar's expressions of obligations to Chaucer are almost symbolic: he praises that mythical figure, 'Chaucer-the-father-of-English-poetry', because he is so aware of his reliance on the traditional genres and styles of English verse.

Gavin Douglas, the third of our poets, seems in some ways to be set apart from Henryson and Dunbar, though this may be partly an illusion arising from the fact that we know a good deal about Douglas's life where we know practically nothing about Henryson's or Dunbar's. Douglas was born about 1475, a son of the powerful Archibald 'Bell-the-Cat', fifth Earl of Angus. After graduating from St Andrews, he took orders, perhaps more because he was a younger son than because of any particular vocation. He rose rapidly, becoming Provost of St Giles' in Edinburgh about 1501, and after Flodden (1513), when his nephew married the widowed queen of James IV, the world seemed his oyster. He became Bishop of Dunkeld, briefly (and perhaps only by his own styling) Chancellor of Scotland, and he had expectations of becoming Archbishop of St Andrews and guardian of the young James V. But his hopes all came to nought, and he died in London, unsuccessfully intriguing, in 1522. So apart from his poetry he survives only as a minor footnote to Scottish history— though it is true that his faction came back into power less than two years after his death, and that if he had lived a little longer he might well have obtained more of his eagerly pursued 'pompe of eirdlie dignitie'.[1]

Both of Douglas's major poems, *The Palace of Honour* and his translation of the *Aeneid*, seem to have some affinities with later English poetry.[2] In *The Palace of Honour* we see a world that is immensely rich but confusing and baffling, a world in which the traditional ways of acting and perceiving no longer appear effective. Dunbar's poems, on the other hand, tend to be either amoral or to follow a simple and traditional morality, while Henryson is an extremely subtle but also very traditional moralist. Douglas's *Aeneid* is in many ways a Renaissance translation: he is interested in Virgil's *Aeneid* as a literary whole, and in Aeneas as 'the mast soueran man', a pattern of conduct.[3] He follows the Latin text conscientiously, although he does not aim at a literal translation: 'Sum tyme the text mon haue ane expositioun,/Sum tyme the collour will caus a litill additioun,/And sum tyme of a word I mon mak thre . . .' (Prologue to Book I, 347-9). Here

[1] Many of the materials relevant to Douglas's life are collected in the introduction to *The Poetical Works of Gavin Douglas*, ed. John Small, 4 vols., Edinburgh 1874. This very unsatisfactory edition is now being superseded by some volumes of the Scottish Text Society. The four volumes containing Douglas's translation of the *Aeneid* have been edited by David F. C. Coldwell, Edinburgh 1957-64, but *The Minor Works*, a volume to be edited by Mrs Bawcutt (Priscilla Preston) has not yet appeared, so my quotations from *The Palace of Honour* are taken from Small's edition. A useful volume of selections has been edited by Coldwell, Oxford 1964.

[2] The only other surviving poem which can safely be attributed to Douglas is the short and trivial *Conscience*, which I leave out of consideration here. The allegorical poem, *King Hart*, has usually been thought to be by Douglas, but it now seems very unlikely that it is really his. See two articles which appeared independently; Priscilla Preston, 'Did Gavin Douglas Write *King Hart*?', *Medium Ævum*, XXVIII (1959) 31-47, and Florence Ridley, 'Did Gawin Douglas Write *King Hart*?', *Speculum*, XXXIV (1959) 402-12.

[3] The Renaissance qualities of the translation have been discussed by Bruce Dearing, 'Gavin Douglas' *Eneados*: A Reinterpretation', *PMLA*, LXVII (1952) 845-62, and by Louis Brewer Hall, 'An Aspect of the Renaissance in Gavin Douglas' *Eneados*', *Studies in the Renaissance*, VII (1960) 184-92.

again, Douglas is very different from Henryson, who allegorises the myth of Orpheus and Eurydice, from Dunbar, with his lighthearted and traditional references to the 'ornate stilis so perfyte' of 'Omer', and, as Douglas self-righteously points out at length, from Chaucer's rather lop-sided treatment of the *Aeneid* in *The House of Fame*.

Douglas's aristocratic, self-seeking and mercurial life is appropriate to his poetry, for with him we seem to have a new image, the poet as gifted amateur, rather than the old image of the poet as a professional and semi-anonymous bard. It is not that his poetry is technically casual or incompetent, but that he gives the impression of writing only at his own pleasure, and only on subjects which interest him. It is curiously fitting, in view of his transitional position in Scottish literature, that his poetry should be exactly contemporary with Dunbar's (*The Palace of Honour* was written about 1501, and his *Aeneid* was finished in 1513), but that most of his public life should take place in the radically changed new world of James V.

The most important thing to say about Douglas's *Aeneid* is what Ezra Pound and C. S. Lewis have already said loudly, just that it is an exceedingly good poem. It seems likely, especially now that a competent edition has appeared, that the poem will in the future be valued for what it is: one of the first and best of the English translations of the Renaissance; a translation of the *Aeneid* which is at least as good as Dryden's; and therefore necessarily an important English work in its own right. C. S. Lewis has helped to clear away two misapprehensions about the poem which a modern reader is likely to fall into. One is that Douglas's language may seem to us quaint and rustic, because 'We forget that in his day it was a courtly and literary language'. The other is that the characters in the translation may seem to us too brisk, colloquial and modern because we have been falsely trained to see them as venerable, antique and stiff. Lewis's point here is surely sound, though perhaps Douglas went a little too much to the opposite extreme from us. One suspects that Aeneas seemed more of a contemporary to Douglas than he did to Virgil.

But there is still a third misapprehension which may block our understanding of the poem. It is easy to think of Douglas as an untaught genius who forcibly, brilliantly and instinctively threw the *Aeneid* into English. But nothing could be farther from the truth, since Douglas's *Aeneid* is an exceptionally self-conscious and rhetorical translation. He warns us of this clearly enough in his prologue to the first book, a critical and polemical general introduction running to more than five hundred lines. The first few lines show both Douglas's opinion of Virgil, as a master of rhetoric, and Douglas's ambition to raise his own language to an equal pitch of eloquence.

> Lawd, honour, praysyngis, thankis infynyte
> To the and thy dulce ornat fresch endyte,
> Maist reuerend Virgill, of Latyn poetis prynce,
> Gem of engyne and flude of eloquens,
> Thow peirles perle, patroun of poetry,
> Roys, regester, palm, lawrer and glory,
> Chosyn charbukkill, cheif flour and cedyr tre . . .

Modern readers have been misled, perhaps, by the contrast which Douglas goes on to draw between his 'blunt endyte' and the 'scharp sugurate sang Virgiliane', between his 'ignorant blabryng imperfyte' and Virgil's 'polyst termys redymyte' ('wreathed' or 'adorned'). But this conventional mock-modesty is of course itself a rhetorical flourish. In the rest of the prologue Douglas demonstrates rather ostentatiously the range and skilfulness of his styles, and at the same time takes up some technical matters. He states that he will use some Latin, French and southern English words, which means that he will use an artificial poetic diction; he discusses, with examples, the difficulty of translating some Latin words; and he derides the blunders of earlier translators. Douglas provides a most revealing image when he remarks,

> Quha is attachit ontill a staik, we se,
> May go na ferthir bot wreil about that tre:
> Rycht so am I to Virgillis text ybund . . .
>
> 297-9

His translation, then, is a green plant winding around a stake, ornamenting and covering it, but attached to it at all points—or almost all, for Douglas says he may 'mak digressioun sum tyme'. The simile also works in a way which Douglas may not have intended, for a plant's stake is designed, of course, to support and guide the plant. Douglas laments that he could have made a poem 'twys als curyus' if he had not been constrained to follow Virgil's text, but if he had attempted to write a poem of this magnitude without a support and guide, the results would surely have been more curious than organised.

Douglas's famous prologues, original poems which are prefixed to each book of the *Aeneid*, offer another guidepost to the nature of the translation. These prologues are in a great variety of metrical forms, and on a great variety of subjects: some provide literary criticism; some are satirical, moral, philosophical, or religious; and some are descriptions of nature at different seasons. Critics have usually concentrated on these last ones, and complimented Douglas on his feeling for nature and his close observation of the Scottish landscape. But this is to put the emphasis on the wrong place, for the prologues are above all a series of set pieces intended to demonstrate Douglas's competence at writing in various styles on various subjects. To be sure, the seasonal prologues are very good, but Douglas wrote them more because the seasons were a standard topic for Scottish poets than because he had any eighteenth-century feeling for nature. The prologues might be compared with the *Shepherd's Calendar*: in both cases there is the same purposive and partly experimental variety of forms, the same self-conscious use, and abuse, of traditional genres, and the same obtrusive concern with poetical techniques.

Douglas's *Aeneid* is so huge and so variegated that it is impossible to treat it in any detail here, but perhaps a single quotation will indicate some of the qualities, as well as some of the problems, of the translation.

> The rage of Silla, that huge swelth in the see,
> 3e haue eschapit, and passit eik haue 3he
> The euer rowtand Charibdis rolkis fell;
> The craggis quhar monstruus Ciclopes dwell
> 3he ar expert. Pluk vp 3our hartis, I 3ou pray,
> This dolorus dreid expell and do away.
>
> I iv 73-8
>
> vos et Scyllaeam rabiem penitusque sonantis
> accestis scopulos, vos et Cyclopia saxa
> experti; revocate animos maestumque timorem
> mittite . . .
>
> I 200-3

One notices first Douglas's characteristic habit of expanding and elucidating his original. *Mittite* is doubled into the downright 'expell and do away'; *accestis* into the explicit 'eschapit, and passit eik'. These expansions seem reasonable enough, but a purist would object that Douglas has unwarrantably introduced Charybdis into the passage, and moreover has mistakenly made Scylla, instead of Charybdis, into a whirlpool (*swelth*). This confusion is unimportant,[1] but the passage shows how he generally takes a freer approach to the Latin than a modern translator would. If one reads Douglas's translation while holding an annotated edition of Virgil, one will find that Douglas incorporates directly into his text many of the modern annotations. Usually, though not always, these additions are correct and helpful. But a modern translator would no more dare to do this than he would dare to insert his own original compositions between each book. Douglas often throws new and valuable light on the meaning of a particular passage, just as his translation as a whole brings out powerfully and unexpectedly some overlooked aspects of Virgil, but he is not a reliable guide to Virgil's actual words. To an unusually large degree, the excellence of Douglas's translation is derived more from the translator than from the original.

This passage also shows some of the reasons for Douglas's excellence. One of them, rather ironically, is precisely the quality which makes him difficult for a modern reader: his vocabulary. In some cases he was simply fortunate in his inheritance: *rowtand*, for instance, is an admirable word for *sonantis*, being more exact than *roaring* and less bookish than *resounding*, while *dolorus dreid* is a very happy equivalent for *maestum timorem*. Douglas is particularly skilful in taking advantage of the flexibility of literary Scots: he moves freely from the most colloquial to the most ornate diction and makes a forceful but never pedantic use of Latinisms and neologisms. The first four lines of this passage, for instance, lead up to the emphatic Latinism, *expert* (which ordinarily meant 'experienced' in Middle Scots, but is here used in a Latinate construction), and then this climax is followed by the

---

[1] The same confusion occurs again in II.I prol 44: Douglas may have been misled by the Latin in III 425 and 557-9.

semi-colloquial *Pluk vp*. Similarly, in the last line the Latinate *expell* is complemented by *do away*.

Douglas's felicitous handling of rhetoric and rhythm is also demonstrated in this passage. There are, for instance, two separate patterns in the first three lines. On the one hand, the first and third lines, describing the dangers, are balanced against the second line, describing the safety. On the other hand, these three lines are divided syntactically into two clauses, each a line and a half long, and arranged in a careful chiasmus: object, subject, auxiliary verb, past participle—past participle, auxiliary verb, subject, object. The next phrase, *The craggis . . . ar expert*, is parallel with the first line and a half, so that the reader expects Douglas to repeat the whole three-line pattern again. But instead there is an abrupt and rhythmically jarring full stop, emphasising the *expert*, and a shift into a broken and colloquial rhythm, imitating the tone of Aeneas's earnest plea. Throughout the passage there runs an alliteration so constant as to be almost structural, but used purposefully to link words together: *Silla— swelth—see, craggis—Ciclopes, dolorus dreid—do away*.

Douglas's *Palace of Honour*, though a less important poem than his *Aeneid*, is especially interesting here because it so clearly stands in the Chaucerian tradition. In genre, it is like *The House of Fame*: a dream-vision about a journey to a lofty and allegorical building. Douglas seems to have borrowed many of the details of his plot from Chaucer, though of course one cannot always be certain that he did not go directly to Chaucer's sources, or on the other hand borrow from *The Temple of Glass* or other fifteenth-century imitations of Chaucer, some of which are perhaps no longer extant. But there are enough verbal reminiscences of Chaucer in *The Palace of Honour*, and enough direct references to Chaucerian characters, to make us safe in assuming that Douglas, most of the time, was borrowing immediately from Chaucer.

By looking at the plot of *The Palace of Honour* one can see not only how much Douglas was indebted to Chaucer, but also how well he understood him—Douglas's poem is a very useful commentary on *The House of Fame*.[1] *The Palace of Honour* has the

[1] Many of the parallels between *The Palace of Honour* and Chaucer are listed in P. Lange, 'Chaucer's Einfluss auf die Originaldichtungen des Schotten Douglas',

same traditional beginning as *The Legend of Good Women*: the narrator goes out on a May morning, sees the spring flowers, hears spring songs, and then has a visionary dream. But Douglas's narrator, like the narrator in *The House of Fame*, dreams that he is in a 'desert terribill'. In both poems, this desert stands for the desolate and barren spiritual condition of the narrator, caught in the wastes of the temporal world, and is equivalent to Dante's *selva oscura* or Eliot's wasteland, though the actual detailed description of Douglas's desert makes it seem oddly like the land- scape in Browning's *Childe Roland*. Douglas's narrator sees Minerva, the 'Quene of Sapience', go by with her train, on the way to the 'Palace of Honour', and then Diana, but he himself remains and does not follow either the way of wisdom or the way of asceticism. Then, after a learned digression on sound waves, in imitation of the lecture which Chaucer's eagle gives, Venus appears, with Mars, Cupid and the rest of the court of love. This court is composed mostly of the heroines of *The Legend of Good Women* and of the figures from the temple of Venus in *The House of Fame*, together with a few characters who are even more Chaucerian: Arcite, Palamon and Emily, Troilus and Criseyde, and Griselda. The narrator finally feels constrained to sing a song, set off from the narrative by being in a different stanzaic form, in which he laments his own woes and denounces Venus. As a result, he is seized by the court, tried and condemned. There is an obvious parallel here with *The Legend of Good Women*, where Chaucer's narrator is condemned by the god of love for having made songs against love, and the parallel is carried on by the sequel. In Douglas's poem the 'court rethoricall' of muses and famous poets appears, and Calliope intercedes for mercy, using the same arguments that Chaucer's Alceste uses: the sin is small, the victim is unworthy of a god, and he won't do it again. So Douglas's narrator, like Chaucer's, goes free after having promised to make poetic amends.

Douglas makes it clear that he is using this material because it is meaningful, not simply because it is traditional. He emphasises, for instance, the difference between sexual love, with its power to

Anglia, VI (1883) 46-95. Some additional verbal parallels are given in the article by Miss Ridley cited above.

brutalise or destroy (the dreamer is afraid that Venus will transform him into an animal or kill him) and the intercessory charity
of Calliope. The complicated relationships between love and
poetry are neatly implied, too: they are at odds, not only because
poetry is often anti-feminist, but also because perfection of the
work conflicts with perfection of the life; yet they are recon-
cilable, partly because poetry celebrates and immortalises love,
and partly because poetry is a parallel but independent road to
the Palace of Honour. So after the narrator is saved by Calliope
and her band of muses and poets, who sweep on stage almost like
a rescuing army, Calliope entrusts him to the charge of a nymph
and they go off together on their way to the palace.

This guiding nymph fulfils the same functions as Chaucer's
eagle and, though less loquacious, shows her similarity to him by
encouraging the fearful narrator and telling him where to look.
Their journey is a terrestrial one, yet no less extraordinary and
extensive than Chaucer's aerial one: 'Now into Egypt, now into
Italie,/Now in the realme of Trace, and now in Spane.' But at one
place there seems to be a humorous glance at Chaucer's air
transport, for the nymph seizes the narrator by the hair and
carries him over a hell-like ditch and up to the palace at the top
of a hill.

The third and last part of *The Palace of Honour*, as of *The House
of Fame*, is concerned with the narrator's adventures at his destin-
ation. Douglas's building is obviously modelled on Chaucer's:
both are very beautiful, are made out of beryl, have intricately
carved golden gates, and have immensely rich interiors which are
full of precious stones. But they are also very different, as the
titles of the poems suggest: 'Palace' is grander than 'House', and
'Honour' less equivocal than 'Fame'. The difference is neatly
symbolised by the hills the buildings are on: both hills appear to
be made of glass, but where Chaucer's turns out to be of ice,
Douglas's is of hard marble, and so equally hard to climb but
infinitely more durable. Chaucer emphasises the arbitrariness of
earthly fame and, with his revolving wicker house, gives an
image of mutability. Douglas's honour is supernatural, just and
eternal (it is always the same season at the palace), and so is
contrasted with earthly mutability: from the top of the hill one

can look down and see the earth, which appears in the guise of a stormy sea filled with drowning mariners.

But there is a curious similarity between the climactic revelations of the two poems. In *The House of Fame*, of course, Chaucer breaks off just as the 'man of gret auctorite' is apparently about to make an important statement. Although *The Palace of Honour* is a finished poem, the climax is almost as equivocal and tantalising: the narrator peers through a hole, sees 'ane God omnipotent', swoons, and is laughed at by his nymph for being such a coward. It would seem as though each poet was forced by the very nature of his poem to produce such an ambiguous climax, or perhaps more exactly such a lack of climax. Dante could end his serious and Christian poem with a Paradiso, but Chaucer and Douglas can only make an ironic gesture towards an ultimate revelation in their half-humorous and ostensibly unchristian poems. Dante, the pilgrim, is educated by his travels so that he can understand the truths of the Paradiso, but neither Chaucer's nor Douglas's narrators are very educable, and perhaps neither the eagle nor the nymph are the best possible pedagogues.

It would be possible to show other Chaucerian borrowings in *The Palace of Honour*—it seems likely, for instance, that there is a bond of relationship between the Chaucerian *persona* and Douglas's narrator, who is shown as being dazed, curious, timid, and, as he himself admits, knowing no more than a sheep. But for all of Chaucer's influence, it must be admitted that the poem seems to a modern reader profoundly un-Chaucerian. In *The House of Fame*, for all its preposterous plot, there is a smooth and plausible narrative line, and the narrator always seems to be present in his flesh and blood. But *The Palace of Honour* is a glittering and artificial poem: Douglas seems to make no effort to preserve any reasonable narrative coherence, or to impart any feeling of verisimilitude.

Douglas's metrical forms are partly responsible for the special quality of his poem, and they also give us an indication of his purposes. The first two books are in the nine-line stanza, rhymed *aabaabbab*, which Chaucer used in *Anelida and Arcite*, and which Dunbar was to use in *The Golden Targe*, a poem very similar to some parts, particularly the prologue, of *The Palace of Honour*.

The third book is in the different nine-line stanza, rhymed *aabaabbcc*, which Chaucer used in *The Complaint of Mars*. In several places Douglas uses a ten-line stanza to mark off rhetorically ornate songs, and at the end of the poem, perhaps taking a hint from the internal rhyme in *Anelida and Arcite*, he has three stanzas, the first with double internal rhyme, the second with triple and the third with quadruple, while he preserves in all of them the normal end-rhyme of the *Anelida* stanza. Douglas's use of the forms of these two poems reminds us of an aspect of Chaucer which was very important in the fifteenth century but which has often been overlooked: Chaucer as a metrical innovator and as a technical virtuoso. And these intricate stanzaic forms show us that Douglas is not trying to conduct a realistic narrative, but to achieve a highly wrought poetic brilliance. The elaborate burst of rhyme with which Douglas concludes *The Palace of Honour* is only an extreme example of the artificial splendour which he has been striving for throughout the whole work.

It is surely no accident that Douglas's narrator is rescued and given a guide by Calliope, the muse of epic poetry and so, as Douglas says, of the 'kinglie stile'. Douglas's narrator rises above the world by the aid of a muse, not by the aid of a philosophical and humanly loquacious eagle: Douglas himself raises his poem off the ground by sheer rhetoric, not by structural design or by sympathetically human characters. Douglas's preoccupation with rhetoric and style is of course very evident throughout the poem. The prologue is a dazzling set piece in the aureate mode, and Douglas begins the first book with a dramatically rhetorical stanza—in which he pretends to disclaim any rhetorical ability. The poem is filled with rhetorical figures and with explicit comments on the styles of Douglas himself, of his characters and of other poets, while at the end there is a three-stanza epilogue that is largely Douglas's mock-apology for his 'barrant termis' and 'vile indite'.[1]

But there is also a connection between the poem's emphasis on rhetoric and its very structure. Visionary poems about allegorical journeys tend to be richly variegated and comprehensive, as if

[1] There are some useful comments on Douglas's rhetoric in the articles by Miss Preston and Miss Ridley cited above.

their authors wished to set up allegorical worlds that were as complex and multitudinous as our ordinary world. Dante and the author of *Piers Plowman* achieve this comprehensiveness by the sheer magnitude and seriousness of their poems; Chaucer, in *The House of Fame*, uses a variety of devices—the re-telling of the *Aeneid*, which brings a metamorphosed classical world into the poem, the exhaustive logical rigour with which the various applicants to Fame are classified, and the stupidity of the narrator, which allows Chaucer to hint at worlds seen but not understood. *The Parliament of Fowls* offers a tidier example, with its three figures of Scipio, Venus and Nature balanced against each other so as to form the corners of an all-embracing triangle. But Douglas has a simpler way to make his poem inclusive. He merely brings every possible sort of subject matter into his poem, fits it all neatly into the tissue of his rhetoric, and passes on. One of the most characteristic parts of the poem is the section where the narrator looks into Venus's magic mirror and sees 'The deidis and fatis of euerie eirdlie wicht': Satan's fall, Noah's flood, over thirty Old Testament figures, about fifty figures from classical history and mythology, medieval falconers and necromancers, and the heroes of contemporary popular poetry.

The basic structural device of *The Palace of Honour*, then, is the list: the different parts of the poem are joined together by simple juxtaposition and these parts are themselves largely made up of catalogues. Chaucer himself is a great master of lists—one thinks of the description of the House of Fame, or of the more brilliant description of the temples in *The Knight's Tale*—but the difference between the two poets is shown by their methods of describing a journey. Chaucer conveys the length and the marvellousness of the flight in *The House of Fame* by letting us see it through the surprised eyes of the narrator; Douglas achieves something of the same effect by simply giving a long, preposterous, but skilful list of the geographical places through which his narrator passes.

One may, if one wishes, repeat the old truism to the effect that medieval critical theories perniciously emphasised rhetoric and ornamentation at the expense of structure and unity. But it is perhaps more helpful to note that Douglas's techniques are justified by their results. The suddenness of his scene shifting, for instance, the quick juxtaposition of apparently disparate passages, works to produce the strange mixture of clarity and lack of causality that is so typical of dreams, and also is used to reinforce Douglas's themes. In particular, the pervasive theme of the contrast between earthly mutability and transcendental perfection is repeatedly brought out by the juxtaposition of contrasting scenes. And even Douglas's catalogues are something more than a medieval vice: it is interesting to observe that Auden, another poet who is fond of allegory and ostentatious rhetoric, uses catalogues frequently. Like Dunbar, who is also addicted to lists, Douglas uses them to group similar or contrasting elements, to balance entities against each other and to freeze them into a comprehensive and rigid rhetorical form. Dunbar's catalogues perhaps reveal a finer ear and a greater meticulousness, but Douglas's are far from slovenly. The following passage, for instance, shows not only Douglas's skilful variation of pace and rhythm, but also his ability to lead a catalogue up to a climax:

> The miserie, the crueltie, the dreid,
> Pane, sorrow, wo, baith wretchitnes and neid,
> The greit inuy, couetous dowbilnes,
> Tuitchand warldlie vnfaithfull brukilnes.
>
> I p. 64

The Palace of Honour is doubtless not one of the world's great poems, but it is, I think, a very deft and interesting piece which has been undervalued because misunderstood: readers have hunted in it for a philosophical richness or a Chaucerian humanity which is not there, and have dismissed as faults and digressions the obtrusive rhetoric and the perpetually shifting subject matter which are actually the poem's essential qualities.

Even if Douglas is not the most typical of Middle Scots poets, he serves well enough as a text on which to conclude. Like the other Scots poets, he can be seen in several contexts. One is the familiar 'History of English Literature'. Here Douglas, Henryson and Dunbar appear as poets inheriting the Chaucerian wealth, partly through fifteenth-century intermediaries, but using it for profoundly un-Chaucerian purposes: there is a vast gulf between *The House of Fame* and *The Palace of Honour*. These poets seem themselves to leave no direct heirs, except for some relatively

minor sixteenth-century Scots, but Douglas, at least, foreshadows
the Elizabethan poets. Just as his *Aeneid* is the precursor of the
Elizabethan translations (and was plagiarised by Surrey), so the
prologues to it seem to point towards the experiments in different
metres and dictions of the sixteenth-century English poets, and so
his *Palace of Honour* makes a bit more evident the connection
between Chaucer and the *Faerie Queene*.

Another context is the general European background, the
tradition that Dante suggested in his famous phrase for Arnaut
Daniel: 'fu miglior fabbro del parlar materno' (*Purgatorio* XXVI,
117). Douglas, Henryson and Dunbar have an honourable place
among the countless medieval and Renaissance poets who tried
to refine their various maternal tongues by concentrating
arduously on perfection of form and rhetoric, and who successfully attempted to produce a literature that could rival their
classical inheritance.

But Dante's phrase, with its use of the word *fabbro*, 'smith,
craftsman, maker', for *poet*, leads us back again to Douglas,
Henryson, Dunbar and the short-lived apogee of Scottish
literature which they represent. The word *poet* itself, of course,
like many of its synonyms in different languages, has an
etymological meaning of something like *maker*, but it is surely
not coincidental that in modern English the term *maker*, in the
sense of *poet*, is reserved almost exclusively for the Middle Scots
poets. Their poetry is a poetry of craftsmanship, and they are
united by their devotion to their craft, even though each poet
manifests it differently: Henryson with his pervading decorum
and his art that conceals art; Dunbar with his succinct brilliance;
Douglas with his gaudy rhetorical flowers. These poets, in their
different ways, all seem to have channelled their passion towards
the idea that a poem ought to be as finely wrought as possible.
This implies their limitations: these poets are not profoundly
interested in philosophy, in nature, or in self-revelation. But their
poems are well made, which is perhaps all the praise that any poet
can demand.

The English Chaucerians

DEREK PEARSALL

THE shadow of Chaucer falls long on the fifteenth century. Critics praise the age for its popular lyric, its drama, its prose, but whatever they praise it for—and it is not much— it is not for its secular non-popular poetry; yet it is this, in effect, that we mean when we talk of the work of the English Chaucerians. Criticism long ago settled into its traditional posture of regarding the continuation of the Chaucerian tradition in England as a long decline and fall. Chaucer was dead: the Renaissance was to come: what else could the fifteenth century be but an age of intellectual blight? Certainly, nothing in the century bears long comparison with Chaucer, nor does the age boast any one great poet such as the sixteenth century finally managed to produce. Reasons for this, if reasons mean much in such matters, can be found: the disruption caused by the Wars of the Roses; the disastrous failure of the wars in France; the grim religious orthodoxy and cramped education which followed the Lollard purge; the emergence of a class of patrons among the aspirant upper *bourgeoisie* for whom literature was a status symbol, and who preferred a big book to a good one. Yet, whatever judgment is made on the century as a whole, we should not let our admiration for Chaucer, and the comparisons we are inevitably drawn to make, blind us to the real qualities of the English Chaucerians: the patient, thorough exploitation of areas of literary experience that he had opened up for them, the blending of Chaucerian with more traditionally English genres and techniques, the consolidation of Chaucer's poetic language, the appropriation to the tradition of new modes of thought as the ferment of the age threw them up, and the final creation of a kind of literature— sober, serious, unironic, preoccupied with moral, social and political issues—which we come to recognise as genuinely of its age. One might say it was the English Chaucerians who made Chaucer English.

The attitude of the English Chaucerians to Chaucer, however, was not the same as our attitude. Modern criticism praises Chaucer for his humour, realism and irony, for his sense of character, for his breadth and subtlety of observation, for his complex narrative attitude and perpetually interesting poetic *persona*; the fifteenth century praised him almost exclusively for his sententiousness and his skill in style, his rhetoric. For Lydgate he is 'þe noble Rethor þat alle dide excelle', and elsewhere

> Noble Galfride, poete of Breteyne,
> Amonge oure englisch þat made first to reyne
> Þe gold dewe-dropis of rethorik so fyne,
> Oure rude langage only tenlwmyne.

For Hoccleve he is 'flour of eloquence, Mirour of fructuous entendement', whose death

> Despoiled hath þis land of þe swetnesse
> Of rethorik; for unto Tullius
> Was never man so lyk amonges us.[1]

Every poet who mentions him, and most of them do, speaks of him in similar terms, which by the middle of the century have hardened into a formula. Their imitation of his work reflects the same attitude: the poems to which they turn again and again for words, phrases, stylistic devices, thematic details, are *The Parliament*, the *Troilus*, *The Legend of Good Women* and *The Knight's Tale*. *The Canterbury Tales* in general are less highly regarded.

One need not see in this difference of attitude a perversity or narrowness of response on the part of Chaucer's immediate successors. On the contrary, *The Canterbury Tales* were widely read, as the number of surviving manuscripts shows, and it would not be too much to assume that they were widely appreciated. Indeed, in the Prologue to his *Siege of Thebes*, in which the monk provides a 'link' for himself to tell a Canterbury tale, we find even Lydgate lumbering in elephantine playfulness after his

---

[1] The quotations are from Lydgate's *Troy-Book*, III, 553; II, 4697-700, and Hoccleve's *Regement of Princes*, 1962-3, 2084-6.

master. Something of rough good humour comes over, though
the language is crude and the character of the Host is coarsened
beyond recognition. It is not well done, but one is surprised to
find it done at all, for, within the then-current system of critical
categories, *The Canterbury Tales* could not, for the most part, be
taken seriously; and it is in terms of this adequation of critical
response to the system of critical theory that the fifteenth-century
attitude to Chaucer is best and most fruitfully understood.
Chaucer is praised for 'sentence' and 'rethoryk' because these
were the twin foundations of medieval poetic theory. Poetry
teaches moral virtue—'All that is wryten is to oure document'
as Hawes puts it (*Example of Virtue*, st. 3), rephrasing St Paul—
and it teaches by sweetening the instruction with rhetoric, poetry
being an ornate form of discourse, a learnt laborious art. As far
as theory was concerned, these were the only terms available for
the praise of Chaucer and it would not be too much to say that
they thus determined the kind of overt response he was accorded.
The same would apply to the critical theories of any age, even
our own. However, in the imitation of Chaucer, as distinct from
the tributes paid to him, there were practical as well as theoretical
considerations at work. He could give to his followers his genres,
his language, his style, his metres, and these they readily took to
do what they could with, but his other qualities, as outlined above
and defined by modern criticism, were more specifically
inimitable and therefore remained largely unimitated as well as
unsung.

It is difficult to move into the fifteenth century without first
understanding the position of John Lydgate (c. 1370-1449), monk
of Bury St Edmunds. Here the usual incantation of names—
Lydgate, Hoccleve, Hawes, Skelton, Barclay—which is what
goes by the name of literary history for the fifteenth century, is
almost totally misleading, since it obscures the overwhelming
importance of Lydgate. His influence on the century, in fact, is
considerably greater than that of Chaucer, and the century's
understanding of Chaucer was largely filtered through Lydgate's
understanding of him. Hoccleve is an exception, but the stature
of Hoccleve as a poet is so immeasurably less than that of Lydgate
that the exception is of no great importance. Yet Lydgate has

hardly been accorded an enthusiastic reception by literary critics; he has on the contrary provided a ready target for the long line of English men of letters who have preferred wit to honesty, the plausible sneer to the painstaking effort at appreciation. To account for this imperfect response, three factors may be isolated: the vast bulk of his work (some 145,000 lines, at the latest count), his metre and his syntax.

That Lydgate wrote so much is to be deplored, though from a physiological rather than from an artistic point of view. What is serious is that so much of what he wrote is worthless. To recognise this, and to discriminate between the good and the bad, is the first step in the proper appreciation of Lydgate, a step which is hardly taken by Professor Schirmer in his careful full-length study of the poet.[1] It would be possible to produce a 10,000-line Lydgate anthology which would show him to be a very considerable poet indeed, though some of the specifically cumulative power of his longer poems, the *Troy-Book* and *The Fall of Princes*, would be lost. Such an anthology would find no place for the *Fabula Duorum Mercatorum*, in which Lydgate's epic techniques of style and amplification operate almost by reflex upon a simple fable, with absurdly pretentious results; for the ponderous *Guy of Warwick*; for the early *Isopes Fabules*, which suffer from the deadly comparison with Henryson's version; for the *Secrees of the Old Philisoffres*, a product of his last years, confused and unfinished; for the great mass of occasional verse, like *The Title and Pedigree of Henry VI*, the verses on *Henry VI's Triumphal Entry into London*, the *Mummings* (though these, like the others, have much historical interest), which Lydgate, as the most notable poet of his day, was called upon to produce. Nor would it find a place for any part of the 25,000-line translation of Deguileville's *Pilgrimage of the Life of Man*, commissioned by the Earl of Salisbury in 1426, a barren waste of words in a genre for which Lydgate, significantly, could find no Chaucerian precedent. Some such surgery is needed before we can see Lydgate in his proper perspective.

Lydgate's awkward metre is a more serious obstacle to appreciation, though careful modern editions have shown that

---

[1] *John Lydgate: Ein Kulturbild aus dem 15. Jahrhundert*, Tübingen 1952. English translation by Ann E. Keep, London 1961.

the fiercest attacks on Lydgate's metre, such as those of Saintsbury, have been based on corrupt and careless texts. The problem of Lydgate's metre needs first of all to be isolated from the irregularity of metre shown by many of his followers, which is likewise made worse by scribes' carelessness but which is nevertheless not their creation. The usual explanation of this irregularity is that it was due to the decline of sonant final -e. Chaucer, in creating the pentameter line, had achieved a balance of alien syllabic and native rhythmical techniques which he helped maintain by the use of sonant final -e, which was in process of disappearing from the spoken language. The balance was, however, precarious, and when the final -e became so archaic and artificial that it could no longer be used, English verse fell back, as it would tend to in any case, on native four-stress rhythms, with or without alliteration, and even on six and seven-stress patterns (as exemplified in the *Tale of Gamelyn*), all with a marked tendency to half-line patterning. This theory seems to account adequately for the practice of poets like Ashby, Bokenham and Capgrave, who would certainly have had contact with native popular verse. Ashby's *A Prisoner's Reflections*, for instance, begins thus:

> At the ende of Somer, when wynter began
> And trees, herbes and flowres dyd fade,
> Blosteryng and blowyng the gret wyndes than
> Threw doune the frutes with whyche they were lade.

The confusion persists in Hawes, Bradshaw and Cavendish, and to some extent in Skelton and Barclay. Against these should be set the large number of more courtly and sophisticated poets whom the loss of final -e seems to have troubled not at all—the translators of Charles of Orleans, of Palladius, and of Vegetius, for instance—perhaps because of a renewed contact with foreign models.

However, this theory has little relevance to Lydgate, who uses final -e under much the same conditions as Chaucer, except in his later works, especially those in non-Chaucerian genres. In fact, Lydgate's versification, in comparison with that of his contemporaries in the early part of the century, Hoccleve, Walton, the author of *The Kingis Quair*, who all combine the use of final -e with smooth, syllabically regular metre, seems to need some special explanation.

It is to be found in his elevation of Chaucerian variants into systematic types.[1] Chaucer's verse was not as syllabically regular as his modern editors would have us believe: in particular he availed himself of two licences, the line deficient of its initial unstressed syllable (the 'headless' line) and the line deficient of the unstressed syllable after the 'caesura' (the 'broken-backed' or Lydgate line), which in modern editions are usually emended out of existence. Whether out of an excess of devotion to his master or because he distrusted his own ear (some of his comments suggest that he thought English verse was quantitative), Lydgate seized on these casual variants and used them systematically, often regardless of rhetorical or rhythmical context. It is this that makes Schick's analysis of five 'types' in Lydgate's verse,[2] which would be meaningless in any other context, pertinent. What Lydgate lacked was Chaucer's sense of line-flow, his subtle variations on the basic pattern balanced against the restatement of the iambic norm, his effective use of the rhetorically underweighted line, his skilful running-on of the line to an emphatic pause in the first half of the next line, his building up of the verse-paragraph with the speech-patterns always in tension against the metrical pattern. Lydgate worked with the line as his unit, weighing each line for its five stresses and measuring it against his own system of line-types. The fault of his versification is not that it is irregular but that it is too systematically, ruthlessly, monotonously regular. Those who have peered into the metrical chaos of John Metham's *Amoryus and Cleopes* (1449) and have recognised his ignorance of the very existence of such a thing as metre, may be inclined to regard this fault as venial.

The peculiarities of Lydgate's syntax can be similarly attributed to the example of Chaucer. These peculiarities hardly need illustration: the long, rambling sentences, the loose use of participial and absolute constructions, the mania for parenthesis, the

---

[1] The explanation adopted here owes much, like the rest of this article, to Eleanor P. Hammond. See her monumental *English Verse between Chaucer and Surrey*, Durham, N. Carolina 1927, pp. 83-6.
[2] In his edition of *The Temple of Glass*, EETS, ES, LX (1891), pp. lvi-lx.

loose subordination which is really a thinly disguised form of parataxis, the inchoate sentences where we wait in vain for a predicate and sometimes even for a subject too. Yet is it only fair to Lydgate to point out that he was trying to imitate Chaucer. There is evidence of this in the deliberate archaism of much of his syntax, archaism clearly modelled on Chaucer's example. We can see him too trying to catch the cadence of Chaucer's sentences, as in the disastrous imitation at the beginning of the *Thebes* Prologue of the long, complex opening sentence of the *Prologue* to *The Canterbury Tales*. If Chaucer was the first to achieve secure poetic control over complex utterances, then Lydgate cannot be harshly criticised if, with the example of Chaucer always before him, he met with but partial success when trying to do the same.

Turning to Lydgate's positive achievement we find an imitation of Chaucer just as close but incalculably more fruitful. Of all Chaucerian genres the most popular amongst his followers was the allegorical love-vision and courtly love-complaint, as represented in his *Book of the Duchess*, his *Parliament*, his shorter *Compleynts* and his translation of *The Romaunt*. Lydgate has four specimens of the type, *The Complaint of the Black Knight*, *The Flower of Courtesy*, *The Temple of Glass* and *Reason and Sensuality*. The *Black Knight*, a conventional love-plaint in a conventional spring and garden-setting, shows us Lydgate at his best and most pervasively Chaucerian. The opening descriptions of May and of the park in which the poet walks, for instance, are a mosaic of borrowings with every borrowed jewel shining brilliantly in its new setting, a studied synthesis, an elaborate interweaving of Chaucerian phrases, images and ideas into a decorative pattern with a beauty of its own. Lydgate always does these descriptions well: in the *Troy-Book* he uses them to punctuate the narrative, and there provides some of the great *loci classici* of decorative seasons-description, serving their narrative purpose but suggesting also, in their scientific-philosophic detail and profound sense of the due order of things, a kind of counterpoint to the swift change of human fortune. Few will think even of looking for realism of observation and 'nature-feeling' in formal and idealised description such as we find in the *Black Knight*. Indeed, we are specifically warned against such un-medieval ideas in the traditional imagery:

the dew shines like silver (l. 26), the water is as clear as beryl or crystal (l. 37), the soil is covered with Nature's carpets (l. 51), the grass is as soft as velvet (l. 80). Nature is controlled, patterned and 'civilised' by being assessed in images of human sway, the trappings of civilised existence, gems and decorative cloths. The imagery, like the style and Lydgate's mind in general, moves always towards artifice. The following passage from the *Troy-Book* clearly shows Lydgate thinking in terms of literary and pictorial convention, not of any real dawn:

> . . . þe larke with a blissed lay
> Gan to salue the lusty rowes rede
> Of Phebus char, þat so freschely sprede
> Upon þe bordure of þe orient.
> I 1198-1201

The sensuous apprehension of reality provides little of the material of Lydgate's poetry: one might even say that, as far as literature is concerned, the world of reality is, for him, non-existent. Everything of which he writes is strained through the medium of literary imagination and literary convention.[1] He is truly, to use a well-tried term, a poets' poet. It is not insignificant that one of the few who have praised him unreservedly has been Thomas Gray.

The lover's complaint is the centre-piece of the *Black Knight*. Leaning heavily on *The Knight's Tale* and *Troilus*, Lydgate has invested it with all the subtle sophistry of *fine amour*, the apparatus of traditional metaphor and classical allusion, the philosophical overtones and carefully pointed pathos. It is conventional in its every detail but the fact that it has been done before should not blind us to the skill with which it is done here. The style is highly wrought and elaborately figured, with repetition, parallelism, antithesis, chiasmus, alliteration, echoing, exclamation, woven into a pattern of complex rhetoric. Chaucer

---

[1] In death, as in life, Lydgate was a strict observer of literary convention. The last line he wrote, at the end of his part of the *Secrees*, was 'Deth al consumyth which may nat be denyed', after which Burgh, the continuator of the poem, adds the rubric 'Here deyed this translator and noble poete'. One imagines the pen slipping limply from the aged monk's fingers as he responded for the last time to the rhetorical cue. But it is Burgh who has recognised the literary commonplace and rearranged Lydgate's stanzas to fit the convention.

is ever-present, providing an image here, a figure there, always
fertilising and stimulating Lydgate's literary imagination. The
very opening:

> The thoght oppressed with inward sighes sore,
> The peynful lyve, the body langwysshing
>
> 218-19

is one of Lydgate's many attempts to catch the exquisite falling
cadence of the opening lines of *The Parliament*. Elsewhere it is the
Troilus that is laid under contribution:

> Lo her the fyne of loveres servise . . .   (end
>
> 400

The passage from the *Troilus* (V, 1849) is imitated, at length, in
at least four other places by Lydgate, always with great effectiveness, as if the very tune of the verse were an inspiration. Most of
Lydgate's best lines, indeed, are cast in some familiar rhetorical
mould:

> God hath a thousand handis to
>   chastise,
> A thousand dartis off punycioun,
> A thousand bowes maad in unkouth
>   wise,
> A thousand arblastis bent in his
>   dongoun,   (crossbows: keep
> Ordeyned echon for castigacioun.
>
> *The Fall of Princes* I, 1331-5

It is a specifically literary inspiration. The convention seems to
release what is best in Lydgate, not inhibit it.

The formal, conventional, decorative style displayed in the
Black Knight is not to everyone's taste, with its classical reminiscences, its elaborate but unostentatious figuring, its polite decorous
diction, its ornamental and strictly limited range of metaphor;
but it is the perfect complement of the formal and patterned view
of life and nature which the poem expresses. As long as Lydgate
holds to the well-trodden Chaucerian ways, comparison is not
always in his disfavour. There is a pressure behind the set forms
in Chaucer, as in *The House of Fame*, which can be disruptive.
Lydgate, being content with less, sometimes achieves more.

The Flower of Courtesy is a much slighter poem, a Valentine to his lady, if anything closer still in style and tone to Chaucer, especially to *The Complaint of Mars*. The bulk of it, over a hundred lines, is devoted to a description of the lady, remarkable as a *tour de force* of non-visual abstraction. Like similar descriptions in *The Temple of Glass* and the *Troy-Book*, it consists entirely of eulogistic topics of surpassing and inexpressible excellence, lists of abstract virtues, praise of Nature's feat of creation, and comparisons with other famous ladies. There is barely a detail of descriptive visualisation. Many hints for the description are taken from *The Book of the Duchess* (817ff.), though the total effect is different, since Chaucer has much more physical detail and varies and individualises the material constantly, as well as breaking it up and embedding it in narrative. Not many today will prefer the morally idealised eulogistic abstraction of Lydgate to the vivid, personalised concretion of Chaucer, but it seems peculiarly pointless to apply to Lydgate criteria of descriptive realism when he has devoted every resource of his very considerable art to the avoidance of such realism.

The Temple of Glass is a more complex and ambitious poem, the narrative of a decorously conducted love-suit, though with far more set speeches, prayers, complaints and descriptions than actual narrative.[1] It is the longest poem in which Lydgate follows no known source, and bears many marks of the care he has lavished upon it, for instance in its cunningly contrived alternation of rhyme-royal and couplet and its unconventional but weirdly effective December-opening. It was very popular and very influential in the fifteenth century, largely, one suspects, as a sprawling anthology of themes which poets could ransack at will. Its best parts are the formal set speeches, especially the Knight's complaint to Venus and his prayer to his lady, which compel respect by their restraint, decorum and sombre weight and unity of tone. Lydgate is at his best thus, when he writes within a strong convention or to a strong source. When he has to select for himself, he is undiscriminating, and the result is flatulence, mere

---

[1] The poem seems to exist in three recensions, ambiguously related. See J. Norton Smith, 'Lydgate's changes in the *Temple of Glass*', *Medium Aevum*, XXVII (1958) 166-72.

accumulation, as in the description of the paintings of true lovers on the walls of the Temple, where Lydgate seems determined to get everyone in, relevant or no. Here, as too often elsewhere, he is driven by a daemon of inclusiveness. The appropriate stimulus undams a torrent of illustrations, examples, parallels and comparisons, as if some psychological congestion had to be removed before he could move on. The sorriest aspect of *The Temple of Glass*, however, is the decline of allegory to mere ornament. The temple itself is carefully described but the description, where it is not totally irrelevant to the theme of the poem, is at odds with it. There is nothing of the luminous allegorical description of the Temple of Love in *The Parliament*, at once meaningful and decorative. Venus in the poem represents no particular facet or synthesis of love, but is merely a mouthpiece for advice and instruction. Personification-allegory has here a purely nominal existence, dependent on the scribe's fondness for capital letters.

Yet, though not itself an unqualified success, *The Temple of Glass* marks a shift of emphasis which makes it more significant for Lydgate and the emergent century than the other two poems. In the *Black Knight* Lydgate had already given expression to a highly attenuated ideal of the service of love; here he makes that ideal specifically moral and didactic. Venus's admonitions to the lovers show love as a test of virtue and an opportunity for virtuous conduct, delay in fulfilment as a form of purification, fulfilment the reward of truth, chastity and patience. Her tone is lofty and serious. What moves Lydgate to eloquence is not the prospect of love's rewards (he was a monk after all) but the satisfaction of duty and service well performed. It is essentially a moralist's handling of the code of love, and very much a fifteenth-century one.

Lydgate is completely at home in *Reason and Sensuality*, a translation of the first part of *Les Echecs Amoureux*, a mixture of morality, love-allegory and classical mythology which gives Lydgate a unique opportunity to be a fifteenth-century moralist in a fourteenth-century 'landscape'. The machinery of the poem is all traditional in the type of the love-vision, decorative, digressive, allusive, in a manner that Lydgate had at his fingertips from his reading of Chaucer, and which he manages here with relaxed ease. He catches too, better than anywhere else, Chaucer's conversational tone of voice: the poem is in octosyllabic couplets, the syntax and rhetoric simpler, and the temperature generally lower. Lydgate appears here in a genial light, indulging to the full his bent for encyclopaedic allusion and for irony at the expense of women. The moralising is moderate, polite and mild, even managing to convey some sense of the potential wealth and range of human experience down the wrong road. The dice are not so heavily loaded in favour of the momentous moral platitude as they were to be twenty years later.

These four poems were probably written between 1400 and 1410. Having absorbed what he could from Chaucer and worked out his own techniques of style, Lydgate was now able to tackle a larger theme, and Prince Henry gave him the opportunity to do this when in 1412 he asked him to translate the story of Troy. The result, after eight years of labour, was the massive 30,000-line *Troy-Book*, which is the cornerstone of Lydgate's achievement. Here, as in *The Temple of Glass*, he is consciously pressing beyond Chaucer, annexing larger and larger territories to the newly defined and newly consolidated poetic language. Chaucer used a vernacular source in his *Troilus* and treated only one episode of the Troy story; Lydgate takes a Latin source, the *Historia Troiana* of Guido della Colonna, and covers the whole range, from Jason to Circe, of this, the greatest epic story of antiquity.[1] What is more, he presses into service every device of medieval rhetoric to amplify and heighten his treatment of the story, to broaden its scope and to draw out its 'sentence'.

Amplification, here seen to be Lydgate's characteristic mode of thought and expression, was the basis of medieval rhetoric, the elaboration of any given subject-matter through conventional techniques of expression. Geoffrey of Vinsauf, the most influential of the medieval rhetoricians, devotes the first and most carefully thought-out part of his *Poetria Nova* to eight techniques of amplification: *interpretatio* (tautology), periphrasis, comparison, apostrophe, prosopopeia (personification), digression, description

---

[1] Lydgate has even the temerity to invite comparison with Chaucer when he imitates the latter's description of Criseyde instead of Guido's (II, 4736-62; *Troilus* V, 806-26). The comparison is sobering.

and *oppositum* (antithesis). Knowledge of Geoffrey in later medieval England is shown by references in Chaucer, Bokenham and the poet of *The Court of Love*, but his influence should not be regarded as necessarily direct or definitive. Brunetto Latini, for instance, a friend of Dante, has a list of eight *colores rhetorici* in his encyclopaedic *Livre dou Tresor*, which are derived from Geoffrey but which show significant changes of emphasis in accord with the fashions of his age. Nor do the rhetoricians do more than allude to the vast body of conventional poetic practice which goes under the name of 'topics'. Rhetorical doctrine of amplification was, in fact, broad, deep and creative, not narrow and pedantic as the categorisations of some of its teachers might suggest, and it was absorbed as much through the example of its great classical and medieval exponents as through academic precept.

Major devices of amplification in the *Troy-Book* include learned digressions, elaborate descriptions of seasons, persons and places, frequent astronomical periphrasis, apostrophes, woeful exclamations, prophetic jeremiads, laments, philosophical and fatalistic disquisition, and endless moral comment and exhortation. Those who read the poem for the story will receive a rude surprise, and will complain, as critics do, of Lydgate's long-windedness, his inability to get to the point, his elaboration of irrelevances. It is, however, rather naive to read a poem of this kind for the story, as if we couldn't wait to find out what happened to Hector or Achilles. The medieval poet had much more complex ideas about the proper conduct of narrative, especially epic narrative, and Lydgate's amplifications here, including both those he introduced himself and those he expanded from hints in Guido, move in three main directions, moral, political and historical. In them we can see Lydgate's poetic personality asserting itself fully for the first time, as his own themes, habits and techniques emerge from those of Chaucer.

Lydgate says in his prologue that Prince Henry asked him to translate the work in order to keep alive the memory of ancient chivalry; but, as he wrote, it was borne upon him that this tale of lust, adultery, vengeance, treason and murder offered less a series of images of true knighthood than a series of *exempla* for the moralist to build on. At first the moralising is mainly factitious, a matter of automatic reflex on Lydgate's part more than anything, but as events move to their climax, Lydgate is stirred to a contemplation of this pagan tragedy in which the inexorability of Fate, the mutability of Fortune, the transitoriness of worldly bliss, the inevitability of retribution, the Christian moralist's anger, outrage and pity, rise in a powerful burden, especially in Book IV. His epilogue, where in a fine passage (V, 3544-92) he concludes that there is little trust in worldly pleasure and glory, our life here being but a pilgrimage, evidently imitates Chaucer's epilogue to the *Troilus*, though it has its own truth and relevance.

Lydgate is also using the Troy story as a political text-book, a Mirror for Princes:

> Þerfor, ʒe kynges and lordis everychon,
> Make ʒow a merour of þis Lamedoun.
> II, 83-4

At every point he indicates the political lesson, making it more effective by interpreting the story in terms of fifteenth-century government, warfare and chivalry. He insists on the necessity for consulting the commons before taking important decisions, on the dangers of envy leading to discord and civil strife among princes (Lydgate wrote a prose pamphlet called *The Serpent of Division* on this theme), on the instability of a reign based on false succession; he draws out examples of chivalry and wise discreet government worthy of imitation, and makes a fierce attack on Achilles for his unchivalric conduct. Lydgate probably had his patron in mind in much of this, though the interest in politics is his own too.

The *Troy-Book*, finally, has its function as an encyclopaedia of history, mythology and science. Lydgate expands and adds to Guido's many digressions and deals at length, for instance, with eclipses, the history of idolatry, dreams, chess, the origins of drama, with a mass of classical and mythological allusion, mostly culled from Ovid and Chaucer. Lydgate's learning was not as extensive as it looks, but his insatiable appetite for facts and names marks him very much a man of his age.

The lower, more strictly verbal and stylistic levels of Lydgate's technique of amplification can be best examined with reference to the *Troy-Book*, though the application is general. Of his use of *interpretatio* or *expolitio*—the variation of the same idea in different words, the elaborately slow unfolding of some simple phrase as if it were revelation, the leisurely meditative habit of mind which can leave no idea alone until it has wrung from it every last drop of meaning, the inveterate assumption that where one word will do the work of ten, ten are better—little need be said, except to point out that it is deliberate. Of more significance is Lydgate's use of the rhetorical 'topics'. These can best be regarded as 'storehouses of trains of thought',[1] sources for the development and enrichment of literary material which are partly conceptual and partly formal. All poets use them, though with widely differing degrees of subtlety. Lydgate generally works from hints in Chaucer, and one of the major distinguishing features of his style is the frequency, length and elaborateness of these topics. There are, for instance, the topics of modesty, usually found at beginning and end of a poem, though they may occur elsewhere: the poet's pen quakes, he confesses his rudeness and inadequacy to his task, begs for correction, apologises for his 'boistous' and 'rurall' terms and his lack of rhetoric, for presuming to tread where others so much greater (Chaucer is often mentioned) have trod before, admits that he never slept on the mount of Parnassus, nor drank at the well of Helicon, nor gathered flowers (i.e. of rhetoric) in the garden of Tullius, and invokes Clio and Calliope to shed their fructifying 'licour' upon his barrenness. The origins of all are to be found in classical literature, though Lydgate himself is particularly indebted to such passages in Chaucer as the *Prologue* to *The Franklin's Tale*. Modesty-topics are a means of ingratiation, of winning favour, and also an opportunity for the immodest display of the very colours which the poet proclaims his ignorance of. Brevity-topics may be genuinely abbreviatory, in which case they serve to give the impression of a swift prosecution of the narrative; or they may be of this type:

[1] Quintilian's *argumentorum sedes*. See E. R. Curtius, *Europäische Literatur und lateinisches Mittelalter*, Bern 1948, trans. W. R. Trask, New York 1953, p. 70 *et passim* for rich and authoritative discussion of topics.

> But ȝif I shulde make descripcioun . . .
> It were to longe to ȝou for to abide
> *Troy* V 352-6

and thus eulogistic in function. Where the brevity-topic is combined with a full description of the thing the poet refuses to describe, that is, in the device of *occupatio*, it provides at once an ornament of discourse, a reinforcement of the quality of descriptive idealisation, and apparent swiftness of movement. The poet may also eulogise by declaring the inexpressibility of his theme: no-one could describe their woe, it would take a whole day to describe the feast, my pen would break if I tried to describe her sorrow, or, with complex elaboration of the topic:

> O, who can write a lamentacioun
> Convenient, O Troye, for þi sake? . . .
> Certis, I trowe, nat olde Jeremye . . .
> . . . nor þou Eȝechiel . . . Nor Danyel . . .
>
> Alle ȝoure teris myȝte nat suffise . . .
> *Troy* IV 7054-95

Or the poet may assert the surpassing qualities of what he is describing: this is one of Lydgate's favourite techniques, and he exploits it with a richness and variety which could be conveyed only by long quotation, though occasionally with some of the desperation of modern advertising:

> Ther may no whitenesse be compared
> To that whittenesse, I dar telle,
> For al whitenesse yt dyd excelle.
> *Reason and Sensuality* 2822-4

He is particularly fond of developing this topic in personal description through a series of analogies: as the sun surpasses the stars, the ruby all precious stones, May all months, the rose all flowers, so . . . (she surpasses all women). Elsewhere in such description he uses topics of comparison, where lists of famous women are given, the virtues of all of whom are enshrined in the one he is describing. This kind of extended allusion is related to the *Ubi sunt* motif, where famous names are quoted as a topic for the power of death.

It is obviously impossible to do more here than merely hint at the richness of this field. Perhaps one topic more may be mentioned, since it is so characteristic of his techniques; it is what we may call amplification by metaphorical analogy, where an idea is developed through a series of contrastive images:

> For he was clos and covert in his speche
> As a serpent, til he may do wreche,
> Hydinge his venym un er floures longe;
> And as a be, þat stingeþ wiþ þe tonge
> Whan he haþ shad oute his hony sote,
> Sugre in þe crop, venym in þe ote . . .
> Liche þe sonne þat shyneþ in þe reyn . . .
>
> *Troy* IV 5215-24

These image-clusters usually occur in certain fixed moralistic contexts, for instance in describing the duplicity of man, the mutability of Fortune, the transitoriness of fame, or the inevitable alternation of joy and sorrow. Such images, like the topics in general, are very revealing of Lydgate's attitude to experience. There is none of the penetrating awareness we find in Chaucer, no variety, nothing unexpected. Every subtle shade of human iniquity, every blend of moral black and white, is compassed for Lydgate in a clockwork sequence of polarised formulae. He can vary but he can never truly develop. He can pile up image upon image, allusion upon allusion, but he can never make any deeper penetration to the heart of any subject than the platitudes Chaucer has provided him with. His style obtains richness by lavish accumulation rather than by any organic density or 'wit'. Style itself is a self-sufficient entity. It is the same with his vocabulary: he can introduce new words but he cannot create new understanding of old ones, as can Chaucer and Henryson. His elaboration of an aureate vocabulary, in which he was again following Chaucer's example, is not so much directed to the enrichment of language-content as the result of a fascinated interest in the shapes and surfaces of words.

Yet, with all this, the topics, along with the larger techniques of amplification and the rhetorical figures with which they are often associated, provide the stimulus for most of Lydgate's best work. For him the evocative impact of the literary convention, with all the rich accretions of centuries of usage, is imaginatively valid in itself, and with the luxuriance of his responses curbed and patterned by the Chaucerian figures, his mind on the eternal common-places, he can, as in the lament for Troy in Book IV of the *Troy-Book* or the great envoy to Rome at the end of Book II of the *Fall*, rise to a solemn, powerful eloquence.

In *The Siege of Thebes*, written between 1420 and 1422, Chaucer is still being laid under heavy contribution: the Prologue is an imitation of the Canterbury links, and the appropriate passages of *The Knight's Tale* are plundered for the description of Theseus' Theban mission. But the poem as a whole, which lacks the high rhetorical colour of the *Troy-Book* and is altogether more sober and down to earth as well as brisker in narrative, is chiefly interesting for its further development of Lydgate's serious moral and political concerns. As in *The Fall of Princes*, and like the Elizabethan dramatists of whom he is a precursor, he is using history (the Thebes story being, for the Middle Ages, historical fact) for the elucidation and illustration of a system of moral and political attitudes. Apart from his persistent moral comment and exhortation, Lydgate is primarily interested in the story as an *exemplum* of unwise government and divided rule leading to political chaos and the horrors and futility of war.[1] Towards the end of the poem there is a condemnation of war as an instrument of national policy which must have seemed peculiarly pointed to Henry V. Criticism which treats the *Thebes* as romance-epic in its own right, like *The Knight's Tale*, can hardly expect to arrive at an understanding of Lydgate's fundamental and characteristic poetic purposes.

The Fall of Princes, written between 1430 and 1436 under the patronage of Humphrey, Duke of Gloucester, is Lydgate's longest poem (36,365 lines of rhyme-royal). Translated and expanded from the French of Laurens de Premierfait, which in turn was translated and expanded from the Latin of Boccaccio, it is a massive catalogue of illustrious men and women brought low by the vicissitudes of Fortune and by their own sin, pride and ambition, narrated with the object of teaching princes to rise

[1] For thorough discussion, see Robert W. Ayers, 'Medieval History, Moral Purpose, and the Structure of Lydgate's *Siege of Thebes*', *PMLA*, LXXIII (1958) 463-74.

above Fortune by the practice of wisdom and virtue. The work has some slight precedent in *The Monk's Tale*, but in its moral, political and historical emphasis it is perhaps Lydgate's most characteristic production and very well suited to the discordant mood of an age on the verge of chaos. On a political level, Lydgate has the opportunity to drive home by remorseless repetition his views on government: the dangers of false succession, of dissension amongst the nobility, of allowing kingdoms to fall under the sway of low-born usurpers, the need for a king to rule with the love and support of his people, and, above all, the chaos brought by civil strife:

> Kyngdamys devyded may no while endure.
>
> I, 3822

These may be platitudes, but such platitudes would appear good sense in the troubled world of 1435, just as they did in the reign of Queen Elizabeth. On a historical level, the poem was for Lydgate a vast encyclopaedia, a dictionary of universal biography: the need for documentation is imperious. But the overwhelming impact of the *Fall* is moralistic. For once, Lydgate must have felt, he had not only an excuse but a veritable obligation to indulge his natural bent, for Gloucester had instructed him to add an envoy to each chapter pointing the moral (as if he would not have pointed it in any case) and offering a 'remedie' against Fortune. These envoys, written in the 8-line stanza within strict formulaic conventions and with deliberate reaching after a richer, more aureate style than the comparatively sober passages of narrative, are the best parts of the poem, amplifications of traditional themes such as the transitoriness of earthly glory, the punishment of pride and the mutability of Fortune, lofty, eloquent, solemn, and technically very impressive.

Apart from these envoys, however, Lydgate does little to vary the monotonous diet of misfortune. He keeps some of Boccaccio's personal and dramatised interludes, such as the lively dispute between the poet and Brunhilde in Book IX or the debate of Fortune and Poverty in Book III, introduces a few personal passages of his own, keeps up his usual running fire against women in a series of heavily ironic asides (as he did too in the *Troy-Book*), and has many fine formal passages such as the complaint of Canacee in Book I, but he fails to enliven the repetitious framework of the processional, as Chaucer would have done. No critical attitude towards such a vast work could be unambiguous: at times it seems that the sheer weight of reiteration is having a cumulative effect of its own, and criticism is silenced as the mind is battered into submission. At others, when Lydgate is dredging amongst the minor Asian kings or the descendants of Alexander, one hears only a wearisome drone, and the mind, having threaded its way through one of Lydgate's toiling sentences, finds it difficult to realise that something has actually been said, and more difficult to care. The whole effect, though, is of a massive mounting threnody, or of some monstrous ruin, the remains of antiquity strewn in apparently indiscriminate confusion, from which gradually a pattern begins to emerge, a vast historic perspective, a dark vision of human history shot through with gleams of garish splendour.

Lydgate's briefer poems have other qualities, and show some versatility. The short love-poems, elaborations of familiar topics, are fluently and gracefully done. *The Churl and the Bird* is a perfect little moral fable on the lines of *The Manciple's Tale*, simpler and unironic, with the dry, terse, colloquial quality which Lydgate could display when he was writing low style. Similarly direct and unpretentious are the gnomic moralising poems with aphoristic refrain such as *A Wicked Tunge Wil Sey Amys*, where Lydgate goes back beyond Chaucer to an older native tradition of clipped didactic utterance. These poems are in a different manner altogether from the courtly and epic poems, with no ornament and little rhetoric. They aim low, but often strike home. The *Dance Macabre*, a translation of French verses designed to accompany frescoes of the Dance of Death, is one of Lydgate's most successful poems, grim, pungent and compact. With a strong source, and within a rich convention, it demands from Lydgate what he can best provide—variation, reiteration, moral insistence —while asking nothing of narrative and exposition. When he is working outside a fixed convention, as in satirical poems like the *Order of Fools*, Lydgate is less successful, though his experiments have importance in the history of literature.

In his shorter religious poems, Lydgate again turns back to non-Chaucerian tradition, though Chaucer's poems to the Virgin in the *ABC* and *The Second Nun's Tale* have influenced him. These poems, especially the Marian poems, represent the most extreme development of Lydgate's mannered art, so richly encrusted with ornament that it is difficult to see whether there is anything else there, and so lavishly aureate that the borderline between English and Latin becomes blurred.[1] Personal religious feeling is here, of course, not in question, nor in the *Testament*, often spoken of as if it were some kind of autobiographical document. What authenticity there is in its conventional conflation of the follies of youth is the result of art, not nature, since self-expression would be as foreign to Lydgate as self-consciousness. His two best short religious poems are *A Valentine to her that excelleth all* and *A Saying of the Nightingale*: the first is an adaptation of the courtly Valentine theme, and the second relies on a skilful twist of the Chaucerian love-vision opening. Even in non-Chaucerian genres, Lydgate runs better in the familiar Chaucerian channels.

Lydgate's longer religious narratives, the two saints' lives (*Albon* and *Edmund*) and *The Life of our Lady*, represent pre-Chaucerian genres, though the amplificatory high style which is adopted in all three owes much to Chaucer's example in, for instance, *The Man of Law's Tale*. Chaucer raised what had been a semi-popular genre to literary status, and Lydgate fixed the type for the fifteenth century. Though these saints' lives are not readily palatable, with their excessive simplicity of outlook and endless moral posturing, *St Edmund* should be recognised for the real qualities of its first two books, which represent one of Lydgate's most considerable narrative achievements. *St Albon*, despite a lofty dignity which is one of Lydgate's most enduring assets, is more pretentious and suffers under the load of irrelevant material it is made to carry. In *The Life of our Lady*, Lydgate surprises us again by his ability to move beyond Chaucerian models, for there is here a devotional intensity combined with a richness of style which Chaucer gives no hint of possessing. In

---

[1] For neat illustration, see Isabel Hyde, 'Lydgate's "Halff Chongyd Latyne"': an Illustration', *MLN*, LXX (1955) 252-4.

itself, it makes nonsense of the epithet 'Chaucerian' as a comprehensive label for Lydgate. It is less a life than a compendium of Mariolatry, a loosely strung series of episodes related to the liturgical feasts of the Church's calendar, each used as the occasion for meditation, exposition, panegyric, doctrinal explanation or lyrical rhapsody.[1] The best writing is in the most formalised passages, above all in the long prologue, one of the peaks of fifteenth-century poetry, where the richly evocative Marian imagery of star, flower and dawn is exploited with transfiguring effect.

Lydgate fixed the modes in which the fifteenth century was to understand and use Chaucer. His influence was enormous, and all his successors pay tribute to his sententious rhetoric, invariably bracketing his name with those of Gower and Chaucer in a formulaic triad. Hawes, indeed, evidently considers him Chaucer's superior and one suspects his views were generally shared. They owed Lydgate another debt in their very language, for it was Lydgate who consolidated the position which Chaucer had won for English as the language of courtly, educated, sophisticated poetic usage, and fixed poetic diction for a century. If Chaucer sharpened the fine blade of language, Lydgate, by sheer constancy of use, wears it down to a solid, commonplace tool of practical expression and workmanlike virtue. No English poet after him did not profit from Lydgate's patient quarrying. But before turning to 'the English Lydgatians', there are his predecessors and contemporaries in the tradition to consider, amongst whom Hoccleve stands foremost.

Thomas Hoccleve (1368-c. 1430), a clerk in the office of the Privy Seal, knew Chaucer personally. In *The Regement of Princes*, in a deeply felt lament for Chaucer, worlds way from Lydgate's conventional tributes, he declares that he will have Chaucer's portrait inserted in the manuscript so that those who did not know him may see what he looked like (l. 4998). He may even have received advice from him about writing poetry:

[1] The edition of *The Life of our Lady* by Simon Quinlan (London diss., 1957, unpublished) has a valuable introduction. I have not seen the edition by J. Lauritis, R. Klinefelter and V. Gallagher, Duquesne Studies, Philological series 2 (1960).

Mi dere maistir—God his soule quyte!—
And fadir, Chaucer, fayn wolde han me taght;
But I was dul, and lerned lite or naght.
The Regement 2077-9

Despite the familiarity of these references, Hoccleve echoes Chaucer less than does Lydgate and writes mostly in non-Chaucerian genres. Yet he represents an aspect of the Chaucerian tradition of which Lydgate offers us hardly a glimpse.

The Regement of Princes (A.D. 1412), his longest poem, is a course of moral instruction for the edification of rulers on the model of the familiar 'Mirror for Princes', dedicated and throughout addressed to Prince Henry. It contains many *exempla* told with brisk verve and welcome brevity, but the moralising lacks the high seriousness of Lydgate and the political and social comment, though often pungent and highly topical, lacks Lydgate's panoramic perspective. But it is preceded by a long Dialogue between Hoccleve and a beggar (ll. 113-2016) which is of a different order altogether, a loosely sprawling medley of autobiography, complaint, social satire and moral reflection stamped with the mark of an individual and arresting poetic personality. Hoccleve's personal revelations, his concern about his job and his future and his wife, his preoccupation with money and the payment of his annuity, his nagging sense that middle age has overtaken him without his having really achieved anything or made any provision for his old age, have a directness and sense of person that we never get from Lydgate, for whom the world of actual experience and personal observation is remote when he writes. Lydgate feels everything through literature: grief, joy, adoration, affection, are meaningless to him until translated into literary formulae. Hoccleve, however, has an eye to see and a poetic *persona* to put over. Like Chaucer, and with much of Chaucer's wry self-mocking irony, he is always talking about himself, but where Chaucer's *persona* is always a laughable fiction, Hoccleve uses Chaucerian precedent and techniques to talk, really, about himself, sometimes with such raw honesty as to be painful. He manages, too, to get some sense of a real dialogue between himself and the beggar, some interchange of personalities. Like

Chaucer, Hoccleve has caught from the taverns and streets of London the tang and cadences of popular speech:

> Now, sone myn, I am a man of age,
> And many wedded couples have I knowe . . .
> But I ne sawe . . .
>
> *The Regement* 1622-5

and Chaucer moreover has given him the means and the example to introduce this into his verse. There is a colloquial ring about his dialogue, a sense of the speaking voice, which makes Hoccleve the only inheritor of Chaucer's well-bred low vernacular.

Hoccleve's style is in perfect accord with his matter. There is little rhetorical colouring, none of the elaborate amplification and figuring of Lydgate, and, though Hoccleve is not frightened of new words, no aureation. The verse is pitched in a low key, with clear, tight-knit, prosaic syntax, and a tendency to terse, pithy utterance. The metre is even and regular, though with an over-careful attention to the syllable count which often results in wrenched stress. To call it a simple style would be the compliment that Hoccleve's skill deserves.

Hoccleve's *Series* (A.D. 1421) is a highly original experiment in framing, in which two tales from the *Gesta Romanorum* and a moral treatise, *How to Learn to Die*, all translations, are integrated into a series of dialogues between Hoccleve and a friend. The translations themselves are rhetorically embellished in a manner others did just as well, but the frame, in particular the opening Complaint and the following Dialogue, is Hoccleve at his best. The Complaint, where he talks of his recent mental breakdown and his struggle to get over it, is ruefully frank, but the Dialogue, in its sense of character, its humour, its cheerful irony, its authentic conversational quality, is Hoccleve's happiest achievement. *La Male Regle* (A.D. 1406) runs it close: Hoccleve here portrays himself as an idle good-for-nothing, lazing about London, eating and drinking more than is good for him, taking time off from the office in the afternoon to go boating, partly because it flatters his vanity to hear the boatmen call him 'Master':

> So tikelid me þat nyce reverence
> Þat it me made larger of despense.
>
> 204-5

Hoccleve is here adopting a Chaucerian *persona* in order to make a potential patron laugh at him as a cheerful rogue and give him money on the strength of his promises of amendment, which gives to his laughing references to his poverty and ill-health a wry pathos.

The Letter of Cupid (A.D. 1402), a translation of Christine de Pisan's defence of women against detraction, shows that Hoccleve could laugh at women as well as himself. The irony, as in many other passages on women throughout *The Regement* and the *Series*, is light-hearted, too full of Hoccleve's characteristic fantastic humour to have Chaucer's cutting edge but delicate enough to make Lydgate look monkish.

Before passing to the love-vision tradition there is need to mention one other immediate follower of Chaucer. John Walton's verse-translation of Boethius (A.D. 1410) provides a compelling illustration of what Chaucer had done for English poetry, for here, in language of perfect fluency, in careful metre and skilfully padded stanzas, an honest craftsman has threaded his way through the complexities of the *Consolatio* with accuracy, ease and dignity. Ironically, Walton had open in front of him as he wrote, Chaucer's prose translation, to which his verse is in every respect superior.

The Cuckoo and the Nightingale, most probably written by Sir John Clanvowe (d. 1391),[1] is the earliest of all 'Chaucerian' poems, and one of the best. The first two lines are from *The Knight's Tale* and the poet echoes constantly the early Chaucer love-visions in his themes, accessories and phraseology. The poem is a debate about love between the two birds, lightly handled, with the balance between the two skilfully held. Clanvowe has caught Chaucer's easy, conversational manner and learnt too the trick of interweaving the personal theme into the allegory, so that the cuckoo's scornful parting 'Farewel Papinjay' echoes painfully in the poet's own lingering sense that there is something to be said for the cuckoo's point of view.

La Belle Dame sans Mercy, the only work reliably attributed to

---

[1] This is the conclusion reached by Mr V. J. Scattergood in his edition of the poem (Birmingham diss., 1961, unpublished), which he and the manuscripts prefer to call *The Book of Cupid*.

Sir Richard Ros (c. 1410-82),[1] is a close translation of the poem
by Alain Chartier (A.D. 1424), and bears obvious marks of
Lydgate's influence only in its conventional frame of prologue
and epilogue, which Ros has added. Chartier's poem is a courtly
sophisticated conversation between a beseeching lover and a
disdainful lady, in which the relationship of the two is eternally
prolonged at a point of no advance, like a game of chess left on
the board for centuries. Rarely had the exquisite refinements of
courtly sensibility been presented with more skill. Chartier works
within very strict limits of theme and style; he is formal, decorous,
rhetorical, and without raising his voice achieves a level muted
tone in which the subtle variations are the interesting ones. Of all
this Ros has managed to preserve a very creditable sample. He
translates line by line, skilfully and systematically padding the
French octosyllabics into English pentameters, and rendering
Chartier's careful variations of stanza-technique with great
precision. On the other hand, some of Chartier's artful rhetoric is
obscured and there are disorders of syntax which show the technical
difficulties Ros was working under. Ros tends to be more
colourful, more vigorous, more obvious, in a sense more English:
he falls easily into a rather inappropriate colloquial idiom which
makes the lady's tone of mocking irony more flippant than it
should be, and he has a native weakness for alliteration. However,
the remarkable thing is that he manages to come as close as he
does to Chartier's manipulation of the controlled, the refined, the
expected. In itself this is the measure of Chaucer's achievement in
giving English a courtly style and diction.

The Kingis Quair is the best of all fifteenth-century love-visions,
a new, rich synthesis in which the lofty moral tone of *The Temple
of Glass* is blended with the wit and wisdom of *The Parliament* in a
complex allegory which answers at every point the structure of
the thought. The poem has hardly been given the kind of
attention it deserves,[2] the question of authorship having diverted

---

[1] Many other fifteenth-century poems—indeed, most other fifteenth-century
poems—are attributed to him in Ethel Seaton's idiosyncratic *Sir Richard Roos:
Lancastrian Poet*, London 1961.
[2] Three recent articles have done much to remedy this situation: John Preston,
'Fortunys Exiltree: a Study of the *Kingis Quair*', *RES*, VII (1956) 339-47; Murray
F. Markland, 'The Structure of *The Kingis Quair*', *Research Studies of the State*

criticism from its main task of elucidation. James I of Scotland is named as the author in the unique manuscript, and the details of the poet's life in the poem are evidently modelled on James's career, though whether this makes James the author is questionable. The details of his life were well known, and could readily be used by someone else as a peg for allegorical discourse, yet the autobiographical element in the poem, which has preoccupied critics so much that they have dismissed the dream of Venus, Minerva and Fortune as an irrelevance, is very small. It is an odd love-poem that contains not a single meeting of the lover and his lady. One is much inclined to dismiss the attribution to James I as an excess of patriotic zeal on the part of the Scottish scribes. But the question, though fascinating, is irrelevant to the poem in itself. More relevant is the fact, proved by Craigie[1] to the satisfaction of all but the most fanatical Scottophile, that the language of the poem is the southern English of Chaucer, and that the Scottish appearance of the text is due to the scribes.

The core of the poem is the dream which the poet experiences after he has fallen in love with the lady he sees from his prison window. In this dream he is first shown the power of love, in the Palace of Venus, and then he is taught, by Minerva, that love must be grounded in virtue and wisdom. Only in this way can man triumph over his bondage to Fortune:

> Fortune is most and strangest
>   evermore,
> Quhare leste foreknawing or
>   intelligence   (Where least
> Is in the man.
>
>   st. 149

In a last vision, Fortune places him high on her wheel, and the poem ends with the winning of his lady, his release from prison, and his realisation that Fortune, which seems so cruel and arbitrary, is no more than the working out of divine will, and that for those who find accord with divine will in virtuous love and wisdom,

College of Washington, xxv (1957) 273-86; John MacQueen, 'Tradition and the Interpretation of the Kingis Quair', RES, xii (1961) 117-31.
[1] In 'The Language of the Kingis Quair', Essays and Studies, xxv (1939) 22-38.

Fortune holds no terrors. The doctrine is that of Boethius, but it is worked out with a keen awareness of the complexities of love and life which sees human business not in terms of categorical imperatives, like Lydgate, but as a series of subtly related contingencies. Every detail of structure and allegory is designed to elucidate the poem's central theme. The mention of Boethius, for instance, in the prologue, which seems at first a Chaucerian irrelevance, is soon seen to be scrupulously functional, and the animal-catalogue in the Fortune-landscape, brilliantly modelled on the tree-catalogue of *The Parliament*, is a poetic symbol of the fertile proliferation of natural life governed by Fortune. The poem could hardly be more deeply indebted to Chaucer and *The Temple of Glass*: everywhere we find conventional themes, descriptions, images and topics, but everywhere the handling is rich, creative and witty. Even in his more specifically verbal borrowings this poet can improve on his original, as in this apostrophe to the restless human spirit:

> O besy goste, ay flikering to and fro
> st. 173

imitated from Chaucer's

> O wery goost, that errest to and fro.
> *Troilus* IV 302

The diction of the poem is a perfect blend of the simple and the elaborate, of the intimately personal and the gravely meditative, which reminds one of Chaucer's achievement but concedes nothing to him in poetic effectiveness.

The Flower and the Leaf is another example of the Lydgatian blending of love-allegory with moral uplift. The courtly cult of the flower and the leaf, mentioned in the *Prologue* to *The Legend of Good Women*, is here used as an allegorical means of illustrating a set of moral antitheses in which true, chaste, virtuous love is set against idle, self-indulgent flirtation, The moral theme is lightly stressed and there is about the whole poem a pleasing air of grave gaiety. The conventional framework and techniques are aptly exploited, with extensive use of the topics of eulogy, and the style, though the metre has suffered somewhere, maybe at the hands of the scribes, is fluent and unpretentious. *The Assembly of Ladies*[1] is equally conventional, though this poet seems to respond only fitfully to the traditional stimuli and Lydgate's sobriety of tone becomes in him mere dullness. The allegorical setting and personifications, and the ladies' complaints at the court of Lady Loyalty, are lifelessly handled. The poet seems more interested in real households than in allegorical ones, and his language, too, betrays a touch of the busy bureaucrat. This poet may be responsible for *Generydes*, a sub-courtly romance in rhyme-royal which may be mentioned here as an example of the influence of the Chaucer-Lydgate tradition of style, diction and metre on a non-Chaucerian genre. The romance of *Partenay* is another example. *Parthonope of Blois*, however, translated from French in an odd mixture of 4- and 5-stress couplets, shows a deeper penetration of Chaucerian influence, particularly in the lively, amusing quality of the poet's personal interpolations about his lack of success in love, and the detailed verbal imitation of the tournament of *The Knight's Tale* in lines 11128-45. The whole romance, for all its length, is brisk and witty and ridden on a very light rein. This is the saving grace also, to return to love-allegory, of the *Isle of Ladies*, a rambling dream-poem in which the author goes back to romance and Breton legend for new motifs, and freewheels along in loose-running octosyllabics which have some of the leisurely nonchalance of Chaucer's poems in the same metre. It is a flimsy airy fantasy which is just saved from being blown away altogether by the gentle amusement with which the poet regards his subject, introducing much sly detail in small matters. This ambivalent attitude towards non-didactic love-allegory seems to be the only one that the later tradition could reconcile itself to, and the last example of the genre, *The Court of Love* (c. 1535?), is something of a pastiche. The poet here is consciously writing within an archaic tradition, as he shows by his ungrammatical attempts to use Chaucer's *-en* inflection and the way he scatters Chaucerian archaisms (*ywis, eke, wight*) like cherries in a

---

[1] This poem and the *Flower and the Leaf* were associated and both attributed to 'a Lady' by Skeat. In my edition of the two poems (Nelson's Medieval and Renaissance Library, Edinburgh 1962) I argue against such an association. My treatment here of the excellent *The Flower and the Leaf* is understandably brief.

cake. He has made his poem an anthology of the traditional themes of love-allegory, his profoundest debt being to *The Temple of Glass*. We find an elaborately rhetorical modesty-prologue, which might well be Lydgate's, description of the palace of Love and of the lady, the prayer of the lover to Venus and his complaint to his lady, allegorical personifications of love, and statutes of love. All this would be of little account were it not for the brilliance with which every convention is handled, the consummate formal decoration of the descriptions, the luminous set rhetoric of the lovers' hymn to Venus, the passionate rhetoric of the lovers' plea for mercy, as well as the force and vigour of the dialogue. Technically, this poet is as gifted as anyone since Chaucer, but he cannot take the convention seriously and his mask slips in the barely suppressed laughter of the statutes, in the pert sarcasm of Rosiall, an early sketch for Rosalind, and in many other revealing details. There is no sense that the poem is a satire on *fine amour*: the poet deploys a masterly talent in the skilful display of many of its traditions, but he cannot suppress a mischievous ironic spirit.

Love-allegory is the dominant form[1] of allegory in the Chaucerian tradition but something needs to be said of the non-Chaucerian genre of didactic allegory, represented in Lydgate's *Pilgrimage* and to some extent in his *Reason and Sensuality*. *The Assembly of Gods*, for instance, once attributed to Lydgate, is moral-didactic allegory of the purest kind, an elaborately contrived *psychomachia* within a mythological framework which, despite the fact that it is in rhyme-royal, is set apart from the Chaucer-Lydgate tradition by its narrow functionalism and almost complete rejection of conscious art in style and diction. More particular mention needs to be made of *The Court of Sapience*, a poem which has been most unjustly neglected. It is in two books, the second being an encyclopaedia of medieval knowledge, in which the poet incorporates catalogues of gems, rivers, fish, flowers, trees, birds and animals, and, as he passes through the courts of Philosophy, Theology and the Seven Liberal Arts, accurate, detailed synopses of the various disciplines with explicit reference to numerous authorities. This appetite for learning is

---

[1] The echo of Professor C. S. Lewis, like the debt throughout this discussion to *The Allegory of Love*, is conscious.

displayed elsewhere in fifteenth-century poetry, especially in Lydgate, but it is never so comprehensively supplied as here, nor with such technical skill. There is a wealth of highly unusual literary experience opened up here for those who are prepared to divest themselves of conventional modern notions of the innate 'unpoetic' quality of certain subjects. The first book explains the condition of man upon earth, the condition which makes true sapience essential for him, and consists mainly of a vigorously dramatic and splendidly rhetorical treatment of the debate of the Four Daughters of God. Far superior to Langland or Lydgate (*Life of our Lady*) in his handling of this conventional theme, the poet here displays the fullness of style, of rhetorical figuring and amplification, which make him Lydgate's truest successor. Peace's farewell to heaven (ll. 428-96) and the prayers for mankind of the three hierarchies of angels (ll. 617-700) are high points in fifteenth-century poetry.

It was left for Stephen Hawes (d. 1523?), Groom of the Chamber to Henry VII, to bring together the didactic allegory of the *Pilgrimage* and the encyclopaedic interests of *The Court of Sapience*, as well as some of the ingredients of popular romance, with the more usual love-allegory. This he does in the *Pastime of Pleasure* (A.D. 1506), in which the hero, Graunde Amour, is subjected to an intensive course of instruction in the Seven Arts, and thereafter in chivalric doctrine, before going out to do battle with vice, in the form of many-headed giants and monsters, having accomplished which quest he wins his lady, La Bell Pucell. There is much that is new in Hawes, and in his attitude towards chivalry and towards the place of the knight in national society he appears as the conscious herald of a new age.[1] He places great emphasis, for instance, on the importance of a liberal education in the training of the knight, and on the function of the knight as the supporter and defender of the commonwealth rather than the privileged member of an aristocratic caste. In this he is anticipating the Tudor ideal of the Governor, though Hawes himself, like Caxton, is concerned for the reinvigoration of medieval ideals of chivalry:

[1] See Arthur B. Ferguson, *The Indian Summer of English Chivalry*, Durham, N. Carolina 1960, pp. 66-8.

> For to renue that hath be longe decayd,
> The floure of chyvalry.
>
> *Pastime* 2985-6

Yet these attitudes are held in suspension and have no issue in the inner logic of the poem. The hero's fights with the giants do not show him, either allegorically or in any other way, profiting by the skills he was supposed to have learnt in the Tower of Doctrine, but are mere concessions to popular taste. The treatment of the Seven Arts themselves, compared with *The Court of Sapience*, from which it is imitated, is thin and tatty and gives no hint that Hawes had ever done much more than read the chapter-headings of books. Hawes is also a very serious poet: he has a high sense of reverence for his predecessors, especially Lydgate, and a carefully formulated view of the moral function of poetry,

> Clokynge a trouthe with colour tenebrous,
> For often under a fayre fayned fable
> A trouthe appereth gretely profytable.
>
> 712-14

He repeats this definition of allegory so often that one suspects he was on the defensive against the new lyricists (see ll. 1387-93) to whom Hawes would indeed have seemed *vieux jeu*. Hawes, in fact, has a place in English literature by virtue of his poetic ambitions alone, for his ambitions ludicrously outran his poetic capacity. It was, for instance, a good idea, though not one without precedent, to introduce a rude character to mock at love and women and by so doing to give comic relief as well as a glance at the other side of the coin; but it is a mark of Hawes' devastating narrative incompetence that he can express this contrast, as it is expressed in the Godfrey Gobelive episodes, only in great undigested gobs of raw obscene abuse. His major failure, however, is a stylistic one. In all his passages of high style, such as his architectural descriptions and his accounts of rhetoric and poetic theory, he is trying to imitate the mature aureation of Lydgate and *The Court of Sapience*, but the best he achieves is a factitious glitter. The rich rhetoric of his predecessors appears in the form of gewgaws, tawdry ornament stuck on the dull threadbare stuff of his native style. Nothing is organic, everything is mechanical: when he uses a rhetorical figure such as anaphora he can only drive it to death by wearisome excess. His hold on the 5-stress line is limp, and collapses when the material is intractable. The best parts of the poem are those where he can lean most heavily on some firmly developed fifteenth-century convention: the descriptions of spring, the astronomical periphrases, the courtly love sequences, and perhaps more than anything the sober platitudes of the conclusion where, in the contemplation of death, time and eternity, we see the decisive assertion of medieval habits of mind.

After Hawes, the vitality of Skelton (1460?-1529) is welcome, but it is a vitality which cracks the mould of courtly allegory. Apart from two early elegies, in which the medieval commonplaces of death and mutability are decorously and skilfully handled, and *The Bowge of Court*, a vigorous court-satire in a parody of the medieval dream-allegory form,[1] his main contribution to the Chaucer-Lydgate tradition is *The Garland of Laurell*. This poem, an allegorical vision of the Palace of Fame, is a typically exuberant explosion of egotism, wit, malice, ostentatious pedantry and half-digested learning. It has many harebrained tirades and displays of colloquial virtuosity, where Skelton tends to drop into the old 4-stress alliterative line of popular verse and drama. Its interest here is that Skelton seems capable at times of working seriously within the fifteenth-century aureate tradition, as in the opening sequence, the description of the Palace of Fame, the garden-scene, and above all in the eulogies of the ladies of the household where Skelton was staying. It may be unfashionable to suggest that Skelton is at his best when he keeps his head and his temper, but in these last there is a genuine enriching of traditional patterns as well as the integration of those patterns, in seven of the eleven poems, into newer, more typically Skeltonic metrical modes.

Allegory, of one kind and another, bulks largest in the Chaucerian tradition, but mention needs to be made of other genres. The English translator of Charles of Orleans, and author of other English poems in the same sequence, whom it is plausible and convenient to take as Charles himself, is certainly influenced by Chaucer, imitates him frequently, and perhaps Lydgate too.

[1] See Judith S. Larson, 'What is *The Bowge of Courte?*' *JEGP*, LXI (1962) 288-95

He could be regarded as continuing the thin Chaucer-Lydgate tradition of love-lyric, were it not for a complex unidiomatic syntax (even in poems which appear not to be translations) a wide and consistent use of non-Chaucerian tags and vocabulary, and a more artificially constructed metrical line, which make the poems appear less Chaucerian than neo-French in inspiration. The poems, mostly ballades and roundels, have also a new, intimate, personal, passionate quality and a stylistic inquisitiveness and wittiness which it is difficult to find elsewhere in courtly lyric before Wyatt. On a stylistic level (the biographical level concerns only Charles' biographers) it is possible to see how Charles has achieved this balance of passion and 'wit' by blending exclamation, question, colloquialism and staccato repetition, all intended to convey force of feeling, with a most elaborate rhetorical artifice (which is often the informing quality of the whole poem), and with a subtle development of conventional thematic imagery. John Donne comes readily to mind as well as Wyatt. The lyrics are set in a pseudo-biographical narrative frame, not translated from the French, which seems to owe more, in spirit at least, to Chaucer. There are two passages, a dream dialogue with Venus (ll. 5053-190) and a pastoral scene and dialogue with his lady (ll. 5191-351), which bear comparison with anything in Chaucer, witty, ironic, dryly observant and with a vein of delightful fantasy.

The poems attributed to the Duke of Suffolk[1] are typical of the many other examples of the type in the fifteenth century. They have a faded sort of beauty but no distinctive lineaments.

The continuation of the hagiographical tradition may be briefly treated. John Capgrave (1394-1464), Austin friar of Lynn, and author of voluminous works in Latin and English prose, wrote a *Life of St Katherine* in rhyme-royal which pays lip-service to the Lydgate formulae but which really represents a resurgence of an older tradition of popular East Anglian legend and romance. This is revealed in the loose 4-stress line, the romance tags and similes, the formulae of oral delivery, the casual disregard of the stanza, and the crude, popular religious tone. There are too many specific echoes of *Havelok* for coincidence. Osbern Bokenham (1392-1447), Austin friar of Suffolk, is more ambitious in his

[1] By H. N. MacCracken, and edited by him in *PMLA*, XXVI (1911) 142-80.

Legendys of Hooly Wummen, in mingled stanza and couplet. His rejection of the high style is explicit, but he rejects it so often and at such length, with so much elaboration of the rhetorical topics and so many references to the Gower-Chaucer-Lydgate trinity, that he seems to be hankering after it. The disclaimers sound as conventional as Lydgate's, but the difference is that Bokenham really means them. He considers the high style inappropriate to his subject and in fact does not use it, but he is not willing to let it be thought that he couldn't rise to it if he wanted to; hence the many references and the occasional examples of fine writing in which he hints at what we are missing.

We come finally to the continuators of specifically Lydgatian traditions. *Fall* literature is represented by the *Mirror for Magistrates*, which lies outside the scope of this chapter since its direct stylistic debt to the Chaucer-Lydgate tradition is small, and by the *Metrical Visions* which George Cavendish (d. 1562) appended to his life of Wolsey. This work may have been prompted by the 1554 print of the *Fall*, for its imitation of Lydgate is close enough to run to the lifting of a whole stanza verbatim, as well as the usual topics, figures and techniques of amplification. The metre is chaotic. The extraordinary thing about the *Visions* is that Cavendish should have bothered to write them at all, when he was the possessor of a prose such as he displays in his life of Wolsey. The pressure of the Lydgate stereotype must have been strong indeed to wean a Tudor writer away from a mode of expression as free and assured as this.

Lydgate's political interests are kept alive in *Knyghthode and Bataile* (1460), a translation of the famous treatise *De Re Militari* of Vegetius, as well as in poems outside the Chaucerian tradition like the *Libel of English Policy*. In his additions to the Latin the Vegetius-translator, who has Henry VI as his patron, reveals two main purposes: the dissemination of Lancastrian propaganda, and the romantic glorification of war and chivalry. Every mention of unchivalric conduct, of the dangers of rebellion, civil strife and treachery, is made the excuse for a covert attack on the Yorkist faction, with York identified as the 'kyng of pride'; the news of the Lancastrian victory at Ludiford is greeted with a rapturous account of the scattering of the rebels, all identified in heraldic terms; above all, the treatment of naval warfare in Book IV is made the opportunity for the introduction of a completely imaginary sea-battle between Lancastrians and Yorkists, powerful, vivid, dramatic and highly coloured. In his enthusiasm for war, whose glories he describes with enormous vigour:

> Lepe o thi foo, loke if he dar abide;
> Wil he nat fle, wounde him; mak woundis wide,
> Hew of his honde, his legge, his thegh, his armys;
> It is the Turk: though he be sleyn, noon harm is
>
> 372-5

the poet reveals the traditional pugnacity of the civilian (he was a priest of Calais at the time). Where Vegetius discusses war with the cool, unemotional practicality of the professional expert, his translator talks of fame, honour, death and glory:

> Here is noo drede of deth or peyne of helle;
> Here or with angelys is us to dwelle.
>
> 2033-4

The style of the poem is fascinating. The influence of the Latin is seen in the many Latinate words and constructions, and may be partly responsible for the contortions of syntax, but there are beyond this qualities—a gnomic compression, an elliptic syntax, an extraordinarily varied and aggressive diction, concatenation and some internal rhyme in the poems, metre of scrupulous precision—which reveal skill and sophistication of a high order. The lineaments of the same poet can be seen in earlier and cruder form in the translation of *Palladius on Husbondrie* (1440) by a member of Duke Humphrey's household. The compression here is achieved at the cost of syntax and sometimes of sense; the Latinity is more extravagant; the attempt at technical virtuosity is more obvious—as in the florid dedication to Gloucester, the incredibly complex patterns of internal rhyme in the epilogues to each book, and the final epilogue, one stanza of which reads the same down as across—but vastly less successful. The metre, though syllabically precise, seems to imitate Latin in its contorted word-order and disregard of natural stress, as if English were innocent of pre-existent rhythmical or syntactic patterns.

The more homely moralistic tradition of Lydgate is represented by two immediate followers. Benedict Burgh (1413-83), a cleric of some standing in his time, was Lydgate's closest disciple, continuator of his *Secrees* and author of a verse *Letter to Lydgate*, in both of which he attempts, with ludicrous ineptitude, to imitate the aureate style of his master and even—dog-like devotion could go no further—his metre. The truer Burgh is shown in the translation of the extremely popular *Disticha Catonis*, where he claims to be, and succeeds in being, nothing more than the humble practical moralist, canny, shrewd and sensible. The style is simple and aphoristic in the manner of Lydgate's didactic refrain-poems, and the metre smooth. George Ashby, clerk to the Signet, is a poet only by courtesy, for he shows no sign of any stylistic gift in his two moralistic poems, *A Prisoner's Reflections* and the *Dicta Philosophorum*, but he is important for the shrewdness and honesty of his response to the social and political problems of his age: the *Active Policy of a Prince* (1470) is in a conventional genre, but his advice in it to Prince Edward contains an assessment of England's ills and the means of remedying them which shows an extraordinary emancipation from the still-dominant concepts of chivalry.

Alexander Barclay (c. 1475-1552), monk of Ely and friar of Canterbury, is a transitional figure of some importance. Though consciously working within the Lydgate tradition, especially in his *Legend of St George*, he moves significantly away from the tradition both in choice of genres and in style. In his translation of the Latin version of Sebastian Brant's *Ship of Fools* (1509) the movement is not completely to his advantage, for here Barclay shows up better as a medieval preacher than as a satirist, and his best passages, such as the exploitation of the *Ubi sunt* or the violent attack on women, are those where he finds, in the near-exhausted mine of Lydgate tradition, some seam which has not yet been completely worked out. His style in this poem provokes mixed reactions. There is, on the one hand, the unsuitability of the fixed cadences of rhyme-royal to his turbulent mind; but, on the other hand, a more positive quality in his tough, homespun language which, despite its Latinity, seems to possess potentialities of development. These potentialities are realised in Barclay's five *Eclogues*, translations from the Latin of Aeneas Sylvius and Mantuan. Here, especially in his setting of the rustic scene, his quick, lively, colloquial exchanges of dialogue, his sharp, observant handling of the satire on court-manners (especially in the second *Eclogue*), Barclay's language has an immediacy which marks the final eclipse of the narrower aureate tradition. The 5-stress couplet is used here in a new manner, with the emphasis on its antithetic quality and the finalising effect of the second rhyme, as opposed to the flowing paragraph construction of Chaucer. Barclay may have had little direct influence, but he is a key to much that was happening in the first half of the sixteenth century.

The Chaucerian tradition in the fifteenth century, it will have been observed, is not simple even when confined to English poets. Probably the most striking single feature of the work of the English Chaucerians is the long continuation of the tradition of formal love-allegory. For a hundred years the love-allegory, with characteristically fifteenth-century modifications, carried a varied load of pleasure and instruction, but at last its machinery proved too antiquated for the changed and increased burdens it was called upon to move. The author of *The Court of Love* shows what could still be done with it by one who could humour its demands, but the work of Hawes suggests that the form had outlived its usefulness. The sixteenth century was far from abandoning the idea that poetry should teach, but it had other ways and other ideas for making it do so. When Spenser came to use the love-allegory again, at the end of the century, he reconstructed the medieval tradition with many new materials.

But this is only one aspect of the Chaucerian tradition. From another point of view the achievement of the English Chaucerians is the continuation and exploitation of the more profound but less palpable tradition of metre, diction and style which Chaucer had established, and if Chaucer does not now appear alien to us it is partly due to their work that this is so. In particular, his 'augmentation' of the literary language was naturalised, and often employed in carrying forward older, non-Chaucerian, poetic genres and attitudes. Augmentation was also developed beyond Chaucerian limits for its own sake; but whereas Chaucer adopted Romance words mainly from French, and apparently through the medium of the language spoken at court—the 'King's English'

—his followers seem increasingly to adopt words direct from Latin, taking them from books and using them often in ways that proclaim their remoteness from speech. But, away from this aureate tradition, which in its turn is a recurring feature in the history of English diction, Chaucer's command of a simpler, living English is never lost in the fifteenth century. It was indeed part of a more general English tradition of popular verse, prose and drama.

From one point of view, it is clearly impossible to say that the Chaucerian tradition ends at one particular point in time, since he made himself, and was made, part of a wider English tradition. The new Italian influences, and the classicist redirection of medieval rhetoric, which bring about such important changes in sixteenth-century poetry, do not constitute a break with that tradition, since they continue broadening processes already at work in the fifteenth century. Yet in a more strictly literary sense it could be said that the history of the Chaucerian tradition continues for as long as poets work within the conventions of Chaucer and Lydgate as a matter of course; for as long as poets take for granted that this, and this alone, is the manner of poetry. When poets begin to imitate Chaucer consciously, as Spenser does, because they think him a great poet and worthy of imitation, the Chaucerian tradition, properly so called, has ended, and the history of Chaucer criticism begins.

Images of Chaucer 1386-1900

D. S. BREWER

IT is well known that a great work of art, or, as we say, the writer (meaning his work), shows different faces to different ages. At one time Chaucer is valued for his extreme artificiality, at another for his childlike naturalness: now he is praised for his nobility and morality, now he is condemned as 'impious and obscene'. One period is apparently blind to his humour, another notices little else. Works of art have much of the mirror in them, too. It is perhaps something to make us a little uneasy that what an age sees in a writer is so like its *own* image. We give ourselves away constantly. Not that it is quite as simple as that. The process of time unfolds further implications in the work of a great poet, so that some new image, that may at first appear to be merely reflection, turns out to be genuinely of the original picture. Without going into the metaphysical problems of what—or where—the poem 'really is' and how we perceive it, we may say that the succession of images that different ages perceive merges into a composite, and our total view is enriched by the succession of time. Even in the study of literature there are objective realities, and some knowledge is cumulative.

One kind of cumulative knowledge will not be dealt with here —the cumulative knowledge of scholarship. Yet it underlies, or the lack of it underlies, most of the critical judgments and general impressions that will be mentioned in this essay. Knowledge of Chaucer's language, life, and the circumstances of history that conditioned him, failed rapidly after the middle of the fifteenth century. By the seventeenth century true knowledge of these and similar matters was almost entirely lacking, and Chaucer's language was far more difficult to men of that time than it need be to us. The texts of his works were also very inaccurate in many cases. The antiquaries of the late seventeenth and early eighteenth centuries began to build knowledge again. Urry's edition of *The Canterbury Tales* (1721), though universally condemned as the worst text of Chaucer ever to appear, at least showed some awareness of the problems. Modern scholarship dates from Tyrwhitt's edition of *The Canterbury Tales* (1775-8). But not much more was done for a long time. It was the nineteenth century that first produced a serious body of work which began to enable men to understand Chaucer rather more clearly in the context of his own times and necessities. The Chaucer Society founded by Furnivall in 1868 first made available in print some of the manuscripts in their original readings, and this made possible the great, though now outdated, edition of Chaucer's works by Skeat in 1894. The Chaucer Society also produced much other material essential to the understanding of Chaucer, while *The Life Records* (1876-1900) made a reasonably accurate biography possible for the first time. In the twentieth century there has been an enormous increase in Chaucer scholarship, mainly in the U.S.A. The inadequacy of scholarly knowledge must excuse, or at least explain, some of the inadequacies and vagaries of critics in earlier centuries. Nowadays we have less reason and less excuse for making fools of ourselves in reading the work of one whom informed opinion for five centuries has agreed must be rated among the very greatest English poets.

A critic must have knowledge, and would do well, also, to know something of the opinions of previous critics. But we need not despair of the possibility of making new judgments and criticisms, and of learning something new about Chaucer. Out of old books, as Chaucer himself says, comes new knowledge. There have been some distinguished original contributions recently to the deeper understanding and enjoyment of Chaucer, and there is plenty more to be said about Chaucer's art, his use of language, the nature of his narrative and characterisation, to go no further. We still lack complete agreement about the nature of his metre. All who have actually handled the manuscripts and undergone the harmless but severe drudgery of editing have become convinced that Chaucer wrote in a metrically regular metre. But the liveliest contributions to the study of Chaucer's metre of recent years have maintained that Chaucer's verse is irregular, or, as they prefer to call it, 'rhythmical'. Again, we still have no definitive treatment of Chaucer's influence on other writers, though up to the early seventeenth century it was considerable.

The first view of Chaucer that we have dates from his own time, testifying to the fact that, like all the greatest artists, he enjoyed a great reputation in his own day as well as later. It is a poem by his celebrated contemporary, the French poet, Eustache Deschamps, which was written about 1386.[1] The text is difficult to understand in some places, and the date and circumstances are uncertain, but some things are clear enough. The poem was apparently the reply to one from Chaucer to Deschamps. Deschamps gives us what may be a glimpse of Chaucer himself, who he says is 'brief in speech', though this may be rather a reference to the brevity of Chaucer's poems compared with those of his contemporaries. Deschamps also gives us a hint of the literary circles of the day, partly in the very existence of this poem, showing as it does the communication and sympathy between the 'new' poets of the courts of France and England, and their recognition of each other. Deschamps says he is the pupil of Chaucer, though this, like the statement that he will remain 'paralytic' till he hears from Chaucer, is no doubt a polite exaggeration. Further, the poem says that 'Clifford' is carrying the poem from Deschamps to Chaucer. This must be Lewis Clifford, a Garter knight, an old companion of the Black Prince (d. 1376), right-hand man of his widow, Joan of Kent, and one of the chief of that group of Lollard Knights, who were old soldiers, courtiers, administrators, literary men, and with whom Chaucer had some close connections.[2]

To turn to the poem itself: Deschamps calls Chaucer a Socrates full of wisdom; a Seneca in uprightness of life; an Aulus Gellius (better known to the Middle Ages than to us as distinguished in both literature and law) in practical affairs; an Ovid great in

---

[1] The text has been reprinted with notes and discussion several times; see especially the works of Deschamps, edited by the Marquis de Queux de St-Hilaire and G. Raynaud, *Société des Anciens Textes Françaises*, vols. II, 138; X, 218, 247; XI, 34: P. Toynbee, *Specimens of Old French*, 1892 pp. 314, 482: and T. A. Jenkins, *MLN*, XXXIII (1918) 268ff. See also G. H. Gerould, *MLN*, XXXIII (1918) 437ff.

[2] Cf. D. S. Brewer, *Chaucer in his Time*, 1963, especially 228ff.

poetic learning (probably meaning classical mythology). Chaucer is brief in speech, wise in rhetoric, an eagle who in his scientific learning has enlightened England. The climax of this first stanza comes, as one might expect from a Frenchman, in the comment that Chaucer has translated into English a French poem, *Le Roman de la Rose*—

> Grant translateur, noble Geffroy Chaucier!

Deschamps goes on to say that Chaucer is the god of secular love in England, who has set up an orchard of poetry, and has asked other poets to contribute some trees, of which this poem is one. Deschamps says he himself is but a beginner to Chaucer, calls Chaucer 'high poet', 'glory of squirehood (?)', and again praises his noble poetry, sweet music.

It is a commonplace that humanist writers of the sixteenth century thought that a poet should be, in Gabriel Harvey's words, 'a curious universall scholar'. The medieval courtly poets of England, France, and Italy thought much the same. In our day of divisions between imaginative literature, on the one hand, and other kinds of writing on the other; of division between the arts and the sciences; between pure science and technology; it is worth recognising both the achievement and the medieval acceptance of Chaucer as a scientist, moralist, man of letters, and poet. No less rationality was attributed to his making poetry than to his science; both science and poetry were welcome, and the whole is crowned with the adjective 'noble'. There is no exaggeration here by Deschamps. Both as scientist and as poet Chaucer was one of the leaders of his times, valued by his contemporaries as such, and royally buried. The whole body of his work bears out Deschamps' praise.

Another contemporary who witnessed to Chaucer was Thomas Usk. He was a city man, under-sheriff, influenced by Lollardy, acquainted with Langland's *Piers Plowman*, and an ardent disciple of Chaucer's. He died in the dangerous political manoeuvres of the times.[1] In his *Testament of Love* he wrote:

> Quod Love . . . 'Myne owne trewe servaunt, the noble philosophical poete in Englissh . . . in a tretis that he made of my servant Troilus, hath this

---

[1] For more details see Brewer, op. cit., p. 60.

mater touched . . . Certaynly, his noble sayinges can I not amende; in goodnes of gentil manliche speche, without any maner of nycete of storiers imaginacion, in witte and in good reson of sentence he passeth al other makers.

III, iv. *Chaucerian and other Pieces*, ed. W. W. Skeat, Oxford 1897, p.123.

Again there is the emphasis on the 'noble philosophical poet', with *Troilus and Criseyde* especially in mind. Usk also emphasises 'the reason of sentence', the rationality of opinion.

Another contemporary who referred to Chaucer in his lifetime was Gower. In his *Confessio Amantis* of 1390, in a passage later cancelled for reasons of space, Gower calls Chaucer the disciple and poet of Venus, and says that he filled the land with 'ditties and songs'. If Gower really meant that Chaucer wrote many short lyrics they have, alas, been lost.

The list of Chaucer's poetic friends, admirers, and disciples could be further extended. They included, among the Lollard Knights, Sir John Clanvowe, presumed author of *The Book of Cupid* (otherwise known as *The Cuckoo and the Nightingale*), and Henry Scogan, tutor to Henry IV's sons, who wrote a moral *Balade* about 1407 in which he refers to 'my maistre Chaucer', 'that in his langage was so curyous' (so elaborate and skilful). Such imitations or brief comments as Chaucer's circle provide reinforce, for the most part, the impression we have from Deschamps' poem. In the view of Chaucer implicit in these poems, besides his interest in the subject of love, his being in the intellectual forefront of his age, etc., there is also the sense of his political and social centrality. I do not mean his centrality between 'right' and 'left', for that would be an anachronism; nor a middle position socially; but that he was at the centre of affairs, and at the heart of society, very much an 'insider', not an 'outsider'. This is taken for granted, but it was rather less true even for his immediate poetic successors in England, surely to their detriment as poets. Perhaps our greatest English poets have always had something of this political 'centrality'—one thinks of Shakespeare and Milton—but it is no doubt easier achieved with courts than with democracies. In Chaucer's case it is in part a product of the unusually high degree of literary culture achieved by the court of Richard II.

The two of Chaucer's younger contemporaries who give us the fullest picture of the way his achievement was understood, are Lydgate and Hoccleve.[1] Hoccleve, a mildly dissolute Chancery clerk (a sort of middling civil servant), living in London and working near the court at Westminster, claimed to know Chaucer personally. Lydgate, a monk at Bury St Edmunds, knew Chaucer's poetry well, but seems only to have heard about the man. These writers illustrate the decline in the status of literature in Henry IV's court, for they were merely on the fringes of that courtly centre of power and prestige of which Chaucer was a full member; nor do there appear to have been any writers, with the minor exception of Henry Scogan, who were closer to the centre. Nevertheless, Lydgate and Hoccleve were effective practising men of letters, and true, if minor, poets. Lydgate himself was something of a scholar, but neither of them had anything like the sheer intellectual power and attainments of Chaucer.

Hoccleve caused a portrait of Chaucer to be made in 1412, twelve years after Chaucer's death, in what is now British Museum MS Harley 4866, containing Hoccleve's *The Regement of Princes*. The portrait accompanies that part of the text where Hoccleve laments Chaucer's death

> O maister deere, and fadir reverent!
> Mi maister Chaucer, flour of eloquence,
> Mirour of fructuous entendement,
> O universal fadir in science! . . .
> 1961–4
> Mi dere maistir—God his soule quyte!—
> And fadir, Chaucer, fayn wolde han me taght . . .
> 2077–8

'Father' is, of course, a title of reverence and honour. Hoccleve goes on to say that Death, in taking Chaucer, has despoiled this land of the sweetness of rhetoric; who was the equal to Aristotle

[1] From this point onwards references to comments on Chaucer are taken from Caroline F. E. Spurgeon, *Five Hundred Years of Chaucer Criticism and Allusion*, London 1925, reprinted 1960. References are identified by the name of the writer (where known), and the year in which the comment was made as it appears in Miss Spurgeon's collection.

in this land but Chaucer? He rivalled Cicero and Virgil, and he was 'The firste fyndere of oure faire langage'. These remarks are the keynotes of the view taken of Chaucer in the next hundred years: his learning; his rhetoric (an important word wrongly used to mean frigidity by post-Romantic writers, but meaning, to Hoccleve, Chaucer's poetic art); and the freshness of his language.

Lydgate has forty years of praise and borrowing from Chaucer, from 1400 onwards. He too gives us just a glimpse of Chaucer the man, in *The Hystorye, Sege and Dystruccyon of Troye*, 1412-20:

> For he that was gronde of wel
>   seying   (founder
> In al hys lyf hyndred no makyng
> My maister Chaucer, that founde
>   ful many spot—
> Hym liste not pinche nor gruche at
>   every blot,
> Nor meve hymsilf to perturbe his
>   reste,
> I have herde telle, but seide alweie
>   the beste,
> Suffring goodly of his gentilnes
> Ful many thing embracid with
>   rudnes.

It is agreeable to think that the calm, balanced, charitable personality implicit in the poems also appeared in the rough-and-tumble of ordinary life.

Lydgate's comments on Chaucer's works are similar to Hoccleve's, but fuller and more frequent. His most characteristic passage is the 'Commendation of Chaucer' in *The Life of Our Lady* (1409-11?):

> And eke my master Chauceris
>   nowe is grave   (buried
> The noble rethor Poete of Breteine,
> That worthy was the laurer to have
> Of poetrie, and the palme atteine,
> That made firste to distille and reyne
> The golde dewe droppis of speche
>   and eloquence

Into oure tounge thourgh his
  excellence,
And founde the flourys first of
  rethoryk
Oure rude speche oonly to
  enlumyne.

I-9

For Lydgate, what Hoccleve called 'our fair language' is 'our rude speech', but exaggeration and excessive humility apart, their view is much the same; Chaucer adorned the language with new and splendid words and eloquence. This may well thought to be the central *literary* fact about Chaucer, provided we remember that we are thinking specifically about the language of high literary culture, and not the common language of all. It is a view that is partly conditioned, however, by Hoccleve's and Lydgate's special interests as English literary men. They add another point, natural enough for clerks, and for the fifteenth century as a whole, but also very true of Chaucer; his devoutness. Hoccleve, in his *Lament*, recalls how often Chaucer had written in honour of Mary. Lydgate, no more than Hoccleve, makes any fuss about Chaucer's piety, but mentions it occasionally and casually, as in *The Pilgrimage of the Life of Man* (A.D. 1426). Lydgate also responds easily to Chaucer's pathos. None of these early writers comments on Chaucer's humour, and indeed the word itself, in the modern sense, did not exist. It is even doubtful whether the concept existed, though of course medieval writers recognised irony and satire. This does not mean that Chaucer's humour was unrecognised. The lightness of tone of Lydgate's *Prologue* to *The Siege of Thebes* and its self-depreciatory fun, like the references of both writers to the Wife of Bath, show that they responded to various kinds of Chaucer's humour, at times with their own elephantine gaiety.

After Lydgate and Hoccleve the fifteenth century added nothing useful to our knowledge of Chaucer the man. The scribe and hirer-out of books, John Shirley, a great admirer of Chaucer, contributed various fragments of ostensible court-gossip, but they hardly reflect a view of Chaucer, and it is very difficult to know how far, if at all, they merit belief. Manly thought Shirley most

9

unreliable. One point Shirley makes, however, in his prose introduction of *The Knight's Tale* (c. 1456) is implicit in his gossip, and perhaps worth singling out. *The Canterbury Tales*, he says, were founded, imagined and made for both the disport and the learning for all those that be gentle (i.e. gentry) of birth or of conditions. No-one in the fifteenth century would have praised Chaucer, as some did in the nineteenth century, for speaking to the people of England, or for representing the *bourgeoisie* (except those who had made enough money to become 'gentle' in their 'conditions').

Almost the only fresh point of criticism that emerges in the fifteenth century is the brief, casual remark of John Metham in 1448-9 that 'hys bokys be rymyd naturelly', because of Chaucer's long practice and use of proverbs. This may not seem to us a very profound remark, but it is the just observation of an independent mind. It is an unusual perception of the delightful sense of ease, and the colloquial vigour of Chaucer's writing, that was not clearly registered till much later, and which rings a fresh note amongst the reiterated praise of, in Caxton's words in c. 1479, 'the worshipful fader and first foundeur and embelisssher of ornate eloquence in our Englissh', who made such noble making, with (in c. 1483) such 'hye and quycke sentence'.

The so-called Scottish Chaucerians, notably Henryson and Dunbar, make the same praise of 'the rose of rethoris all', with his 'fresch anamalit termes celicall', as Dunbar wrote, outdoing his master, in *The Golden Targe* of 1503.

With the beginning of the sixteenth century a new literary climate began to develop. Many religious, educational, and consequently literary problems had to be met, and it was inevitable that the greatest English writer so far should be called in evidence in controversy, and seen in terms of the preoccupations of the age. (It was the same set of forces that in the early sixteenth century led to the beginning of studies of Old English.) In Chaucer's case it must be remembered that especially in the sixteenth century, in Thynne's editions of 1532, 1542, etc., and Stowe's of 1561, a number of poems were printed that were not by Chaucer, but some of which were attributed to him. He was thought, for example, to have written *Jack Upland, The Pilgrim's*

Tale, and *The Plowman's Tale*, all of which are sixteenth-century anti-papal satires, very different from Chaucer's own work, though, indeed, inspired by his genuine anti-clericalism. He was also often thought to have written Thomas Usk's *Testament of Love*, and it was this attribution, in fact, which led some later biographers to attach Usk's recantation of Lollardy and betrayal of his friends to Chaucer. (*The Flower and the Leaf* was also thought to be Chaucer's, and this pretty poem was warmly praised by critics as unlike as Dryden, Hazlitt, and Keats, until it was expelled from the Chaucer canon, and so failed to attract the notice of critics.) Such accretions, and others, rather blurred the outline of Chaucer as known to the sixteenth century, and caused him to appear more of a religious reformer than he was. By the early twentieth century there had been a complete reversal of judgment. To Miss Spurgeon, in the Introduction (p. xx) to her collection of references to Chaucer, it seemed merely 'quaint' to think of Chaucer as 'theologian, reformer and moralist'. Yet in *The Parson's Tale* he is consciously all three. Even the poems that are most obviously designed primarily for comic effect depend on the recognition of a firm system of values, a concern that good should prevail, and a faith that it ultimately will. A writer whose chief mode is narrative or dramatic, who is intensely aware of the actualities, and especially the incongruities of human existence, may well be aware of two sides to every question. His work is not therefore to be denied its serious implications. Even in his most ribald satire, one may well say *especially* in his most ribald satire, Chaucer can be seen to be concerned with moral and theological questions, and to wish to improve the world. The sixteenth century was not 'quaint', nor grossly mistaken in its view of Chaucer, and Thomas Lodge summed up neatly in 1579 when he said that 'though he be lavish in the letter, his sense is serious'. Chaucer, therefore, was often cited by the Reformers, as Miss Spurgeon noted. The great humanist and reformer Ascham, who would allow short shrift to the 'manslaughter and bold bawdry' of Malory's *Morte d'Arthur*, for its usurpation of the Bible's place in kings' chambers, was fond of referring to Chaucer, 'our English Homer', as a moralist. Foxe the martyr-ologist took Chaucer for 'a right Wycliffian', and he may well have been right in detecting at least Lollard sympathies in Chaucer.[1]

Literature of the depth and complexity of Chaucer's writing, however, is not simple enough for propaganda, and there were plenty in the sixteenth century who read Chaucer rather differently. There were first those who disdained the frivolity of 'Canterbury Tales', and though they may have been thinking of light reading in general, they certainly meant to include Chaucer. Sir Thomas Elyot, a good Humanist, but a rather severe moralist, compared *Troilus and Criseyde* with the New Testament, of course to Chaucer's disadvantage. Even so, one cannot but be struck by the number of times Chaucer provides casual but apt quotations for serious writers and pamphleteers up to the end of the seventeenth century. Such casual quotation, with all that it implies of well-remembered reading, is the mark of a poetry which has entered the texture of a whole culture.

As well as a religious problem, the sixteenth century had a language problem. Compared especially with Latin, the uses of English were limited, its range narrow, its vocabulary inadequate, its prestige low. It will be remembered that even as late as the third quarter of the next century Milton felt he had sacrificed his European fame to his patriotic duty in writing *Paradise Lost* in English. In the sixteenth century most serious writers wished to improve the English language, and it was especially the concern of those who may be thought of as Humanists—men who had a specially vivid sense of the importance of language and literature. There was continuous debate on the deficiencies of English, and how they might be cured. Chaucer was therefore often cited as the outstanding English poet, whose writings gave some measure of prestige to the language. He was often bracketed with Lydgate and Gower, of course, in this connection. Having been praised throughout the fifteenth century for improving the language it was natural that such praise should continue throughout the sixteenth century. The antiquaries and scholars Bale and Leland both drew a picture of Chaucer in the image of the humanist and reformer, learned and fundamentally serious, devoting himself earnestly to the study of literature, and aiming above all to enrich

[1] Brewer, op. cit.

the English tongue with polished verse, as Dante and Petrarch had studied to enrich Italian. This picture has no doubt much truth. A great poet does not become so by accident, and Chaucer himself witnesses to his own passion for study in *The House of Fame*. The most complete expression of the Humanist, Reforming and patriotic view of Chaucer, and his improving the language is to be found in Sir Philip Sidney's *Apologie for Poetrie*, c. 1581.[1] Sidney refers as usual to Dante, Petrarch, and Boccaccio, who made their language aspire to be a 'treasure-house of science' (i.e. knowledge in general), and compares with them Chaucer and Gower, whose example others followed to 'beautify our mother tongue'.

Sidney, however, is one of the last to mention Chaucer in this way. Another response to Chaucer was growing up throughout the sixteenth century—the very natural one of Chaucer's sheer difficulty, due to the lapse of time. Chaucer was becoming obscure, and even in 1532 a glossary of hard terms was provided. This was connected with an acute problem of the time, that may be phrased as the problem of 'purity of diction'. It particularly centred on whether foreign words should be 'borrowed', or old words revived. The extreme opposition to 'borrowing', as represented by Sir John Cheke, said that if the language borrowed too much, it would go bankrupt, and he went so far as to translate part of the Bible using only originally English words. In contrast, not only scholars but the ordinary people were often enamoured of strange and foreign words. Most of these came from Latin, and because of their learned origin were known as 'inkhorn terms'. Chaucer entered this controversy in two ways. First because of his increasing obscurity, whereby his old English was becoming as strange as foreign terms or Latin terms newly introduced; and second because his English, being 'old', could legitimately be regarded as more authentic than new terms. One would have expected a third way in which Chaucer might have entered the controversy; after all, he was a very notable user of new foreign words in his own time, and in his learned works had also introduced 'inkhorn terms'. Chaucer's

---

[1] A full account of Sidney's position will be found in the edition by G. T. Shepherd in Nelson's Medieval and Renaissance Library, London 1965.

Host is the first of a long line of ordinary people who are made fun of by English authors for their proud and loving misuse of long words. Dogberry, Mrs Malaprop, and the elder Weller are in this respect his direct descendants. But no reflections of this kind seem to appear in the sixteenth century.

As to Chaucer's remoteness and hence obscurity, Sidney himself had touched on this with his customary courtesy, praising Chaucer for seeing so clearly, though in that 'misty time', and pointing out that he had great deficiences 'fit to be forgiven in so reverent antiquity'. This criticism of Chaucer's obscurity had begun in the beginning of the century, strangely enough, for in his praise of Chaucer in *Philip Sparow* (1507?) Skelton goes out of his way to answer it:

> And now men wold have amended
> His English, whereat they barke
> And marre all they warke:
> Chaucer that famous Clarke,
> His tearmes were not darcke,
> But pleasaunt, easy and playne.

It is astonishing to think that there appears to have been some attempt at *modernisation* of Chaucer, if Skelton is to be believed, even at this early date. If there was, it has not survived, unless some bad late manuscripts can be accounted for in this way. Throughout the century, as late as Spenser, it was customary to compare Chaucer with Virgil, but in 1565, and occasionally later, the sense of Chaucer's extreme ancientness was conveyed by comparing him with Ennius, traditionally the 'father of Latin poetry', of whose work only fragments survive. In 1546 Peter Aston, who had translated some Chronicles of the Turks, said that he had tried to use 'the most plain and familiar English speech', not using inkhorn terms, and not using Chaucer's words, 'which by reason of antiquity be almost out of use'. In 1553 Thomas Wilson in his celebrated *The Arte of Rhetorique* also condemned inkhorn terms, and advised men to speak 'as commonly received'. He complained that Englishmen back from foreign countries 'powder their talk with oversea language'; lawyers and accountants use their own jargon; 'the fine courtier will talk nothing but Chaucer. The mystical wise men, and poetical clerks will speak nothing but quaint proverbs and blind allegories'. It is interesting that it is courtiers, and not poetasters, who affect Chaucer. Nothing illustrates more clearly the central courtliness, the high breeding, the political centrality of the Chaucer tradition. When a poet like Wyatt was much influenced, as Wyatt was, by Chaucer, it was a tribute as much to his social status as to his poetic sensibility. Wilson's comment also shows the conservatism of the high culture of literacy in the royal courts of sixteenth-century Renaissance England. To recognise this is largely to explain why Spenser practised an archaic, 'Chaucerising' style. It was a political and patriotic, as much as a poetic, choice. But to mention the ambitious Spenser is to anticipate the other side of the controversy over 'pure English', as it affected the view taken of Chaucer.

It is interesting that all the dominant figures in the mid-century controversy over the purity of English diction were Cambridge men, often associated with Peterhouse. They were Humanists, Reformers, and Chaucerians, almost to a man, and though Ascham and Cheke seem to have been their leading lights, their circle certainly extended to Sidney and Spenser. To go back to one of the earliest of them, one Peter Betham in 1544 also condemned terms borrowed from other tongues, but, he says, 'I take them best English men which follow Chaucer, and other old writers, in which study the nobles and gentlemen of England are worthy to be praised, when they endeavour to bring again his own cleanness, our English tongue, and plainly to speak with our own terms, as our fathers did before us . . .' This seems to be the first time that Chaucer is praised *not* for adding 'terms borrowed from other tongues', but for the original purity of his diction. This is obviously absurd in itself, but significant because it was taken up by Edmund Spenser, who was thus able to hitch this Cambridge fantasy to his ambitious courtliness, and immortalised this entirely erroneous view of Chaucer in his splendid line,

> Dan Chaucer, well of Englishe undefiled.
> *Faerie Queene* IV, 2, xxxi, 1596

This is not a practical judgment, as Lydgate's opposite and more accurate judgment was; it is an expression of political, patriotic and poetic self-confidence, which is projected back on Chaucer. Then, in the passage from which this is taken, further poetic use is made of the idea of Chaucer's greatness, for just as age has destroyed his work, so age will destroy the work of the present day. So we return to the theme of Chaucer's ancientness and obscurity. Spenser, like most authors of the end of the sixteenth century, has a very strong sense of how far away Chaucer is.

Before partly losing Chaucer like this, however, the sixteenth century had added one further trait to the image of Chaucer— his humour. The first to make clear mention of it seems to be Skelton, who in *Philip Sparow* (1507?) relishes his tales of Canterbury, 'Some sad stories, some merry', and refers to that perennial favourite, the Wife of Bath. Increasingly throughout the century writers refer to his 'merriness' or 'pleasantness'. Spenser's friend Gabriel Harvey (1585-90?) seems to have taken particular pleasure in Chaucer, and notes his comedy, though Chaucer 'is excellent in every vein'. Some writers seem to have dismissed Chaucer on grounds of triviality, while Sir John Harington in 1591 pushes further the slowly increasing charges of various degrees of indecency by accusing Chaucer of incurring 'the reprehension of flat scurrility'. This is, however, chiefly in order to excuse his own grossness. As a whole, the sixteenth-century view of Chaucer is quite well summed up by Sir Francis Beaumont (father of the dramatist), whose letter on Chaucer was printed by Speght in 1598. Beaumont defends the present difficulty of Chaucer's language by pointing out that languages inevitably change; Chaucer's words were pure in his own day. He also refers to Spenser's adornment of his own style with ancient words from Chaucer. Beaumont defends Chaucer from the charge of being 'somewhat too broad in some of his speeches' by pointing out the dramatic propriety of such speeches in the mouths of the Cook, the Miller, etc., and by saying that anyway Virgil and Ovid are worse. It is an interesting comment on the changing tone of the age that what the monks and friars and ladies of the late fourteenth and fifteenth centuries were apparently able to swallow without much trouble, the learned judge of the sixteenth century has to apologise for. Beaumont sums up by calling Chaucer 'the pith and sinews of eloquence', thus praising him, like Skelton and so many others, for never writing emptily. Finally, Beaumont refers to the group of 'ancient learned men in Cambridge' who brought him and Speght first to love Chaucer when they were undergraduates, and which may have even included Archbishop Whitgift.

In the seventeenth and later centuries Cambridge's interest in Chaucer, as in other early English literature, declined. Interest revived towards the end of the seventeenth century in Oxford, where it has never quite died out, and where the foundations of the modern study of Old English were laid. In general, the references to Chaucer in the seventeenth century are the least interesting of any period. The most representative poet of the seventeenth century is Cowley, and Cowley found it impossible to read Chaucer. We owe this information to Dryden, but Dryden also tells us, in the *Preface to the Fables*, 1700, that Cowley's patron, Lord Leicester, was an enthusiastic reader of Chaucer. Here perhaps we see the survival of the old courtly tradition, and the difference between courtiers and clerks that Thomas Wilson noticed. But no doubt temperament and personal attitudes entered in. It is clear, for example, that Shakespeare and Dryden were both in their different ways fairly considerably influenced by Chaucer, while Ben Jonson and Milton, for all their respect, were less interested in him.

In the seventeenth century the language difficulty increased. By the end of the century even Shakespeare seemed not only antiquated but remote. Modernisations began. *Troilus and Criseyde*, as in the preceding centuries, was considered Chaucer's greatest achievement, and was the first of his poems to be so rescued, about 1630, by an unknown writer who paraphrased the first three books. Five years later occurred one of the curiosities of literary history, when Sir Francis Kynaston translated the first two books into Latin, on the perfectly true grounds that up till then Latin had lasted much longer, with less bewildering change, than had English, and that it was understood all over Europe. Milton's similar views have already been mentioned. Bacon, ten years before Kynaston's translation, had had his great philosophical work translated into Latin in order to preserve it, while many years later Pope was to write, 'Short is the date of modern rhymes'. None of this was likely to lead to a clearer understanding of Chaucer's language, or of the nature of language in general. Ben Jonson made some sensible contributions, as one might expect, in *Timber* (1620-35), but as he considered that 'the chief virtue of a style is perspicuity', and thought Chaucer's style 'rough and barren', he was not very enthusiastic for Chaucer. Chaucer continued to be praised for his matter, and sympathised with for being born in so barbarous an age, but he was increasingly difficult to understand. Incomprehension reached its depth in finally denying both praise and sympathy. Addison wrote in 1694

> In vain he jests in his unpolish'd strain
> And tries to make his readers laugh in vain.

This is the low ebb of the understanding of Chaucer, but almost immediately the tide began to turn.

Probably there were more admirers and readers of Chaucer in the seventeenth century than has been allowed; but they were not literary men. They were courtiers like Lord Leicester, and Pepys's elegant and inefficient superior, Sir John Minnes; or men of affairs like Pepys himself; or obscure professional men, doctors, lawyers, clergy, who rarely published, and who, when they published, wrote on serious matters of religion and politics, where only a passing allusion to Chaucer, the odd quotation, reveals their interest. Such writings are of course in the stream of literary culture as a whole, but they do not much follow the immediate fashions. In the seventeenth century the fashion was for Cowley. But fashions change, and the type of verse represented by Waller and Dryden became popular towards the end of the century, after the 'strong lines' of the middle part of the century. To a modern eye there is much that is similar in the type of writing of Dryden and of Chaucer. But they are superficially different, and there is, of course, the actual change in vocabulary and grammar, which was so much more apparent in Dryden's time. Yet nothing shows Dryden's depth of judgment, and his clear-sighted independence, than his championing of Chaucer in the Preface to *Fables Ancient and Modern*, 1700; for it was, at the time, a very unfashionable view. The *Fables* were verse translations and modernisations of Ovid, Boccaccio, Chaucer. The Preface, as everyone knows, is one of the great pieces of English critical writing, and there is a fine appreciation of Chaucer. Dryden's bold preference of Chaucer to Ovid clearly encouraged several later writers in the eighteenth century to stand by their natural enjoyment of Chaucer in the face of indifference or contempt. At first sight, however, Dryden seems to do hardly more than rehearse the traditional views of Chaucer's achievement. He calls him, as so many others had, the Father of English poetry; he praises his versatility, his achievement in refining the language. He praises the noble epic *Palamon and Arcite*, and of course notices Chaucer's satire. He condemns his metre and his ribaldry, and says that his sense' is scarce to be understood'. Dryden sums him up in phrases of characteristic genius—he is 'a fountain of good sense', 'a rough Diamond' (the first time this latter phrase is used in this brilliant metaphorical sense).

To have said so much, so well, at such a time, was a fine achievement. But unassumingly and almost as it were unconsciously Dryden also set out the lines along which the understanding of Chaucer was to proceed for the next two centuries. He notices as common to Boccaccio and Chaucer that they both wrote 'Novels', and resemble each other in their familiar style and manner of relating comical adventures. He also comments on the dramatic realism of the descriptions of the clothing, manners, and passions of Chaucer's Characters: 'We have our Fore-fathers and Great Grand-dames all before us.' Furthermore, he says that Chaucer wrote 'with more Simplicity and follow'd Nature more closely' than to use such verbal conceits as in Ovid destroy the illusion. Unlike Chaucer, Ovid 'would certainly have made Arcite witty on his Death-bed'.

Dryden acts as a bridge between the old image and the new. The old is the medieval and Renaissance poet, learned, noble, artistically sophisticated. The new is the 'natural' Chaucer, who writes novels. By 'novels' Dryden himself of course meant short stories, but it was a prophetic use of the word. The eighteenth century saw the rise of the novel proper, with its claim to represent life with realism, its opportunities for vicarious experience, its unqualified demand for sympathy with people whom the novelist pretends are more or less ordinary. In the eighteenth century Chaucer's poems begin to be read as novels, the tendency increases in the nineteenth century and in the early twentieth century, and it is only recently that some of us have tried to get out of the habit.

The various novelistic traits of Chaucer, therefore, began to be discovered. In 1739 George Ogle found Chaucer particularly happy in 'Characterising'. In 1740 a pseudonymous Astrophil asserted in verse that when Chaucer recites some scene of tragic woe

> Our pity feels the strong distress he writes,

and having mentioned with good sense many of Chaucer's recognised characteristics, he adds

> Meer fictions for realities we take.

Such a response to literature is especially characteristic of the young and of the novel-reader. Not to respond at all in this way, on the other hand, is probably impossible. Some such sympathy is probably the foundation of all desire to read imaginative literature, but when nothing more sophisticated is built upon it, this simple response is dangerous for literature. Especially when it is represented as the only necessary response it encourages the serious man's view that all literary experience is merely an indulgence in irresponsible feeling, a weeping for Hecuba—and 'what's Hecuba to him, or he to Hecuba?' Novels have always been liable to such contempt, and have often deserved it. Literary studies in England today suffer from it, for it is widely held, even by those who teach literature, that literature is only private pleasure. The full understanding of Chaucer has suffered from it. We have all been told, for example, that *Troilus and Criseyde* is the first psychological novel. This means that we should try to read it identifying ourselves with the characters, trying to see the characters as rounded, 'real' people. In consequence our responses have been distorted; with this novelistic expectation it is natural to be bored by the reflectiveness, discursiveness, and lack of incident in the poem; we end up with describing the ending as 'artistically a sorry affair'. Thus Godwin in 1803 complains of barrenness of incident, lack of visible images of nature and life, insufficient 'vicissitudes of fortune'. 'Add to which, the catastrophe is unsatisfactory, and offensive . . .' Godwin eloquently praises the nobility and sensibility of the lovers, but all is felt in novelistic terms. Thomas Campbell, in a careful essay of 1819, emphasises Chaucer's interest in characterisation, but finds *Troilus and Criseyde* languid. Campbell in 1830 seems to be the first critic actually to call *Troilus and Criseyde* a novel, and it is therefore not surprising that he seems to be the first to criticise Chaucer in this poem for providing no sufficient cause that should prevent Troilus from marrying Criseyde. He also shrewdly compares the pathos of *Troilus and Criseyde* with that of Richardson's novels. Throughout the nineteenth century there is increasing comment on the vividness of Chaucer's characterisation, the realism of his settings, his liveliness, and what Case in 1854 called his 'naturalness', his lack of artificiality.

Dryden is at the beginning of all this development. He had emphasised that Chaucer 'followed Nature', though 'Nature' could mean almost anything he approved of at the moment, for Dryden. Here, however, it probably means his sense of the 'naturalness' or realism which he seems to be the first to isolate as a special quality in Chaucer's work, and which, though it does indeed seem to us to be genuinely there, came to recognition through the view of Chaucer as a novelist. There is, however, another idea of 'Nature' overlapping with 'naturalness' but slightly different. This is the 'Nature' that is the essential truth of things. Thus in Dart's life of Chaucer, prefixed to Urry's edition of 1721, we are told that Chaucer 'discovered Nature in all her appearances, and stript off every disguise with which the Gothick writers had cloathed her: He knew those Dresses would change as Times altered; but that she herself would always be the same . . . and therefore despising the mean assistances of Art, he copied her close'. Here is probably the source of Blake's criticism in 1809. 'Of Chaucer's characters, as described in his Canterbury Tales, some of the names or titles are altered by time, but the characters themselves for ever remain unaltered, and consequently they are the physiognomies or lineaments of universal human life, beyond which Nature never steps. Names alter, things never alter . . .

Chaucer's characters are a description of the eternal Principles that exist in all ages.'

There is another sense of Nature that appears in Dart, though not in Blake; that is, the opposition of Nature to 'the mean assistances of art'. Here Dart is much closer to Addison and all those who think Chaucer 'rough'. Only Dart is inclined to praise what Addison condemned. Dart also gives the first hint of the sentimentalised, artless, naive, and childlike Chaucer who was chiefly the creation of the nineteenth century, but is still, alas, occasionally with us. Yet another sense of Nature was also discovered in the eighteenth century—that which applied to natural scenery, especially in its grander and rougher aspects— and even this, with associated elements, became part of Chaucer for Thomas Warton. In 1754, besides praising Chaucer's humour, pathos, invention, painting of familiar manners, and moralisation, he also attributes sublimity to him; in 1762 Warton further found 'romantic arguments and wildness of painting', transporting us into a fairy region. In 1774 Warton went on to praise Chaucer's representation of the beautiful or grand objects of nature with grace and sublimity. One suspects that Warton had not read Chaucer very often over those twenty years, and that memory had somewhat adapted him to Warton's characteristic interests. But Gray, in 1760-1, found Lydgate far behind Chaucer in 'images of horror and in a certain terrible greatness'. This aspect of eighteenth-century Gothick Horror can be found in Chaucer, but has been little noticed, before or since.

There was another different and new trait in the image of Chaucer that the eighteenth century began to build. It is found in that 'biographical part of literature' which was what Samuel Johnson best loved. The earliest conscious example of this interest that relates to Chaucer seems to be an unknown publisher's advertisement in 1753, in which earlier biographers are condemned for considering poets 'merely as such, without tracing their connections in civil Life, the various Circumstances they have been in, their Patronage, their Employments'. There had been plenty of such fact, or rather, what passed for fact, in earlier lives, but what seems to be hinted at here is a closer connection between such facts and the poet's work. The extreme to which such a

connection could be stretched is found in Godwin's life of Chaucer
published in 1803, in two large volumes. Godwin believed that
'the full and complete life of a poet would include an extensive
survey of the manners, the opinions, the arts and the literature of
the age in which the poet lived'. There was much irrelevance in
his book, and the reviewers rightly condemned it. In our day we
have been rightly taught, especially by the New Criticism, to
look into a poem, not all around it, for its meaning and value.
Yet Godwin, and others before him, like Johnson, perceived two
genuine sources of legitimate interest. First, the whole mass of a
great poet's work unquestionably gives those who know it well
the sense of being in contact with a great mind. That mind has
its own characteristic configuration, which can be shown in the
patterns and structures of the work. In this sense it is not foolish
to talk of the poet's own 'character', the sort of person he appears
to be in his poetry. Blake, in 1809, in this way makes some very
acute criticisms of Chaucer. It is then natural, following this, to
be interested also in the character of the poet as the world saw it,
and in the forces and experiences which formed both the man and
the poet. To deny such interests is to cut literature off from other
human interests and experience. The second source of interest in
biographical aspects of literary achievement arises from the first.
It now seems reasonable to assume that a great poet can only arise
when the general culture is propitious to genius. That is, granted
the genius, which is rare, standards of education must be high, at
least for the relevant audience; the status of literature must be
high; there must be good means of communication. A sense of
the relationship between literature and the general culture, though
crudely expressed, appears in the biographical and broader
cultural interest in the past that began to be felt in the eighteenth
century. It developed in the nineteenth century. After Godwin's
mainly unsuccessful effort the first clear expression of cultural
interest comes from an unknown reviewer in *Blackwood's* in 1819,
who wrote, 'The existence of the works of Chaucer changes, it
may be said, to our apprehension, the whole character of the age—
raising up to our mind an image of thoughtful, intellectual
cultivation, and of natural and tender happiness in the simplicity
of life, which would otherwise be wanting in the dark stern

picture of warlike greatness and power'. For the nineteenth century the Middle Ages, and especially the English fourteenth century, became a potent image of a natural simplicity and tender happiness, as we see in William Morris's *News from Nowhere* and other works.[1] Fewer readers and scholars were so struck by the 'thoughtful, intellectual cultivation' seen in Chaucer, and so to be attributed to the general culture of his time. But another unknown reviewer, this time in *The Retrospective Review* of 1824, did take up the theme of intellectual cultivation, when he described Chaucer's works as part of 'the history of the national mind', and bringing a genuine picture of the age before us. A. H. Clough and Andrew Elgar each made a similar point independently in 1852, which did not of course prevent many others reiterating the old view of the barbarous unfit time in which he lived, as some still do today. But perhaps the sense that those times could not have been unredeemably bad if they could produce a Chaucer reinforced a certain historical sympathy and patriotism that, fed from several sources, becomes increasingly common in the nineteenth century, when the Englishness of Chaucer comes to be something to take pride in.

The account of the characteristic traits and images of Chaucer that began to be drawn in the eighteenth century has constantly taken us beyond that century into the nineteenth century, and this continuity is worth remarking. All the same, it was often continuity with a difference. The various changes in literature that became noticeable in the view of Chaucer are often only ripples from the great wave of Romanticism—or Romanticisms —that was sweeping Europe in the eighteenth century. In so far as these affected the literature of England they culminated about the end of the century, as everybody knows, in a period of rapid change with a number of writers of extraordinary brilliance. There were many changes, but one of the most important, as well as the most relevant here, was the rapidly developing breakdown of the 'rhetorical' view of literature.[2] Instead of literature being thought of as artistically formed, a pleasing persuasion, or instruction, or diversion, for its audience, it began to be thought

[1] Cf. Raymond Williams, *Culture and Society*, 1958.
[2] For these matters see M. H. Abrams, *The Mirror and the Lamp*, 1953.

of as an expression of its author's own important thoughts and feelings. 'Sincerity' therefore came to be thought of as one of the chief criteria of literature. There was an increasing tendency to divide verse from prose, poetry from the novel, in thinking about literature. The novel's status was low. Poetry's status was high. Those attributes of the poetry of earlier ages, such as the rendering of character, narrative power, which were now found in the novel, tended to be denied to poetry. Poetry therefore became narrowed in definition to the expression of feeling, and to be valued rather from sympathy for what was expressed than from recognition of verbal skill. (Paradoxically this is a close parallel to valuing the novel for its capacity to render vicarious experience.) The poem was valued as a personal statement, and its importance lay in its revelation of the mind of the poet, 'the main haunt and region' of Wordsworth's song, though he claimed a larger representativeness.[1] Some of the effects of this development, so crudely summarised here, have already been suggested. Others may be guessed. If most of Homer, according to J. S. Mill, was mere narrative, and therefore not poetry at all, Chaucer could hardly hope to escape. Chaucer came again, for different reasons than had affected Addison, to be regarded as simply not a very poetical poet. Richard Wharton (1804-5), who modernised some poems, thought Dryden and Pope more poetical than Chaucer, in whom he found some 'dryness'. Anna Seward, in private letters before and after 1800, made a series of egregious denials of all but trivial merit to Chaucer. Byron in 1807 thought him not only obscene, as did many eighteenth-century writers, but also contemptible. Such negative judgments would be out of the path of this essay, save that they often spring from the expressive view of poetry, which has greatly hindered satisfactory criticism of Chaucer's poetry until the last few years, just as it has hindered satisfactory criticism of the novel. But also, such condemnations of Chaucer were in their day the negative side of the beginning of a positive recognition of two important qualities of Chaucer which

[1] The classic expression of these views is in J. S. Mill's essays 'On Poetry' and 'What is Poetry?', 1833 (ed. J. W. M. Gibbs, 1897). Some of what he says is a remarkably close adumbration of some of T. S. Eliot's most famous pronouncements.

had not before received adequate recognition; the plainness of his style, and the rationality of his poetry. The latter had indeed been accepted in his own day, but as part of his general achievement, and in association with his scientific and religious writing. Chaucer's plainness and rationality are largely the product of the rhetorical, ratiocinative poetic tradition which Romanticism challenged, and some Romantics did not like it, but even their dislike may have sharpened their awareness of these qualities.

Chaucer's writing is rarely evocative, lyrical, 'mysterious' in the way nineteenth-century poetry often is, and even more as nineteenth-century critics thought poetry ought to be. In a word, his style is often plain, or, as Richard Wharton seems to have thought, dry. The great Romantics did not always condemn him for this, but Hazlitt seems to be a little uneasy, and to have felt this plainness when, in *The Characters of Shakespeare's Plays*, 1817, he found Chaucer's ideas 'hard and dry' and contrasted him with an intuitive Shakespeare, full of 'romantic grace'. Coleridge, in *Biographia Literaria*, published in the same year, also noticed Chaucer's mastery of the plain, unaffected, 'neutral' style in English, to which he attached some considerable importance, quoting in support *Troilus and Criseyde* V, 603ff. In 1818 Henry Hallam found that Chaucer 'wanted grandeur', a Romantic judgment, though at variance with that of eighteenth-century romantics like Gray and Thomas Wharton, and suggesting Hallam's reactions perhaps to a plain style. In 1836 Southey, no bad critic, and a great reader and admirer of Chaucer, wrote that Chaucer's language was 'what he had learnt in the country, in the city, and in the court . . . what every one could understand, and everyone could feel; it was the language of passion and of real life, and therefore the language of poetry'. This is a good example of the way contemporary concerns are reflected in ancient poetry, for Southey's remarks are clearly reminiscent of Wordsworth's Preface to *Lyrical Ballads*, with its demand that poetry should be written in 'the real language of men'. On the same occasion Southey perceived that the 'ornate style', of which, like a good Wordsworthian, he of course disapproved, also began in Chaucer's time, though he will only allow its appearance in Chaucer in some of the smaller and later pieces. Lydgate, that Southey of the fifteenth century, would have been surprised! The plain style, decently neat, not gaudy, seems to be what an unknown reviewer of 1837 in *The Edinburgh Review* is reflecting on when he says that Chaucer voiced the literary spirit of the English people, vigorous, simple, and truthful—he wrote for the people, but in the style of a gentleman. Across the Atlantic, Emerson, in 1856, attributed to Chaucer as to the English people generally 'a taste for plain strong speech, what is called a biblical style'. Matthew Arnold in 1861-2 found in Chaucer 'a sensibly lower style' than Homer's grand manner, while in 1863, Alexander Smith found it difficult to account for Chaucer's charm, lacking as he is in fine sentiments and bravura passages. (One cannot help wondering occasionally if critics always read what they talk about.) Smith notes, besides Chaucer's humour, irony, conciseness, and that he 'was a Conservative in all his feelings—not the stuff martyrs are made of', that he used a 'short homely line'. J. R. Lowell noticed Chaucer's 'plainness and sincerity' in 1845, and in 1870 (in the deservedly famous essay reprinted in *My Study Windows*, 1871, which has set the key for so much American criticism since), though he found an 'elegance of turn' and a breaking away from the 'dreary traditional style', he still found Chaucer's 'key so low that his high lights are never obtrusive'. It may be that it was partly Arnold's sense of the plainness of Chaucer's style that led him in 1880 to deny him greatness, as Hallam had at the beginning of the century. For Arnold, Chaucer has not the 'accent' of Shakespeare and others. The great American scholar Lounsbury repeated some of Lowell's phrases, and continued, in 1891, with a comment on 'the uniformly low level upon which [Chaucer] moves. There is no other author in our tongue who has clung so closely and so persistently to the language of common life'. Here are Southey and Wordsworth again, of course, and it is not surprising that a reference to Wordsworth follows within a couple of sentences. This same theme, pursued with more subtlety, and in contrast with Chaucer's more elaborate styles, has been developed with distinction in recent scholarly American criticism to good effect. The tendency today, however, is to generalise from Chaucer's realistic or low style to see him almost in terms of the late nineteenth-century French naturalism, which is rather fashionable today, complete with its squalor and symbolism. It is, of course, the dominant mode of the American novel.

The 'intellectual' Chaucer, the idea of whom is in origin associated with an anti-Romantic rationalism, and the plain style, has already been slightly touched on. It points to an aspect of Chaucer still perhaps neglected. Crabbe turned to Chaucer as early as 1812 for support of his own poetry, asking if we do not feel Chaucer's satirical character-drawing to be poetry? Crabbe has the sense of going against the Romantic stream, refusing to admit in the preface to some of his poems that some 'poets should so entirely engross the title [of poet] as to exclude those who address their productions to the plain sense and sober judgment of their readers, rather than to their fancy and imagination'. Crabbe is no doubt hinting against Wordsworth and Coleridge here, but Chaucer had no warmer admirer than Wordsworth in any century. Wordsworth, indeed, must be thought of as only half a Romantic—he had one foot very firmly planted in the eighteenth century. And it is he who early emphasises Chaucer's reason. His recognition of Chaucer's rational power is no doubt based, like Crabbe's, on Chaucer's anti-clerical satire, for in one of the *Ecclesiastical Sonnets* of 1821 he praises Chaucer's 'lucid shafts of reason' shot against 'Papal darkness'. Anti-clerical satire had of course been noticed long before, but Wordsworth gives it a deeper sense, for there is no poet who stresses more than Wordsworth the necessity of right reason. Hazlitt in 1818 said that Chaucer delighted in 'severe activity of mind', and the intellectual Chaucer, often in connection with religious Reform, or seen as an influence towards Reform, reappears sporadically throughout the century, usually, of course, noted by serious-minded men like F. D. Maurice who had similar concerns themselves. That the quality of intellectuality felt in Chaucer is not only the result of religious conviction, however, is shown by the Roman Catholic Bagehot's fine comment in 1858 on the symmetry of Chaucer's mind, his healthy sagacity and ordered comprehension.

Perhaps this vein of criticism is not the most typical of the nineteenth century's discoveries in Chaucer. There were, anyway, others. The end of the eighteenth century had seen the invention of the concept of 'naive' poetry in Schiller's essay *Über naive und sentimentalische Dichtung* (1795). Schiller meant something different from what we now normally mean by 'naive'. Hazlitt's interesting characterisation in 1818 of Chaucer's 'downright reality', which exhibits 'the naked truth', though principally describing 'external appearances', and which is specially notable for its 'intensity', reminds one of Dart's life of Chaucer, but is also a fair description of some elements of Schiller's 'naive'. In addition, according to Schiller, in 'naive' poetry the poet is elusive.[1] Whether by coincidence or not, we have in 1812 the first description in English of Chaucer as naive, by John Galt. It is not quite easy to see how Galt uses the word. Like Anna Seward he will admit little merit in Chaucer. All he will admit is that 'there is a little sprinkling here and there of *naiveté* in Chaucer, but his lists and catalogues of circumstances are anything but poetry'. Here *naiveté* seems to be faint praise. Another version of *naiveté* was offered by an unknown writer in *The British Quarterly* in 1846. In Chaucer's age writers had 'to drive the plough of their ideas through the stubborn soil of an unformed language. And therefore it is that the word *naiveté* becomes less applicable to the productions of English writers after the age of Shakespeare'. Here the idea of *naiveté* seems unquestionably patronising and depreciatory. The naive Chaucer is still not quite expelled from criticism even today, but in the middle of the nineteenth century he began to have a competitor in the tender and childlike Chaucer, though for some writers, like the Kenelm Digby of 1826, who was perhaps a Roman Catholic, Chaucer remained 'impious and obscene'. Coleridge, though he had also called Chaucer 'manly', emphasised in 1834 Chaucer's 'exquisite tenderness', free from 'sickly melancholy or morbid drooping', and of course Chaucer's pathos had always been recognised. But a powerful creator of the tender and childlike image of Chaucer emerged in Thoreau, who unconsciously saw very much of himself in Chaucer. In 1843 he wrote that Chaucer's poetry is youthful; Chaucer had the habits of a literary man and a scholar, though surrounded by active men. Chaucer helped to establish the literary class. He was full of good sense and humanity, though the *Prologue* to *The Canterbury Tales* is not transcendent poetry. Delicacy and essential purity of

[1] For Schiller cf. M. H. Abrams, op. cit.

character are Chaucer's with a simple pathos and feminine gentleness. He has a pure, genuine, and childlike love of Nature. J. R. Lowell, in the essay of 1845 already referred to, followed up; Lowell almost heard 'the hot tears [of Chaucer] falling, and the simple choking words sobbed out'. 'His chief merit, the chief one in all art, is sincerity.' The tenderness of Chaucer's heart is now insisted on, rather than the pathos of his poetry. For Meredith in 1851 he is 'tender to tearfulness—childlike, and manly and motherly'. (No doubt there is something sentimental in this insistence on tears, which reflects the sentimentality of the nineteenth century, but the nineteenth century was hardly more sentimental—though about different things—than the fourteenth. Chaucer's own heroes are often tearful, and it is clear from contemporary records that men did indeed often and easily burst into tears.) Chaucer's childlikeness continued to be dwelt upon. Landor, in a poem published in 1863, averred that 'The lesser Angels now have smiled/To see thee frolic like a child/And hear thee, innocent as they . . .' Even F. J. Furnivall in 1873 contributes to the image of a 'gentle and loving [Chaucer], early timid and in despair', though he balances it a little with a reference to 'the most genial and humourful man' that Chaucer was. In the same year an unknown writer in the periodical *Temple Bar* writes, 'He talked, a child, to children . . .' Everything, included his long-windedness, is attributed to his childishness and to the period—'It was the childhood of poetry'. According to this writer Chaucer treats everything in a 'childish, simple, superficial way'. It is all very silly, but it is worth remembering that something rather similar has always been said of Dickens, at that time in his hey-day. Dickens scholarship and criticism has recently woken up, but it is still not unreasonable to speak, with due respect and caution, of a certain childlikeness in Dickens's view of people, places, and things. Chaucer, after all, is unique in his century, and for centuries to come, for the relative prominence he gives to children. But not till the nineteenth century do we find anything like a full treatment of children in literature.[1] In the

---

[1] Cf. P. Coveney, *Poor Monkey*, 1957, and D. S. Brewer, 'Children in Chaucer', *Review of English Literature* (1964).

nineteenth century treatment of children in literature is usually
sympathetic and even sentimental, like Chaucer's. They still bear
traces of the clouds of glory. In the main they are good and pure
victims of the world of adults, or of brute necessities. To call
Chaucer childlike may have been patronising, but it was well-
meant as praise of certain qualities of goodness and freshness. The
twentieth century, creator of all sorts of *Enfants Terribles*, no
longer sees children nor Chaucer so.

The nineteenth century made some other critical discoveries
that were less widely taken up than those already mentioned, but
some of which have received much emphasis in the present
century. The most notable quality of the modern image of
Chaucer is perhaps his irony. It seems to have been first picked
out by Isaac D'Israeli in 1841, when he remarked that Chaucer's
'fine irony may have sometimes left his commendations, or even
the objects of his admiration, in a very ambiguous condition'. A
sense of Chaucer's 'ambiguities' was shown by John Payne Collier
in 1820. Considering the universality of comment nowadays on
Chaucer's ambiguity and irony, it is salutary to notice that they
were not remarked on till the nineteenth century, and rarely then.
They are very much of our own time, and irony and ambiguity
as the essential ingredients of poetry are decidedly post-war
products. Yet we think we truly see them in Chaucer.

Another important idea about Chaucer that has been further
developed lately is rather characteristic of the latter part of the
nineteenth century, and first appeared then; the idea of the middle
class and of Chaucer as a representative of it. It seems to be noted
only in 1880 by Swinburne, a rather special, but not altogether
uncharacteristic product of the nineteenth-century English middle
class. He will not admit Chaucer's equality with Shakespeare,
Milton, and Shelley, our first dramatic, epic, and lyric poets,
because mere narrative is essentially an inferior form. But he
makes a sensitive appreciation of Chaucer, and says that 'Dante
represents, at its best and highest, the upper class of the dark ages
not less than he represents their Italy; Chaucer represents their
middle class at its best and wisest, not less than he represents their
England . . .' (Villon represents the lower class, even more than
he represents France.) We have learnt to distrust these threefold

simple class-divisions that originate in the nineteenth century,[1] and in the first essay (pp. 1-38, above) there has been an attempt to show the inadequacy of the concept as applied to Chaucer's linguistic, literary, and social situation; but Swinburne has here detected an element in Chaucer's work that certainly seems to exist. Of course, Swinburne is not condemning the middle class; he refers to the English middle class of Chaucer's time as 'the wisest and happiest'. In modern times the word, especially in the French form, *bourgeois*, has usually been used pejoratively, to describe coarseness and 'bourgeois realism'. It will be noted that the 'middle-class Chaucer' is a product of the latter part of the nineteenth century; earlier, it had been explicitly stated, as must have been tacitly assumed in previous centuries, that he 'wrote like a gentleman', which in fact seems to be the truer description. But we have lost the idea of the gentleman in the twentieth century.

This concludes the variety of images of Chaucer drawn by centuries before our own. The nineteenth-century images are much more diverse than those of earlier centuries, and it may be that this diversity will even increase with the progress of education. There is, however, one great difference. The mass of scholarship already accumulated in the twentieth century, is, like that of other branches of learning, far greater than that of all previous centuries combined. Whatever our critical fashions, the solid basis of knowledge continues to grow. It may be that a consensus of opinion will be reached about Chaucer, and about other great writers. So far, however, this seems unlikely. It seems to be the quality of a truly great writer to arouse a response from each succeeding generation that is a product of the interaction of the writer and his readers. When the readers are always new, and the writer of sufficient complexity, there is always something of new interest born of the marriage of true minds. And the values and interests, and sheer appearances, of the past of our race, especially as represented in great literature, are worthy to be carried forward into the future, however we must modify them. Knowledge of them, like all true knowledge, can well be, in Bacon's words, 'for generation, fruit, and comfort'.

[1] Cf. J. Hexter, *Reappraisals in History*, 1961.

INDEX

This includes the titles of Chaucer's works and those by anonymous authors. Other works appear in the entries for their authors.